Chapter 1

The hundreds of red ... were an unwelcome sight ... another thoroughly ... ce again Martin Francis ... At last reaching the bro... ie traffic crept past the 40mph sign where the road widened to two lanes. Forty yards per hour would be more like it!

Mucklow Hill is the gateway to Halesowen. A small unremarkable town in the Black Country that is an area near Birmingham that got its name during the Industrial Revolution due to the widespread pollution caused by heavy industry. Then, in 1990 during the first Gulf War, Halesowen shot to fame when it came to light that a local firm was producing sections of the barrel for Saddam Hussain's top secret super gun. For a short while, the little town was placed firmly on the map as arguments raged over whether anyone knew exactly what they were making. The owners of the firm maintaining it was part of an oil pipeline and nothing at all to do with a massive cannon capable of wiping out important chunks of Iraq's neighbours. Now some thirty years later, Mucklow Hill is home to the area's two largest DIY stores where that proud tradition is still staunchly upheld. Every weekend, DIY-shy males strenuously deny that they know what it is, how to assemble it or even if they can get it home in the car. No doubt the Butcher of Bagdad would have been delighted by his legacy.

After almost fifteen minutes of entirely tedious nose to tail driving, Martin eventually made his way around the clogged mini roundabout and pulled into the staff car park. He disliked his job at the DIY centre, but admittedly for a man in his early fifties, anything was preferable to the frosty winter mornings on a desolate building site. The claggy mud, everything you touched being wet and wearing three layers of clothes that the biting wind still found a way through. Those were the days he didn't miss. So now he spent his days helping clueless DIY enthusiasts negotiate the complexities of home electrics for thirty-nine hours a week. On the upside, it was a regular wage in a clean, dry and warm environment with a cast iron pension plan. The downside was he spent much of his time trying to prevent kamikaze handymen electrocuting themselves or incinerating their home and everyone in it. This had taught him that the internet had a lot to answer for and that a YouTube video was definitely no substitute for a trained professional.

At long last, as he walked up to the front door, he could see Nigel the store supervisor lurking beside a large display of BBQs. He knew that the rules meant he should use the entrance from the staff car park. But there didn't seem a lot of point, as he already had his uniform on and the walk around to the back of the building would only make him later. His assumption that Nigel was waiting to intercept him proved to be correct, as he shot from his charcoal lair the second his foot crossed the threshold. Nigel was a big timekeeping enthusiast and annoyingly enthusiastic about rules and regulations in general. A man that found endless pleasure in the trivia of day to day employment and enjoyed reading memos from head office aloud, in probably much the same style that Moses read the Israelites the ten commandments.

"Martin, a word," trilled Nigel, his clipped nasal tones instantly forming an irritant in Martin's ears.

He reluctantly lolloped over to the seasonally optimistic selection of outdoor cooking apparatus to receive work-life counselling from a man infinitely more irritating than fibreglass underpants.

"What time do we begin work?"

"9 am, but the traffic was terrible."

"Is this a one-off phenomenon, Martin, or is the traffic generally pretty bad on The Hill?"

Nigel always referred to it as 'The Hill'. Mainly because he was a massive bell end who was desperate to be seen as a trendsetter.

"No Nigel, the traffic is usually bad, but unfortunately today it was worse than usual."

"Then in the future, might I suggest you anticipate the traffic situation and maybe leave the house a little earlier? So that then the worst-case scenario is arriving at work sooner than expected. You then might enjoy an excellent free coffee from the machine and plan your day. Before beginning work, both relaxed and energised."

Nigel could often be seen sat alone in the staff room drinking coffee at 8.30 am. Martin felt sure that an early morning conversation regarding the latest developments in microbore plumbing over a lumpy powdered cappuccino wouldn't be a day well started. He'd rather listen to Ross in the wood yard ramble on about how he would never tire of the smell of natural wood, and that was saying something. Ross loved his wood more than any man should and could often be found with his nose pressed up against a pine plank, taking slow inward breaths and shuddering deeply. Understandably, female members of staff were reluctant to venture in there alone whenever Ross was on duty.

"I will bear that in mind" lied Martin, smiling. Knowing that Nigel was so desperate for a mate at work, just appearing to consider it would be enough to get him off the hook.

"Off you go then!" trilled Nigel once again like a young mum dropping her child off for the first day at nursery. Then casting his eye across the shop floor to see who might have witnessed this textbook display of correctional encouragement.

Martin didn't need telling twice. He hastily beat the retreat past several pairs of sympathetic eyes and along the front aisle to the electrical section. Here he would spend the next eight hours utterly bored out of his mind tidying stock or putting it away. Whilst being regularly interrupted by attempts to keep the store's more electrically inexperienced customers out of the crematorium.

Upon reaching his workstation, he found a customer already lurking by the cable racks holding a piece of tired flex in his hand. As he approached, the man quizzically held it up for his expert appraisal. Martin lost the next three hundred seconds of his life, never to return, selling three quid's worth of twin and earth for a vintage kettle.

As the customer wandered off, Derek from goods inwards arrived with a cage full of fresh stock for his section. He was a good-natured bloke who loved his football, which held very little interest for Martin. So sometimes it was a struggle to find common ground during their conversations. But this morning, Derek had some hot gossip.

"Did you see all that crap on the car park this morning?" he laughed.

"No, I was late. What sort of crap?"

"There was all kinds of stuff. Somebody obviously decided to do a bit of fly-tipping last night. Mainly things you wouldn't show your mother!"

"Such as?"

"How about a quantity of women's underwear and a carrier bag full of jazz mags?'"

"Ugh! That's one pair of rubber gloves that won't find their way back into stock. Do people still have printed porn? I thought all that was on-line now?"

"This was all vintage stuff, I would say 1980s from what I saw. Guess whose car boot that's all safely stowed in now?"

"Umm let's see? Does he have sawdust in his hair?"

"Bang on! He scuttled out of his 205 like a little pervy porn crab and gathered it all up before anyone else got a look in. I bet he's up there in his lair now. Charging up his batteries with massive lungful's of wood sap in eager anticipation of home time. He'll go across that car park faster than Linford Christie when his shift ends."

"Yes, home for his very own Olympic event. The hundred beaver shaft stroke!"

"Ha-ha! He might have to dry them out first!"

"Not a good time to be on Economy Seven storage heaters. Gonna need a decent boiler for that!"

They both laughed at the thought of Ross attempting to dry out the rain dampened adult literature on the radiators around his home. Then sadly, it was back to reality and the cage full of stock that wouldn't put itself away. Derek gave him the paperwork and returned to goods inwards to collect another cage for another section of the store. Martin enviously watched him go. Wishing that he had a job that allowed him to socialise across the entire store. Being stuck in one area under the nerdy gaze of Nigel was like serving time in prison. Then again, he thought about the rain outside and the wet ankle-deep mud covering any building site at this time of year. Perhaps working in a DIY warehouse wasn't so bad after all!

From his workstation on the bottom corner of the row, he could see the girls in the store's little cafe. The coffee in there was altogether better than the instant muck from the machine in the staffroom. This area was sometimes the setting for heated exchanges between partners over a microwaved sausage bap and a flat white. Tempers sometimes ran high when newly cohabiting couples discovered that they didn't share the same taste in wallpaper or bathroom tiles. So a shaky relationship loudly disintegrating amidst the wipe-clean tables and special offer posters wasn't altogether unusual. Providing him with five minutes of free entertainment during an otherwise dull working day.

Martin had a well-practised routine to order a coffee from the girls without approaching the counter and risking a lecture from Nigel. Once their counter was free of customers, he gave a low wolf whistle. When Debbie looked over, he gave her the signal for a flat white, a straight arm across the chest. A Cappuccino was a hand through the hair and a latte was two hands making horns like a cow.

With his coffee ordered, his attention returned to the cage of stock that would form the bulk of that morning's labour. Martin had a system, he always put the big stuff away first. To the casual observer that made it seem he was making far better progress than he was. The smaller stuff took ages and was always fiddly. Threading blister packs onto hooks and observing stock rotation with any overstocks on the top of the shelves was extremely tedious. But Nigel was obsessive about checking batch numbers against the stock inventory to ensure Martin had followed correct company procedure. So it wasn't a surprise to anyone in the store that he still lived with his elderly mother and conducted his last serious relationship via the internet with a woman he never met who worked in a salami factory in Gdansk.

Several consumer units, a few drums of cable and a bulk box of sockets later, Martin was making progress. He had checked the end of the row several times to see if Debbie had left his coffee in the usual place, but as yet he was still caffeine-free. That probably meant that Nigel was lurking somewhere in the coffee shop's vicinity. As he had a thing for Magda, Debbie's Polish colleague. Who, in turn, had a fairly obvious preference for rather tall black men. But then it was still fun watching him try out his awful Polish and making endless salami based double entendres.

"Well, look who it ain't?" said a voice out of nowhere from behind him.

Martin physically winced. When you work in a DIY store, old acquaintances can sometimes be an issue. Former school mates, long-forgotten neighbours, ex-girlfriends and old drinking partners all mean the same thing. Painful stunted conversation, ancient anecdotes and last but not least, DISCOUNT! The natural assumption being that the staff get enormous discounts they can pass on to anyone of their choosing. Sadly, that's not the case as they warn every new employee about abusing their discount privileges and not everyone takes a polite refusal all that well. But when you haven't heard from someone for over a decade, what's another two between old friends?

Martin turned, expecting to see someone whose name he would struggle to recall throughout their forthcoming conversation. One where his brain would work in two halves. The first half carrying on a bland conversation, asking and answering the usual boring questions about life in general. While the other tried hard to remember who they were from their answers. On this occasion, he needn't have worried. Stood before him was his old pal Craig Allen. Now gently greying around the temples and wearing glasses. A smart suit replaced the baggy rave gear and bucket hat he was rarely seen without in their heyday. Yet still unmistakable as the keyboard player from The Party Faithful, the band who shared a rehearsal room with Martin's band Fizzy Orange during the acid house years of the 1990s.

"Shit me! How are you?" exploded Martin, grateful that it was someone he didn't mind talking to.

"Not bad. Taking a lot of no notice as usual."

"I remember you were always good at that," laughed Martin.

"I had my moments. How long is it since I've seen you?"

"Well, let's see. Probably your wedding, I would guess? So that must be around 1996. How is Cheryl?"

"Sorry to say I wouldn't know. She left me for a teacher from our lad's school about five years ago. Never saw it coming, but then she was always at PTA meetings, so I suppose I should have in hindsight. I think a lot of the time she just meant he was giving her a 'meating'. But then, she never was that good at spelling. What about you?"

"I was married for a time, but it didn't work out. I spent a lot of my time working away, so that probably didn't help. We just drifted apart. She remarried a few years back. I still see her in here sometimes. It's all very amicable. I've even done a couple of jobs at her house for her new bloke."

"Wow, very modern. We went down the more traditional route of total hatred, solicitors, custody hearings and financial meltdown. Just about over it all now. But then it's nice to bring it all up again in such pleasant surroundings. So how come you're working here?"

"Ah, you know. Got sick of the travelling, the early mornings, crap digs, muddy vans and working for firms that only pay you when you threaten to go back and rip it all out. What's with the suit then? Last I heard you were planning a European Tour."

"Well, that never came off. We ended up having a big row in a motorway service station over a stolen sausage and split up. Before you ask it wasn't my sausage and I didn't nick it while he was in the toilet, but I know who did! These days I'm a Funeral Director. Please no jokes, I've heard them all,"

"So you're currently between bands then, I'm guessing? Still got your Korg keyboard?"

"No, the Korg is long gone. Sold it when we were getting a deposit together for a house."

"Same here. I sold all my gear when things got tough work wise in the early noughties."

"Well, I suppose I better get what I came in for and let you do some work."

"I suppose, but it's been great to see you after all these years. Fancy a drink one of the nights?"

"Yep, why not? It would be great to chew over the old days again. People we knew, places we played."

Before they parted the two old friends swapped numbers and made promises about getting together soon. As Craig strode off looking every bit the polished funeral professional, a flustered Debbie finally made it across with Martin's flat white.

"Sorry it's late, Nigel was lingering. Your mate's a bit of all right!" she said nodding towards Craig who was now examining an electric fire display out of earshot.

"And I thought you only had eyes for me?" he laughed.

"Bugger off," replied Debbie. "I would rather do a shift with Ross in the wood yard wearing a bikini!" then winked suggestively, her smile saying otherwise.

Chapter 2

Two days later Martin sat waiting for Craig in the Struggling Man at the top of Mucklow Hill. The Struggler as it was known locally specialised in the 'can't be arsed to cook tonight' end of the gastronomic market. Boasting a fully equipped kitchen with non-beeping microwaves and grill extraction that you could easily smell over the petrol in the garage across the road.

Their impromptu meeting had sparked a flurry of texts and both men found that they had very little to do in the evenings except microwaving a meal for one and ignoring the ironing. So it had been a simple matter to decide on a 'two for the price of one' reunion meal in a convenient local hostelry. Martin had enjoyed the brief walk from his rented studio flat where he had lived his life for the past six years with the pause button firmly down. Anything that broke the monotony of his middle-aged singleton life was always welcome. He'd tried internet dating with little success apart from a few casual encounters and one slightly longer affair, which eventually fizzled out when she met a dentist. He didn't blame her. He had made apathy into an art form by unconsciously foiling her attempts to move their relationship on. So she had fast-forwarded straight to the dumping stage. Granted, it was a difficult text to read, but he didn't bother replying. Which sort of proved her point.

Martin closely studied the wipe-clean menu, which ironically didn't seem to have been wiped for quite some time. A splodge of what resembled brown sauce grimly gripped the area covering the limited salad selection. He considered cleaning it off but decided against it. As in all honesty, it didn't make a strong case for the popularity of their salads. He reasoned that people didn't come to a pub for health food in February. They came for steak, burgers, chilli or curry and the physical condition of much of the clientele reflected this as the constant creaking of their overburdened wooden chairs echoed HMS Victory in a round the world yacht race.

As Martin tortured himself between the sensible option of lasagne with a side salad and the dietary irresponsible Death By Meat Mixed Grill, the door swung open and in walked Craig. The barmaid immediately looked up from her phone and passed a hand through her hair. Annoyingly, he had always been the kind of man that women noticed. It wasn't something he did purposely, he just had it. A poor man's Johnny Depp without the poxy rock star jewellery, matt black serial killer car and the aftershave with its name corrupted to SAUSAGE on a thousand bus stop posters.

Martin wondered if he should wave, but then decided it would be funnier to shout "Yoo-hoo" in a faux camp sort of way. The barmaid looked utterly dejected as Craig joined in by flamboyantly waving back. Then sashaying over to their table by the window and flopping himself down as if made entirely from wafer-thin boiled ham falling off the slicer.

"Don't you bring me to some lovely places? Last time I was in here they had a pool table and a Dave Lee Travis quiz machine."

"Yes, as I recall, almost entirely populated by violence specialists, long before Fight Club became popular."

"So what does sir recommend from the menu?"

"I'm torn between the artisan lasagne featuring a rich béchamel sauce, herby Italian tomatoes and Aberdeen Angus beef mince served with herb dusted fluffy garlic bread and side salad"

"Frozen then?"

"Almost certainly… and the Death By Meat Mixed Grill. Which whilst I agree is unlikely to be frozen, I wouldn't want my GP to walk in and catch me eating."

"So basically the dilemma is death or boredom?"

"In a nutshell."

"Death it is then!"

Two and a half hours later they rose from their table after eating more red meat of questionable origin than a one-eyed pregnant lion in a hard-up safari park. Washed down with three pints of lager bearing an exotic foreign name but, in fact, brewed under licence in Smethwick. Linking arms to further depress the barmaid, they laughed their way to the door. Having spent the time recalling a thousand escapades and episodes. Broken down vans, faulty gear, dodgy girlfriends, drugs, impromptu piss stops but not forgetting the endless arguments.

Many see disagreements as an essential element of the creative process, and the carcasses of those who got carried away litter our musical heritage. Lennon & McCartney, Simon & Garfunkel, Gallagher & Gallagher, Peters and Lee to name but a few. Predictably, when a van full of adolescent males travels the nation's highways, lack of sleep, jealousy and money soon place a hand on the wheel of fortune. Then all it takes is a stolen sausage and all you're left with is a greasy plate, the long walk home and your memories.

Out in the car park, the two old friends cheerfully said their goodbyes and promised that this should be the first of many nights enjoying their rekindled friendship. Walking back to his former marital home, Craig continued to think about his life in the band. The Party Faithful had played several high profile gigs back in the day and had eventually come to the attention of Anchovy Jam. A father and daughter management team that scoured local gigs for talent with a following. That they would sign, repackage and present to their London based A & R contacts hoping to hit the big time.

Now with another can of lager left open on the dining table, Craig was negotiating the ladder up to the loft in search of a box that he hadn't seen in many years. Cheryl had always loftily dismissed his musical career. After The Party Faithful had imploded in an avalanche of acrimony he had tried hard to find another band. But after a lot of disappointment and soul searching, not to mention the relentless nagging from his then fiancé about houses and weddings, he gave up. Now the only remnants of that time that didn't live inside his head were somewhere in his roof space. Finally, after much searching, he found what he was looking for. A Barratt's shoebox that hadn't seen the light of day in the best part of two decades.

After descending the loft ladder one-handed, he placed the box on the table next to the open lager and sat down. Taking a long slug from the can, he prepared himself to undertake an emotional journey back in time. Emotions were something he was used to dealing with every day. But then those were other people's, not his own.

Removing the lid, a thick wad of 6 x 4 glossy photographs confronted him. Shot after shot of smiling mates taking life by the balls, who felt they were going somewhere. Shaky low light backstage shots of dilated pupils set in sweaty teenage faces. Rusty old vans with beer mat tax discs and moody MOTs. Grotty rehearsal rooms filled by expensive blue smoke and ashtrays of ripped cigarettes. Just like the memories of generations of council estate kids playing battered ex-catalogue guitars and dreaming about rock star tomorrows.

Further down in the box were the professional shots paid for by Anchovy Jam. Most were black and white headshots. The classic 'all look different ways' pose, looking moody on a derelict street and messing around on the swings in the park. The same corny, industry-standard images that spewed from a thousand band promo packs in a million record company offices . Until websites, My Space and social media took it all on-line and photos started gathering dust on hard drives instead of in old shoe boxes.

Digging yet deeper, he found a CD, labelled "Demo Master" in red marker pen. Three tracks, five hundred quid and a lost weekend at a studio in Malvern. This should have been their ticket to the big time. Instead, it had been two nights on an icy floor, fried breakfasts in the café over the road and a lot of heated discussion about levels, mixes and song choice. When at last the finished product had arrived in the post two weeks later, it surprised them how good it was. But as time wore on and they listened more closely. They found fault with everything, especially each other, and eventually critiqued themselves into extinction.

Craig crossed the room to his ancient black tower Hi-Fi system, also recently liberated from the loft. As Cheryl liked nothing she considered 'too manly'. Except for macho games teachers, apparently, for which she had made an eager exception. Instead preferring her music blue toothed from her phone to tiny portable speakers. Craig had always considered that to be a soulless way to enjoy music. Nothing span or moved. No whirrs or clicks. No static or scratches. Just pin perfect sound that was as dreary as Cheryl herself. A woman who had systematically sucked the colour from his life until all that remained was beige. She loved the colour. Walls, carpets, kitchen. They even had a beige fucking car!

He pressed play, and the ancient technology made the pre-play noises that had once seemed so modern. Then stood in the centre of the room, eyes closed, arms stretched aloft, waiting for the massive rush that he knew was coming. The soaring symphonic chords that opened 'Holy Crook' poured from the speakers. Announcing to everyone present that they would probably die dancing. He felt the adrenaline kick in and a tingle that started in the base of his skull and travelled all the way down his spine. The shuddering beat crashing through his chest as his heart began to thump in a way he could feel right down in his feet. God, how he'd missed the power and the glory. The power to make people dance and the glory of being able to.

When you see a brother
Who maybe needs your cover
Never turn your back and walk away
'Cause the power that we proffer
Has everything to offer
To rest your weary ass along the way

Friendship health and rapture
Things hard to manufacture
Could be yours in just a little time
Like stories from a book
Written by some holy crook
All covered by a simple golden sign…

To anyone peering through that living room window, Craig was a fifty-something man dancing like a lunatic to rave music with a can of lager in his hand. To the man himself, it was a rebirth; the phoenix rising from the ashes. He had rediscovered what life was all about, and there definitely wasn't any fucking beige in it!

Chapter 3

A bilious Martin was trying to decide which particular brand of indigestion medication was most appropriate for his symptoms. He settled on his old faithful Andrews Liver Salts and quickly mixed a spoonful into a glass of water before drinking it down in one. Nervously lingering by the sink knowing that the seconds immediately afterwards could often prove to be explosive. Before letting go an enormous hippo belch and lying to himself, that felt much better!

He had tossed and turned all night as his middle-aged belly struggled to deal with the kilo of grilled meat in a lager and ketchup sauce that he had ingested the night before. At least he wouldn't be late for work today as it was only 6.45 am. So he had plenty of time to get ready and avoid the traffic. Reaching for his phone he once again played the video Craig had sent him at midnight. He smiled warmly at his old friend dancing around his living room to a relic from their past. Then promptly ran to throw up in the bathroom.

Martin arrived at work way ahead of schedule but was neither bright-eyed nor bushy-tailed. The gastric grumbles had given over to a massive headache beautifully blended with a severe lack of sleep that didn't make eight hours of electrical trivia particularly appealing. So when he lurched into the usually deserted restroom, he wasn't entirely delighted to see Nigel sat at the table with a full cup of coffee in front of him.

"Early bird catches the worm eh? Far less traffic on The Hill at this time of the morning, ay mate?"

Nigel's chirpy early morning nature was one of the things that made him so massively aggravating. That said, he had a wide range of other annoying character traits which made it a photo finish to decide which of them won overall. Martin simply grunted his agreement and tried to focus all his attention on the coffee machine. Punching in 1966 for a cappuccino, extra sugar, extra cream, whipped. Knowing that it wouldn't be great, but it was all that was on offer until Debbie opened the coffee shop at 9 am. Now he really wished that he had made the effort to stop for a newspaper on the way to work. Then at least he would have something with which to deflect Nigel's entirely unwelcome attention. He cursed himself for not thinking ahead, as now he would almost certainly have to endure another of his motivational pep talks.

"So how are you finding things?" inquired the nerdy supervisor using his stock conversation opener. "Very different from a building site I would imagine?"

"Not bad, beats being up to my ankles in mud and frozen stiff this time of the year."

"As a fell runner, I can relate to that. Though I imagine that the scenery isn't as stunning."

This attempt at humour perished on stony soil. Other staff members had warned Martin to be aware of Nigel's fell running obsession. Like any zealot, he was always looking for converts. If working with him was bad, running with him up wet hills in the middle of nowhere would undoubtedly be far worse.

"No, mainly brownfield sites around the Midlands. I usually worked on factories and new industrial estates."

"So what do you do for fun when you're not providing our customers with excellent service?"

Martin heard a loud warning klaxon in his head. It was easy to guess what the next question would be. If he admitted to spending much of his time horizontal in front of the telly with a can of lager, he would be easy prey for the 'Billy No Mates' fitness geek.

"Err, I play in a band with a mate of mine."

"Wow, I didn't realise you were a musician. I suppose that explains the timekeeping."

Martin looked at him quizzically.

"The late nights lugging gear and all that," he expanded,

sensing Martin's bewilderment.

"Oh yes, it's a lot of work. Rehearsing, gigging and travelling." Martin was trying hard to kill the conversation, but now Nigel was enjoying digging for detail. He was desperate for someone else to walk into the restroom and rescue him.

"So what do you play? Which instrument?"

"Keyboards mainly and some vocals if we're pushed…"

'Please, for fuck's sake somebody save me!'

"I had a keyboard…"

'Oh balls, he plays keyboards!'

"… once for Christmas. Never got further than playing all the effects and doing the racing car going past impression."

'Thank you, God!'

"So what sort of music do you play?"

"Just covers…" said Martin desperately trying to be as vague as possible. Hoping that Nigel wouldn't declare undying love for whatever genre he lied about playing.

"What sort of covers?"

"Mainly old chart hits from the late 1980s & 90s. A fairly mixed bag."

This was beyond stupid. Being vague was one thing, but being too vague was just as dangerous. Martin watched with horror as Nigel's face lit up like a badger eating Chernobyl flavoured earthworms.

"Maybe you could play at our Spring works social. That would be a brilliant team-building exercise, wouldn't it? Maybe we could do something for charity?"

"It would depend on the dates," lied Martin, trying to play it to the floor in the desperate hope that he would take the hint from his absolute lack of interest in the idea.

"Oh, we haven't set a date yet, so just give me a Saturday in April that you're free and I'll start looking into venues."

Martin was now utterly screwed. In less than a minute, before his very eyes, Nigel had transformed into an orange-clad Bob Geldof. Eternally obsessed with increasing his popularity within the workforce, he was now planning out loud a massive works party entirely based around Martin's totally non-existent band. He sat and listened helplessly as he fantasised about venues, getting approval for corporate branding from head office and seeking sponsorship deals with the company's big suppliers.

Finally, five minutes too late, Barry from building supplies walked into the restroom. Instead of an opportunity to escape, Nigel forced him to listen as he relayed their entire conversation to him. Barry nodded enthusiastically and unhelpfully agreed it was a marvellous idea. Martin just sat aghast in shock watching as their mouths moved and his nightmare grew legs and ran. Then panicked, realising that Nigel had just asked him a question.

"Sorry I was miles away…"

"I said. So what's the band called?"

Martin had no idea. The band didn't even fucking exist! How in the name of God had this happened? Now he risked total humiliation in front of the entire workforce. Plus possibly head office too, just for good measure! With two expectant faces gazing at him, the unanswered question hung in the air like yesterday's fish stew. Feeling the pressure to throw out the very first thing that came to mind, he desperately scanned the room for inspiration. Eventually, his eye fell on the vending machine behind Nigel's head, which held a wide range of overpriced snacks and confectionery. The Flakes obviously didn't work, and Salt and Vinegar sounded far too much like Salt-N-Pepa. He was reluctantly considering 'The Double Deckers' when he spotted a Dairylea Dunker.

"The Cheesy Dips…"

"The Cheesy Dips" repeated Nigel slowly. "Cool man…"

At 5 pm Martin sat alone in his car on the car park, phone in hand. It had been an exhausting day. Pretty much everyone in the store had inquired about his imaginary band, and now it was becoming impossible to keep track of the tangled web of lies he was spinning. A harmless fib he told to evade an obvious attempt to press-gang him into becoming an unwilling running partner had created a monster he had no longer had any control over. People were recommending local charities that might welcome a donation and asking about bookings for parties. If he had to confess that the whole thing was a fabrication, he would be lucky to keep his job, let alone still have any friends at work!

An elated Nigel had spent much of the day haranguing head office for permission to stage the party as a corporate event. This would then allow him to use the company's social media channels to increase the exposure for what he was now calling 'TOOL AID'. A once in a lifetime opportunity for Do It Yourself to change the world. Exactly who would benefit from any money generated hadn't been established, but Nigel would make it his business to save someone!

Martin sat looking at Craig's number on the screen, convinced that this would be a difficult call to make. It was less than a week since their first meeting. Now he would ask him if he would mind saving him from utter ruin by retrospectively forming a band to play a major one-off gig for a local DIY chain store. "Oh, and by the way, it already has a name inspired by a cheese spread based savoury snack."

He wisely decided than given the magnitude of the favour he was about to ask, it might be an idea to start with a text.

"Hello Mate! Really enjoyed last night. Hope the neighbours are still talking to you. Can you give me a ring when you get a moment?"

He pressed 'send' and took a deep inward breath just as

Debbie from the coffee shop passed in front of his vehicle on the way to her own. Noticing him, she mimed someone playing a keyboard before grinning. Martin waved back and tried his hardest to appear the consummate professional when in reality that was the last thing he was. As the day had worn on, a seismic change in his level of popularity had become apparent. Colleagues from other departments that he had previously only been on a casual nodding acquaintance with in the past, had not only stopped to speak to him but also now knew his name. Even Debbie had been more flirtatious than usual if such a thing was possible. It might have been his imagination, but he was sure he had caught her gazing in his direction several times through the day. Not that he was complaining. Female attention of any kind was more than welcome. If that just happened to come with a side order of free caffeine, then who was he to argue?

Just as he was considering turning the ignition key to drive home, his phone rang. He tried to play it cool by letting it ring a couple of times before answering. But the level of anxiety he was experiencing, coupled with his increased coffee intake, made being cool a rather tall order. He answered after half a ring and Craig was happily chattering away before he even had it to his ear.

"Hello, Marty! No problem with the neighbours. One side is empty due to repossession and the lady the other side is stone deaf. Before you say what you need me for I have something to ask you. As you know when I got home last night I got some old stuff out of the loft from my time in the band. I've realised that's what's missing from my life…music! Now I'm on my own I can choose what I do with my life. Doesn't matter what time I roll in, how many hours I practice, or even who I talk to at gigs. So how do you fancy taking a trip back in time and giving the music one last go for old times sake?

"Erm…"

"I know what you're going to say. Who would be interested in two old codgers playing keyboards? Well, I've considered that. There's a lot of electronic duo's in the charts these days and have been for many years. So why don't we create a set list of covers based on suitable chart acts? We're both men of substance these days, so buying the gear we'll need won't be a problem. We can hire a van for gigs and get paid for enjoying ourselves. What do you think? Great idea or what?

Martin could scarcely believe his ears! As his heart rate returned to something resembling normal, he explained that morning's unfortunate conversation with Nigel. The fast-expanding lie regarding the band and his now mounting problems with integrity, charity and the recent emergence of TOOL AID. He tried hard not to sound like a desperate man, but viewed from any angle it was obvious that's exactly what he was. He had decided in advance that if Craig was reluctant, then he would bypass gentle persuasion and go straight to begging. He honestly didn't expect laughter, but that's exactly what he got. Craig laughed and when he'd finished, he laughed some more.

"So what did you say we were called again?"

"The Cheesy Dips…"

"Sounds like something out of a kid's lunchbox."

"It's funny you should say that…"

"So how long have we got to get a set together?"

"About seven weeks."

"And not a keyboard between us."

"Or a set list."

"Are you working this Saturday?"

"No, I have this weekend off."

"What time shall I pick you up then?"

"Where are we going?"

"Keyboard shopping!"

When the call ended, the enormity of the situation finally dawned on Martin. They had less than two months to master enough songs to form a ninety-minute set whilst still working full time. A truly Herculean task. Right there in his car he swore he would never touch grilled meat and lager again!

Chapter 4

It was bang on 9 am when Craig blew his horn outside. Martin had initially woken early but snoozed until 8.25 am. During which he had experienced several short nervous dreams which all ran along the same dismal theme - musical Armageddon.

Upon rising he had practically run through the shower, thrown on his clothes and was now leaving the house with wet hair and a slice of toast held in his mouth while he locked the front door. He wasn't a well-dressed man. At home, he lived in jeans and a sweatshirt. His wardrobe hadn't actually changed that much in twenty years. Except for the sizes were now bigger, and the names on the labels didn't seem quite as important as they once did. That was one thing that he liked about his job, the uniform. Which conveniently removed the need for him to separate home and work clothes. Making life altogether easier for a middle-aged sloth.

Craig was quite the opposite. He dressed with the style of a man who continued to follow trends. He had his hair cut every two weeks, always on the same day, by his regular barber. His clothes were designer and based around a colour palette which flattered his naturally toned physique. Giving him the appearance of a man who had just jumped out of a catalogue rather than a charity shop. He also possessed one or two well-practised signature moves. The hand through the hair that needed no product to hold its style and the rub of the lightly stubbled chin whilst slowly nodding that created empathy with his clients and put them at ease. If you had to sum him up with one word, it would be 'smooth'. If you used two, it would be 'smooth prick'.

Martin climbed into the Jaguar and quietly admired the sumptuous leather upholstery as they pulled away. It smelt so great inside he wasn't sure if it was an air freshener or Craig's weekend cologne. The car was fragrant and automatic, much like Craig himself. He smiled to himself, inwardly enjoying his own joke.

"What's so funny?"

"Nothing. Where are we going then?"

"I thought as we have no time to waste, we would just head up to Jed Rooney's shop in town. He always had a big range of new and used stuff back in the day. So we can try out a few boards before making a final decision. That way we stand the best chance of coming back with what we need rather than coming up empty-handed."

Jed Rooney was a legendary figure in the Birmingham music scene, having been a founder member of several successful bands. A multi-instrumentalist who had always slotted himself right into the middle of whatever current musical trend was in vogue. Like a fat Brummie Madonna with a ponytail, he had made a thirty-year career out of getting down with the kids. He had a massive showroom spread across two floors and several departments. Whatever you played and regardless of your budget, the chances are you would find what you wanted at Jed Rooney's.

The traffic into the city centre was unusually heavy, even for a Saturday. Despite Craig using several rat runs to circumvent the worst of it. But to his annoyance, the journey still took thirty-five minutes. However, they spent the time constructively shuffling through tracks that Craig had on his phone as potential choices for their set list. As both men had been reasonably proficient vocalists first time around, they decided that they would split the singing duties equally. Martin gave a fairly rousing version of 'Altogether Now' by the Farm. Which Craig tried hard to top with 'We Call It Acieed' by D-Mob holding a woman in the car opposite transfixed as he threw in all the arm movements for good measure. Once again reminding Martin of his pal's effortless ability with women and making him wonder how he ever got involved with a miserable medusa like Cheryl.

The lights in Jed Rooney's empire blazed in the late Winter gloom as they stepped from the car in the poorly maintained municipal car park opposite. Martin wondered if it might have been a better idea to come in his seven-year-old Citroen rather than risk any damage to the Jaguar while they attempted to re-launch their music career. But Craig dismissed his concerns with his usual cavalier confidence, blipped the alarm, and they walked towards the light.

The man himself was standing in the middle of the showroom floor talking to a member of staff as they entered. Nowadays the shop did much of its business via the internet, so it was quieter than they remembered. In the nineties, it had been a popular weekend hangout for budding musicians. Who came to lay greasy fingerprints on stuff they couldn't afford and enjoy the artistic buzz that hung around the place. In those days the staff were all in bands, just biding their time until they made it. Rather like the budding actors that wait on tables in Hollywood restaurants performing the day's special menu like a sonnet. Making contacts and mixing with the stars while praying for good fortune to deal them a winning hand. Martin soon recognised some who had clearly never hit the big time, and now this was their only stage. The cool tour t-shirts and acne were long gone. Replaced by embroidered polo shirts and carefully positioned ponytails designed to conceal their hair loss. He felt sure there was also a gigantic box in the stockroom marked 'Broken Dreams', that they all took turns to cry into.

Jed instantly finished his conversation and turned to greet his customers in the style of a Texan used car salesman. His great gift was treating everyone like he knew them personally. Making people feel special made them come back. Yes, there were cheaper deals on the internet and sometimes people would try, then buy on-line. But the 'Jed Factor' often closed the deal, and many years of instrument sales stood testimony to that.

"Good morning fellas, what can I do for you?"

He stopped for a moment and stared hard at Craig before his face broke into an enormous grin.

"Is that you Craig all grown up?"

"Yes, Jed, it's me. How are you?"

"Mustn't grumble. The ears aren't what they used to be and I can't do the splits on stage any longer. But apart from that, I'm fine. How are you? I thought your band was going places, then you vanished. What was it called now?"

"The Party Faithful. Well, you know the story. You pay your dues, nothing happens, people get tetchy, it all kicks off and then you get married."

"And now you're back here after all these years…"

Martin was fairly pissed off that Jed didn't seem to remember him too. He'd spent more hard-earned cash in here than Danny La Rue threw at Max Factor. He sighed quietly as he waited patiently for the old man's attention to switch to him. But he was far too interested in Craig. It was like knocking around with George Michael. Blah, blah, blah!

"… yes, we've got seven weeks to get a ninety-minute set together. We will need everything for an electronic duo. Keyboards, sequencer, drum machine and a PA."

Jed licked his lips. If there was one thing he liked better than running into an old friend, it was meeting one who needed a truckload of pricey gear.

"Well, I guarantee we can offer you an amazing deal and I will put my best man on it. As you might guess, I'm a little behind the times on the electronic stuff. So I will hook you up with Nick, who's always got his nose buried in something stuffed full of silicon chips. He will work out exactly what you need and get you the very best bang for your buck."

Jed produced a small black walkie-talkie from his pocket and requested that Nick should meet him in the main showroom. It was a piece of theatre that had become a tradition in the shop. A few moments later they heard the thunder of running feet descending the stairs and Nick appeared through an archway, bounding over to them like a teenage game show host on kid's telly.

"Nick, this is Craig Allen, an old friend of mine…"

"Jesus, so I don't even get a mention!" thought Martin. "No wonder Andrew Ridgeley gave it all up to go car racing."

"… he's looking to reboot his musical journey. I need you to hear what he's planning and show him all the good stuff. But before you make the final bill up, let me see it first."

This was Jed's well known final discount pledge that he had been doing for more years than anyone cared to remember. The final act of which was a rather theatrical wink in Craig's direction. Before bowing out to intercept a couple and their daughter who were paying a lot of attention to some flutes in a display case in the next room.

"Right guys, what are you planning?"

Martin disliked Nick right off the bat. He looked like the lovechild of Des O'Connor and Tony Blair, which gave him far too much charisma for someone working in Birmingham.

"Well, I'm sure you know who the Chemical Brothers are?" said Craig, smiling.

"Do they come in here?" replied Nick looking puzzled.

"I wouldn't have thought so..."

Martin wanted to laugh, as Craig appeared fairly deflated by the generational marker that had just been hammered into place. He then explained at length their need to create a ninety-minute set in record time. Nick listened politely without butting in while he droned on about staying true to the music. But when Craig finally paused for a breath, he jumped straight in.

"So what do you guys know about the Mikinoyati Gigmaster?"

"I know I can't spell it," said Martin, who decided if Nick called them guys once more he would call him Prickolas a few times once they had paid.

"Good one!" said Nick, raising a clenched fist for a bump. It hung there until Craig mistook the gesture for Rock, Scissors, Stone and covered it with his hand. Martin massively enjoyed the resulting moments of intense awkwardness as a bewildered Nick slowly withdrew his hand.

"Guys, technology has monstered along at an incredible rate in the last 10 years. The Mikinoyati Gigmaster has now combined all the separate pieces of technology that people used to drag from gig to gig. It's a keyboard, synthesiser, sequencer and drum machine in one easily portable unit. Which lets you worry less about the equipment and gives you more time to concentrate on your performance."

Martin decided that Prickolas definitely suited him as he led them through the archway to climb the same stairs he had descended for his earlier introduction. At the top, they reached the showroom that was obviously Nick's domain. Row upon row of expensive-looking electronics with large hanging labels bearing descriptions that sounded more like computers than keyboards. With a flourish, Nick stopped in front of a unit half the size of a dining table and held out his arms in deference.

Martin sneaked a peek at the price tag and tried hard to look unconcerned about the vast number next to the pound sign. It was more than a month's wages and made his heart physically lurch. He quickly calculated in his head that if he maxed out his credit card and ate a lot of cheap canned stuff on toast for a month, he could just about run to it. As his ears faded back into the room following his panicked internal budget meeting, Nick was giving it to Craig with both barrels.

"… it can pretty much run the whole gig for you. You can preload everything you need into it in advance. It has a battery backup and internal memory so you don't need to carry anything else that you might lose, such as USB pen drives or memory cards. It's entirely portable and will link wirelessly to any PA system and has over one million pre-installed keyboard sounds and the same again in synth settings. It can also process and compress your vocal and mix it internally with all your other outputs. The drum machine is able to record then decode the drum pattern from any piece of music it hears in learn mode. Which you can then modify to avoid any potential copyright issues…"

At this point, he smiled and raised his hands to do rabbit's ears around the word 'issues'. This made Martin want to provide him with his very own personalised issue. In the form of a cut lip and a chipped tooth. But finally, the smarmy git wisely stopped talking and just turned the unit on. Which instantly lit up like the control panel of a nuclear power station, before taking a few seconds to settle. A bewilderingly fast tour of its capabilities, options, settings and sounds consumed the next few minutes. After which Nick paused expectantly to take questions.

Craig appeared suitably impressed while Martin tried hard to not look like a potential bankrupt. After a few seconds passed without comment, Craig nodded knowingly and said 'nice' really slowly.

"Shall we get one each then?"

"Well, we'd look pretty fucking stupid, both playing the same one…"

An hour later, The Cheesy Dips were loading two enormous boxes onto the back seat of Craig's Jaguar. Which amazingly hadn't come to the attention of any passing car thieves. Collectively they had just spent a little over £4000 on two keyboards that were so complex they came with an instruction manual thicker than a flood-damaged bible.

It could have been far worse as Craig had negotiated a reasonable discount with Jed at the till as they paid. Made entirely possible by a lot of ego-stroking and suitably exaggerated tales from their collective past. Martin considered that it would be much cheaper and far less hassle to just admit he was lying and get a new job. But then he admitted to himself that he would miss Debbie's free beverages and their stolen glances across the coffee shop. Plus, he was secretly enjoying the elevated status that their musical venture offered him within the store. Nigel didn't seem so precious about his timekeeping and hadn't allocated him any late shifts at all for this month. Allowing them ample opportunity to rehearse late into the night.

The traffic was far lighter on their return journey. Singing had now given way to earnest discussion regarding a rehearsal venue.

"Well, we can't do anything at my flat, it's just too small and the neighbours would get the hump as there's very little soundproofing in the place. If the bloke upstairs gets up for a wazz in the night, he wakes me up scratching his arse."

"Can I offer you my warmest thanks for that image I doubt will ever leave me in my loneliest hours. I've got the room, but once we cranked the volume up there would bound to be complaints."

"OK, so we need somewhere cheap and easy to get to. No point trekking into town when we only live a mile apart."

"What about your works? Is there a room or something that we could use there?"

"You must be joking! We're supposed to be a fully functioning band! People might ask questions when we're trying to suss out how our instruments work!"

"Then we need a proper rehearsal space. Do you want to block rent a room so we can leave all the gear up there? Rather than having to drag it all home after each session?"

"As long as it's properly secure and they have insurance. I might have to sell my last kidney if it all gets nicked."

"OK, why don't we see if Wally is still in business at Make It Big!"

"If he is, it doesn't say a lot for his business plan."

"Well, you'd have expected him to have had made it big by now, wouldn't you?"

"Maybe he's renamed it, Failed Miserably To Make It Big."

Martin Googled 'Make it Big Rehearsal Studios Oldbury' on his phone. Sure enough, he found a live Facebook book page that declared it to be Oldbury's premier rehearsal studios with live recording facilities and a full range of rehearsal rooms to suit every budget. Martin attempted to find more information regarding cost. But remembering Wally's pricing structure from the 1990s, he guessed it would be based on his tried and trusted 'what you might be able to afford' tariff. He dialled the number stated and waited to be connected. After several more rings than a reasonably motivated business professional might consider appropriate, his call was answered.

"Make it Big!"

Martin instantly recognised Wally's dulcet tones. It wasn't tricky, as Wally was a Welshman. Who, for some reason that even he probably couldn't remember, had decided to establish his cut-price conservatoire in the least musical town in the entire country.

"So Wally, has anyone actually made it big in the last twenty-five years?"

This was an ill-judged attempt at humour. An opener to a light-hearted and spontaneous conversation during which Wally would regale him with tales of his near misses with musical stardom after instantly recognising his voice. Sadly for Martin, he had forgotten what a miserable twat Wally was and how many crank calls he entertained during a typical working week. Plus, everyone sounded the same to Wally, as in 'not Welsh'.

"Is that meant to be funny? Fuck off!" replied a less than amused Wally, and the line went dead.

Martin had one job! Until now Craig had created most of the forward thrust for their imagined enterprise. If he let on to his driver that Wally had dumped the phone on him, it would irreparably confirm his position as the junior partner. Leading to another opportunity for Craig to exercise his considerable charisma whilst Martin was again the bystander.

Instead, he improvised an imaginary one-way conversation where both he and Wally enjoyed jokes about sheep interference, the likelihood of Welsh Independence and Boy George. The latter being inspired by a kid they drove past who had a big daft hat on. Bringing the call to a close by making an imaginary appointment to pop round for a coffee in twenty minutes, praying that Wally would still be there. Martin hadn't done a lot of lying until very recently. If he practised more, he might have improved. As it was, he remained firmly rooted to the bottom rung of the Ladder of Deceit.

"Straight round to Wally's then?" said Craig, who had been more than impressed that Martin could enjoy such controversial banter with a man that neither of them had spoken to for over two decades.

"Yep, the old sheep shagger is expecting us."

A puzzled Craig seemed to recall an incident where Wally was once addressed as a 'sheep shagger' by a band member with whom he was having a heated exchange regarding late room rent. Which resulted in Make it Big's highly strung owner throwing all the band's equipment off the fire escape while they watched from the safety of the car park below. He decided that Wally had definitely mellowed over the years.

Popping in for coffee required a slight deviation to their planned route home as Make it Big was located on a run-down industrial estate just out of Oldbury town centre. Some unloved commercial premises can develop a sophisticated patina over time, which only adds to the allure for aspiring musicians. However, this couldn't be said for the Brian Bentley Trading Estate. It resembled some bullet weary areas of the Balkans just after the Yugoslav War. Except Bono had neglected to write a song about it as evidently Miss Oldbury hadn't got the same ring to it.

As they drove on to the estate, Craig did his best to avoid the worst of the broken glass as they passed a still smouldering skip and a showroom's worth of dumped settees. Given their surroundings, it didn't seem prudent to leave their newly acquired electronics unattended on the back seat of the

Jaguar whilst entering negotiations with Wally on the price of a lock-up.

"I'll stay here with this lot while you go up and see him. You still seem to have a good rapport and I strongly suspect that we left owing rent last time," said Craig, who felt sure that Wally would remember such a detail.

That suited Martin as he was unsure how well the 'spontaneous' meeting would go if Wally recognised his voice from the phone. He climbed out of the car and strode confidently across the weed-strewn car park. It was just as he remembered it, right down to the faded laminated sign that declared Make It Big Studios occupied the third floor of the building. A sign that spoke volumes about the likelihood of anyone using its services fulfilling such a prophecy.

Pulling the concertina door shut behind him, Martin punched the button for the third floor and the lift lurched into life. Its ancient mechanism screaming for lubrication as it rose slower than you could climb the stairs on crutches holding a laden tea tray. He felt relieved when at last he could alight and made a mental note to make use of the stairs in the future.

As he walked along the short corridor that led from the lift to what could only be loosely described as the 'reception area' his ears were viciously assaulted by the sound of a no-hope band rehearsing 'All Right Now'. The vocalist had a unique style, which delicately danced through the air like the screams of a someone having their genitals nailed to a wooden chair with vinegar-soaked nails.

Martin found Wally sat in his office, which had a slide open window with square wired glass that formed a counter of sorts facing into the reception. He was hunched over a laptop as Martin entered and didn't bother looking up. Around him stuck to the walls were a gaggle of luminous yellow star-shaped tickets that offered a range of low-quality microwaveable foodstuffs for the 'band on the go'. From the smell he could surmise that someone had recently indulged in a curry-based delicacy, no doubt classically followed by an out-of-date Mars Bar and washed down with a can of warm full fat Tango. He stood for a few seconds, not sure of how to gain Wally's attention without annoying him further.

As he pondered his phone rang. He pulled it from his pocket, expecting to see Craig's name on the screen. He peered at the number displayed, puzzled for a moment, then realised Wally was no longer at his desk. Instead, he now stood glaring at him through the glass, with the handset of the office phone in his hand.

"I thought it was you."

"Hello Wally," responded Martin, blushing and pushing his phone back into his pocket. Wally turned and dropped the phone from standing height onto the desk and continued glaring. "Sorry, I was trying to show off to my mate in the car and got carried away."

"Let me guess? You're freshly divorced, stuck in a dead-end job and you've recently been following Britain's Got Talent with renewed interest. So now, like a born again biker you want to rediscover your youth and stage one last assault on the charts. Hoping that somehow Simon Cowell will raise his hand mid-song and tell you some old bollocks about how your struggle is over and that the world needs to hear your talent. Only for you to lose out in the final to a man who can pull his ball bag over his head like a hairy pink swimming hat while playing the mouth organ. But then console yourself with the notion that Simon will somehow continue to be your mentor and propel you onto the world stage to sing shite covers and tunes he bought at knockdown prices from Mickey Mouse writers. But just a month later the mobile number he gave you during the heats no longer connects. So you wind up singing to backing tracks in provincial shopping centres and selling signed CDs from a trestle table. Whilst sighting artistic differences as the reason you're not the one singing his utterly forgettable Christmas number one?"

Martin instantly gathered from this monologue that the current state of the British music scene might have had some effect on Wally's mental health. He had never been the happiest of people. But now stood in his booth surrounded by packets of overpriced guitar strings, add to water beverages in paper cups and signs stating that 'The use of illegal drugs in this establishment is strictly prohibited'. It wasn't difficult to sense his toes were clearly curling over the cliff edge of sanity. So it seemed somewhat unwise to disagree with his rather inaccurate assessment of events so far.

"Err, something like that…"

"So now you're here to pull the old mates routine to secure a lock-up rehearsal room at a bargain rate. Based on a former business relationship that you have neglected to maintain with any contact whatsoever during the last twenty-odd years. Whereupon, after a three-month honeymoon period, you will consistently pay me late and run up an enormous tab for microwave lasagne and chicken curry. Which will end with you emptying your room while I'm on a low season package holiday in Zante. And me returning to discover that the PA amp is fucked and a million complaints about the stench from the prawns you've hidden behind the radiator."

"Have you got anything available then?" said Martin, smiling weakly.

Wally removed his bottle bottomed NHS glasses and furiously rubbed them with a handkerchief he produced from his trouser pocket. They didn't look any easier to see through when he replaced them on his nose. Martin felt glad Wally wasn't the pilot of a plane he'd just seen through the cockpit window as he boarded for the holiday of a lifetime with the excited residents of an orphanage trailing behind him.

"I have one lockup available. What do you need in it?"

"Just a PA and two keyboard amps."

"How would you be paying? Cash, cheque or direct debit?"

Martin got creative. "Direct debit."

"Sixty quid a month, with a month in advance."

"Ah, OK. What if it's cash?"

"Sixty quid a month, with a month in advance," replied Wally tersely.

"What about fifty quid a month and a 20% discount on any DIY materials you need?"

"As I'm not planning to add a decked roof terrace to the facilities, I will have to decline your generous offer. And just for the record, if I wanted fifty quid a month, I'd have said fifty fucking quid a month!"

It didn't seem wise to make a counter-offer, as Wally didn't seem in any mood to indulge in further negotiation. So Martin nodded in agreement and Wally passed him the key to room seven through the hatch, closely followed by a pre-printed direct debit form.

Chapter 5

"So where exactly is your brother?" inquired Tony Chapman to one half of Electric Fondue his star act.

"I don't honestly know," lied Dominic Dafoe who just minutes ago had left his twin brother Declan in an incoherent mess on the bathroom floor of the flat they shared in Canary Wharf. He had himself only just made the meeting regarding the continuing lack of progress on their forthcoming sixth studio album. Ironically titled 'Unimpressed By Your Attitude' by getting a stopover guest from last night's 'party' to drop him off on his motorbike.

Tony surveyed the obviously still intoxicated mess that had poured itself into the chair in front of him. Exactly seventeen minutes later than the time they agreed upon when the brothers cancelled their last meeting at a moment's notice. He bore no resemblance to the clean-cut twenty-two-year-old kid he had signed to his management company a little over ten years previously. Back then, both brothers had lived with their mom in a little council flat in Haringey. She had done a marvellous job of keeping their feet on the ground and their noses out of the powder for the earlier part of their career. Unfortunately, since she had passed away, the hangers-on, party girls and drug dealers had become their new family. Now just trying to get them together in the same room to discuss business was proving to be impossible.

He stood up and walked to the window to survey the stupendous view of London's skyline that making a lot of right decisions in the music business had bought him. Once he felt calm enough to speak, he turned away from the window to enjoy his other view of success. The entire wall of gold and platinum discs from his portfolio of artists that continued to dominate the charts year upon year under his guidance. Yet here he was again, wasting his time with a pair of lazy junkies who couldn't even manage to attend a meeting in any fit state to talk business.

In the old days, that had been a joy to work with. Always brim-full of creative ideas and fresh angles. Bombarding him with lyrics and melodies that reflected the current state of the nation's challenges. Tunes that instantly connected with the music-buying youth. Reflecting their hopes and struggles in a way that they understood and appreciated.

Some artists spent nearly as much as their album would make from sales during recording. Often forcing them to tour to see even a modest profit. Whereas, Electric Fondue's albums cost very little to make and yet were still immensely successful. This attention to the bottom line had brought massive profits from the music they released. The media loved them as they were always bright and engaging. They remembered regular interviewer's names and made a point of asking after their children. Happily signed autographs in the street whilst posing for a million selfies and shared thoughts and snippets of their jet-set life on social media. Regularly delighting their loyal fans by reaching out to people having a tough time and sending merchandise for charity auctions benefitting worthy causes. Two working-class London boys who had done well, but hadn't forgotten their roots. However, in recent months all that had changed.

Tony had tried everything to reboot their work ethic. Threats of detox, therapy, withholding funds, minders, life coaches and personal trainers. All had come and gone, seeing no real long-term improvement. Sure they would shape up for a month or so, then slowly but surely they would sink ever deeper into the feckless, powder clouded lifestyle that their immense wealth had allowed them to create.

Dominic took a slug of the strong black coffee that Tony had made him upon his arrival. His head really hurt as last night their dealer had bought something new for them to try. He had introduced it like a waitress at The Ivy explains the dish of the day. Waxing lyrically about the mellow high and the elevated state of consciousness. But had somehow neglected to mention that the next day the entire cast of Gremlins would be Spring cleaning in his head equipped with Brillo pads. Bright lights greatly hurt. Quite honestly, any light at all fucking hurt! Now he could sense that Tony was working himself up to delivering the mother of all bollockings. In recent months he had experienced the rest of the Bollocking family, so now it was only fair that mother should get her turn. His substance addled brain searched for some nugget of information that might be available to deflect the expletive peppered onslaught that he knew was coming. But the cupboard was bare. They had got no fresh material, as all they used their home studio for these days was hiding drugs. Dominic couldn't honestly remember the last time he laid his hands on any electronic equipment with artistic intent. So he mentally tensed and waited for the storm to begin.

"We really can't go on like this. I can't spend my time trying to be the father you never knew while you continually ignore me and let me down."

Dominic noted that Tony's approach was different today. More melancholy than usual.

"I have a lot of artists on my books now, some that are not as successful as you. But if I spent more time on their careers and less time on yours, they could be. You're both obviously unhappy and your attitude to your work demonstrates that. The problem is with 'unhappy' is it's a virus. If I catch it from you, then I will transmit it to other people. If you cannot take the necessary steps to stabilise your lives, then I will have to isolate myself from you. Not to be ruthless, but to protect me and the other artists. If Tony gets sad, then we all lose. Because I'm the one making all the play. Do you understand what I'm saying to you, Dominic?"

It was a good try, but Tony knew it was all cobblers. Electric Fondue was by far his highest-earning act. The income from licensing alone made him six figures annually. More than all his other artists put together. They used their music on TV commercials worldwide for everything from cornflakes to condoms. Sometimes he got massive royalty payments for agreements that even he had forgotten they had made. They were an absolute fucking goldmine!

Dominic listened with due reverence and thrust his hands deep into the pockets of his £700 designer jacket whilst trying hard to look remorseful. He knew Tony was telling the truth, but he also knew they were having the time of their lives. Living with their mother had been like living with Michael Jackson's dad. Once it became apparent at five that the twins had a God-given talent, Diana Dafoe had become a musical tyrant. In the beginning, they had shared the Casio keyboard that she bought from a car boot sale for them to play about on. But when their obvious gift for music became apparent, she had bought two far better ones from her catalogue. From the day they were delivered, she made them practise day and night with the constant threat of repossession if she didn't make the payments. So during the long sweltering summers, she forced them to rehearse jazz standards from old sheet music books the thrifty Diana bought from charity shops. Whilst the other lads in the block played football on the grass below, rode bikes, made dens and kissed girls. Now, with Diana gone, they were making up for lost time. They weren't playing a lot of football or making dens, but they were kissing a lot of girls and definitely riding more than their fair share of bikes.

As Dominic's fingers fished around in his jacket pockets, they brushed past a familiar form in the lining. As Tony droned on and on, he attempted to gauge the snap bag's width and to his delight realised that it wasn't empty. Taking his hands from his pockets, he clasped them together in a praying motion and made full eye contact with his desperate manager.

"Tone, Tone, I know what you're telling me is the truth. We had a chat the other night and we realise that we are letting you down. We know how hard you work for us and that we should start cleaning up our act and taking better care of ourselves. The label won't wait forever for us to deliver the album, and they can't promote it unless they have a video. Let me just go outside and ring Declan. I'll relay what you've said and tell him we really need to sort ourselves out this time."

This was music to Tony's ears. At last, he was getting through to one of them. If they carried on the way they were going one or both of them would become a statistic.

"Not a problem, take all the time you like. I'm here to help you with whatever you need to make it happen."

Dominic rose from his seat and took out his phone. Opening

the door, he walked out into the main office, past Tony's secretary who had heard it all before and didn't even bother to look up from her nails. But then instead of dialling his brother, he made his way along to the Gent's toilet. Once safely tucked inside a cubicle, he took the small bag of white powder from his pocket and sprinkled the contents on to the top of the cistern. All he needed was a little bump just to get him through another session of Tony's inspirational horseshit. Then he could get a cab home and go to bed. As he bent his head, one nostril closed and the other with a fifty quid straw sticking out of it, the cubicle door exploded inwards behind him.

"You lying little fucker!" roared Tony. Grabbing Dominic's hair and smashing his head off the now powdery white porcelain.

Declan Dafoe was enjoying a late breakfast of cold pizza and potato wedges after seeing off last night's 'girlfriend' in an Uber just after midday. When their still extremely irate manager burst into the spacious kitchen holding his now bruised brother in a one-handed chokehold. He instantly rose from the table and raised his hands in surrender.

Before his time as a musical Svengali, Tony had been a moderately successful boxing promoter and prior to that, a slightly less successful boxer. Chinner Chapman was never a contender, sometimes barely even a competitor. But what he had was a nasty temper and fists like cauliflowers. Part of the reason he had done so well in the music business was that people felt disinclined to cross him. In the early days, his office had been in a tough part of North London. During the crossover period between boxing and music, he had used some fighters on his books to ensure that he got his 20%. This had left him with a reputation for physically expressing his displeasure when pressured, and right now he was steaming.

"Sit back down and you sit right fucking next to him. I've had enough of the lip service and soft soap bullshit that I've got from you pair of ungrateful little tossers in the last few months. I've been patient and I've tried hard to be sympathetic. I know that your mom had you on a fairly tight leash and now that's she's gone, God rest her soul, you fancy a bit of fun. Well, the fun needs balancing with some actual work. You pair will give me a fucking stroke. The world and his auntie are ringing me about this album and I'm getting bored with having to lie to them. You're not grieving from your mother's death. You're wrecking your careers and fucking up my business, all at the same time!"

At this point, Declan's phone rang on the table. Terrified of Tony's reaction, he just moved his eyes to look at it. Tony grabbed it from the table, smashed it against the back of a chair, then threw the battered mobile at the wall with considerable force. It exploded on impact and shards of silicon chip and LCD screen found their forever home in the corners of the rarely cleaned designer kitchen.

"Yours!" he thundered, holding out his hand to Dominic who reluctantly passed him his phone and winced as it received much the same treatment.

"Right, that's all the dealers and slags off your radar. The only phone that you pair will use for the foreseeable future will be one with a curly fucking wire sticking out of the back. You stay here. You go to your shithole room and pack a bag, but leave it open so I can check there's none of that white crap you're so fucking fond of in there."

Declan rose from the table and ducked his head, fully expecting a smack as he passed his furious manager. Tony had gotten a little shouty in the past, but nothing like this. He was beyond blue. He obediently left the room and made his way to the health hazard that passed for his bedroom. He supposed he had a point. It was a complete pigsty with traces of white powder on most of the horizontal surfaces and a bed with sheets bearing more stains than the Turin Shroud. Five minutes later he had thrown together a sports holdall full of nearly clean clothes that he had collected from the floor and chairs dotted around the room. When he re-entered the kitchen Tony had made three cups of steaming hot coffee and everything that had formerly occupied the kitchen table was now in a broken pile on the floor.

"Right! you do the same. You! Sit down, drink the coffee and put the bag on the table for me to check."

Declan rolled his eyes to his brother across the table as he sat down. Just the way he had when they were kids and their mother had an issue with something or nothing. That was a colossal mistake. Tony wasn't their mother. She was an eight stone woman with a hairbrush. Tony was a fifteen stone silverback with a history of casual violence and a gift for improvisation. Who promptly smashed his head off the table in pretty much the same fashion that he smashed his brothers off the cistern.

"I hope that you both appreciate my fantastic parenting skills."
"What fucking parenting skills?" screamed Declan, who now sincerely regretted paying £2500 for an antique solid oak 18th-century dining table and wished he'd bought a flat pack one instead.

"I'm treating you both the same. He's got a lump on his head and now you have one too. Admittedly, there might be a slight size discrepancy, but I can always keep smacking away to ensure they match if I have to."

Half an hour later, the bags had been thoroughly checked, coffee drunk and head injuries compared by a slightly less enraged Tony. Declan had got the worst of it and now had an apple-shaped swelling in the middle of his forehead. His brother had caught more of a glancing blow from the cistern and so only had a slightly bruised temple to show for his duplicity.

"Where are we going, Tony?" whined Dominic as the large mirrored lift took them down to the basement car park.

"Somewhere where there are no grasping slags, coke or booze! Just get in the car and shut the fuck up!"

"So is this a substance intervention?"

"It will turn into a boxing exhibition if you don't stop asking me stupid fucking questions!"

After two hours on the M1, Tony needed to refuel. The journey

North had been a quiet one as the twins had dozed off not long after they left London. The excesses of last night's party and the trauma of being manhandled by their manager had been too much. Now they slept huddled together on the back seat like two seven-year-olds in dad's car travelling home from a day trip to the seaside. Even as two chemically imbalanced thirty-somethings, they still looked cute when they were asleep. As probably only twins can. Had they set out on the usual path through life, they would most likely be married now and living separate lives. Maybe even with a kid or two. Instead, their journeys were still unavoidably entwined as they continued to meander through the toxic adventure playground that is the music industry. Whilst insulated from the real world in a great enormous bubble of everything poisonous. A path that often leads to death or glory. The outcome of which entirely depends on how quickly you wise up and realise that just because you can, it doesn't always mean you should.

As he indicated to take the slip road to the services, Dominic stirred from his slumber and declared that he needed the toilet.

"Give your brother a nudge too. We could all use something to eat, I reckon. It said there's a burger place here on the sign a mile back."

"Magic, I could murder a couple of cheeseburgers and a milkshake."

"Give your brother a nudge and we'll have a little party."

Declan woke with a start when his brother stuck his finger so far down his ear it entered his dream.

"How old are you?" he said wearily, without bothering to fully open his eyes. Then followed that with "Where are we?"

"Just outside Northampton on the M1. Fancy a slash and a burger? Just like the old times. Do you remember? Before we got all those fancy discs and people started kissing our arses everywhere we went. Three mates on an adventure."

Tony pulled into a parking space and turned off the engine.

"Do proper mates bang each other's heads off fixtures and fittings?"

"I suppose not. But then do they tell blatant lies and disrespect each other by not taking their commitments seriously, leading to severe tension within their relationship."

"Come on, let's have a burger, bro. Tony's paying!" laughed Dominic.

"He'll have to! He made both of us lock our wallets, cards and cash in the safe before we left."

"Do you ever stop fucking moaning?" said Tony shaking his head.

"This is a kidnap situation. You've taken us prisoners against our will!"

"It's a matter of opinion. I would guess that one man's kidnapping is another man's rescue. It just depends on your viewpoint. Look on the bright side! Just think it will be an amazing story to put in your autobiography when the times right. Come on, let's have something to eat like adults and a friendly chat about the future. However, I'm warning you! Go anywhere near a phone or try to leg it, we will engage in another cleansing session of Impact Therapy and you'll spend the rest of the journey locked in the boot. Do I make myself clear?"

The 2Ds nodded moodily. Until now they had only heard of Tony's 'emotional' outbursts second hand from people that had dealt with him in the earlier days of his agency. Now they had experienced a couple first hand, it would be far less painful to just go along with whatever he had planned.

Chapter 6

Despite their age, two hours later the twins had regressed into childhood. Repeatedly asking Tony if they were nearly there yet, as they continued their journey north on the A1. Jetsetters they might be, but they had spent very little outside London. The rest of the British Isles was a mystery to them. Rarely travelling further north than Manchester, and that was usually in a helicopter.

The traffic on the old two-lane carriageway got lighter as they moved up past Newcastle and they made better time. The rain that began when they left their second service stop had finally petered out. Replaced by a clear sky and a near-full moon and around sixty miles later Tony turned East off the A1 at Beal Crossroads and the twins peered at the road sign for a clue about where they were going.

"Is that where you're taking us Holy Island?" laughed Dominic. "Are you going to get us cleansed by a priest?"

For the umpteenth time that day, Dominic instinctively reached for his mobile to Google it. Once again momentarily forgetting that he'd left it lying in component form on the kitchen floor back in London. Now the only source of information regarding their final destination lay with their driver. Word of mouth, the time-honoured method of sharing information. Before you could punch three words into a phone and become an expert on pretty much anything in life. Providing if what you read online was actually true. Which, as a man who sleeps standing up with a weight tied to his dick will tell you, isn't always the case…

Tony had rehearsed this moment in his head numerous times in the previous seven hours. Hoping to deliver an answer that provided both intrigue and mystery. But now he was tired, and so most of what he had composed fell by the wayside as he explained their destination to his passengers.

"In a nutshell, it's an island that lies three miles off the coast of Northumberland out in the North Sea. Which can only be accessed by road using a causeway that entirely submerges twice a day. Making it an ideal location to ensure that two gifted, yet chemically distracted musicians get their heads down and write the album that the record company continues to breathe down my neck about on a daily basis."

"Genius plan! But how exactly are we going to do that without a studio and equipment?" inquired Declan.

"Whilst I am aware I once had a profession that required me to be repeatedly punched in the head in exchange for money. I can assure you that the area of my brain required for logical thought and planning remains entirely unscathed. Sadly, I know the same can't be said for my nose or left ear, which admittedly has somewhat curtailed my modelling opportunities."

"Had you bothered to grace me with your presence at today's meeting, I would have explained that I have hired a residential studio complex on the island for eight weeks. Along with the option for another four if you rediscover your love of music. I have also arranged for a delivery of your preferred sound-making apparatus to be waiting for us upon arrival. To further ensure the project's complete success, I have engaged the services of Hugh Hunt as engineer and producer. As you may remember Hugh previously provided his expertise on your first two best-selling albums. Long before you began powdering your noses several times a day and ordering late-night companionship via an app on your phones. You might also remember that he possesses a legendary work ethic, is completely teetotal and even agonises about taking an aspirin for a fucking headache. Making him an entirely suitable choice of project manager, slash baby sitter, for a pair of lazy twats who would probably smoke Tutankhamen's dick if they could find a big enough Rizla."

By now they were crossing the poker straight, post lined causeway. Salt spray from the puddles already creating feathered patterns on the side windows of the car. Tony was no fool, he had deliberately sought a musical Alcatraz for the wayward twins. His confidence in their ability to deliver was now returning along with the strong urge for another piss. He was hoping for future positive updates from his re-energised electronic maestros that he could then pass along to the record company. Instead of avoiding their frequent calls and being imaginatively evasive about a firm delivery date for the completed album.

As the straight road gave way to a gentle right-handed bend, the brothers got their first view of Lindisfarne Castle majestically rising out of the North Sea mist. Even for two Londoners more accustomed to the Golden Arches than ancient monuments, it was an impressive sight.

"Nothing here but fresh air, beach walks and work. Just what you fellas need to reconnect with the music."

"Is there even a pub?" whined Dominic

"Actually, there's two plus a hotel. But you won't be setting foot in any of them. The licensees all have your photo and strict instructions not only to refuse to serve you but also to ring the number on the back of the photo should you even dare to set foot in any of them."

"You can't do that! We're not fucking children! We're platinum-selling artists with over five million followers on Twitter," raged his brother.

"Quite right. In London, it would be virtually impossible. However, this is the North East and here it's no problem whatsoever. If you can find one person here willing to kiss your fancy London arse and sell you a drink, I will eat my fucking hat. You're here to work and if you don't, you won't just need to wear your animal heads on stage. You will need to wear them 24/7 to hide the bruises. There's a great deal of medieval stone here that I can enjoy bouncing your heads off so I will be entirely spoilt for choice. So pipe down and realise that I'm doing you both a favour. In one fell swoop, this will save your careers and quite possibly your lives. Plus, the price of coke down South will plummet with your snouts out of the trough for a while. With the way you've been putting it away of late, some of your so-called mates might experience a temporary 'overstock' situation."

Tony easily dismissed their remnants of verbal resistance as he picked his way through the narrow stone-lined streets of the tiny hamlet that is Lindisfarne. He smiled at the familiar terraced cottages he remembered fondly from his childhood. Back then, his parents had brought him and his brother here many times during the Summer holidays. A time when a seven-hour journey required an overnight stop and a car capable of making the lengthy trip. Round past the priory ruins, still stubbornly casting their strong gothic shapes in the brilliant moonlight. Then in through a five-bar gate and up to the courtyard as granite chips pinged from beneath the tyres on the gravel drive. The slate sign on the wall lit by a single bulkhead lamp proudly declared that 'Priory Studios' would be Electric Fondue's base of operations for at least the next two months.

Just as their eyes grew accustomed to the inky darkness, the heavy wooden door flew open and the unmistakable figure of Hugh Hunt stood framed in the flickering firelight pouring across the drive. He was a bear of a man. Not at all typical in the world of weedy record producers. Famous for not only being a keeper of his word but also for taking no shit whatsoever from over pampered chemically dependent pop stars. It made no matter if it was your first album or your fiftieth, the work always came first. Hangers on were despatched without ceremony, attendant girlfriends strongly discouraged and the only drug available in plentiful supply was caffeine. Just what the 2Ds needed. Eight weeks of early mornings, fried breakfasts and long days in the studio.

The brother's initial silence gave way to an audible groan as their taskmaster approached the car with his enormous arms outstretched in greeting.

"Welcome lads! Hello Tony! Delighted to have the opportunity to work with you again in such beautiful surroundings. How was your journey up?"

"Fucking awful! We were kidnapped at fist-point by our domineering surrogate father figure who even insisted on waiting in the bog with my brother while I had a crap!" whinged Declan.

"That must have been truly traumatic," laughed Hugh. "Did you have to breathe through your mouth, Tony? Or did you just put Vicks over your top lip like they do at an autopsy?"

Hugh's well-chosen retort broke the tension, and all four men laughed.

"Come on in, I have good food on the way, a roaring log fire…"

"… and lashings of ginger beer?"

"Only the non-alcoholic stuff."

Tony opened the boot of the car and took out the 2Ds bags. For now, they were friends again. Once they forgot all about London and fell back in love with music, the hits would return and so would the green. But then it wasn't all about the money. He had made them into the stars they had become, so the responsibility for their wellbeing was his. And hopefully removing them from temptation for a while would at last make them see sense.

When Hugh said roaring log fire, he wasn't exaggerating. The large open stone fireplace had two huge pine logs that crackled loudly, perfuming the smoky air as they entered. Two large high back oxblood leather armchairs sat either side of the fire with a matching chesterfield set further back from the fire on the ancient herringbone parquet floor. The walls were bare stone dotted with numerous photos of the acts that had previously recorded there. With no one there to impress, the 2Ds dropped their artist personas and swooned like excited kids over some of the other famous musicians drawn there to resurrect their careers. Tony and Hugh left them to it and walked through to the spacious kitchen. Knowing the photos formed as much of the treatment as the simple surroundings.

Hugh made them both a cup of coffee and they settled on the breakfast stools surrounding the tiled island. The large kitchen window offering a panoramic view of the moonlit priory from a different angle. Making it the perfect spot for a heart to heart between old pals.

The 2Ds long-suffering manager had already appraised Hugh on the current situation within the band. Who, fully appreciating the seriousness of what he had been told, generously agreed to postpone a long-held recording commitment in the States in order to be available for the project. Tony had offered him extra money for the inconvenience, but Hugh was no longer motivated by wealth. During his career, he had seen many of the talented kids that passed through his studio fall victim to the excesses of the music industry. Attending more star-studded funerals than he cared to remember. If his influence could see two bright lads live into old age instead of spending years bouncing in and out of rehab. Before finally succumbing to their demons when the world stopped caring and the money ran out, then so be it.

"So have they got anything at all down ready to mix?"

"Nothing as far as I'm aware. I checked their home studio before we came away. All I found were a thousand roaches and a stack of dirty glasses. Looked to me that all they've used it for lately is impressing girls."

"OK, so we're starting with an entirely blank canvas. Nothing at all on their phones?"

"Search me. I smashed them to stop them ringing for help."

"No problem. I'll get them up tomorrow and walk them across the beach. See if the stunning coastline and the history of the place can't kick start something in their heads. No one will care who they are up here. So that'll help to give them back a sense of perspective in their lives. But right now I think what we all need is a decent meal and a good night's sleep. When are you planning to go back?"

"I'm leaving first thing in the morning. I'm meeting a team of specialist cleaners at their flat the day after tomorrow. The place is a pigsty and I need them to return to a new reality if I have any hope of getting them back on the straight and narrow. Plus, I will put a security team in place to dissuade any undesirable callers who might decide to pop round in the meantime."

"Sounds like you've got your end of it more than covered. Don't worry! I'll have them back at their musical best within a week. Once their mojo returns, we'll kick some rough tracks down to you for a listen. Then I'll mix the ones you like and make 100% sure that they can play them live ready for the festivals."

Suddenly the Victorian sprung doorbell loudly interrupted their train of thought…

"That sir will be our dinner. I've ordered three options in serving dishes from the hotel with accompanying vegetables. Good old-fashioned, stick to your ribs, British food that'll soon get some weight back on those bones."

Forty-five minutes later, the mess on the kitchen table bore witness to the culinary carnage that had just taken place. Each of them was now thoroughly stuffed, having enjoyed a choice of braised beef in local beer, roast pork and stuffing or local sausages in onion gravy. Accompanied by a selection of fresh seasonal vegetables and followed by homemade apple pie and custard.

"Right lads, so how are you enjoying Holy Island so far?" inquired Tony, sitting back in his carver chair and patting his belly like Henry VIII.

"It's definitely growing on me," said Dominic, smiling, which earned him a caustic glance from his brother. He had always been the playmaker who dragged his brother along. Tony knew from experience that if he could get one brother onside, then the other would always follow.

"So lads, do you want to go and discover the studio while we wash the dishes and drop them back round to the hotel? Just go out of the door you came in, across the courtyard and in through the door opposite. The control room is upstairs and the performance area is through the door to your left. I think you'll find that everything is in order."

The 2Ds rose from the table, lingering long enough to help gather the washing up together whilst trying hard to not look too interested. Then quietly melted away out of the door and into the courtyard. Their frantic chatter betraying their true level of excitement when they thought they were out of earshot.

Tony and Hugh had stopped to listen hard and smiled to each other when they heard the twin's conversation bouncing off the old stone walls surrounding the courtyard. Maybe this wouldn't be such an uphill battle after all.

Chapter 7

Martin's leaden legs slowly climbed the stairs to Make It Big studios. It had been a tough week as working all day and rehearsing all night was taking its toll. When he walked into the reception area Wally had his head in the back of a broken amplifier checking its workings with an electrical test meter. He barely looked up as he passed. So Martin didn't see the sense in disturbing him with an unwelcome greeting. But as he continued on his way down the corridor to room seven, Wally lifted his head unexpectedly and called after him. At first, Martin wasn't sure if he was just cursing the broken amplifier. But turned back when he realised that Wally was attempting cordial conversation. Not something he was usually associated with.

"I listened at the door for a while last night. You were playing some quality stuff from what I could hear. I'm amazed that you've got so good in such a short space of time. Just goes to show that talent never dies. You've either got it or you haven't."

Martin offered gracious thanks, as Wally wasn't a man to distribute idle flattery. Many of the bands using his rehearsal facilities didn't make any progress at all in six months. They came in once a week, set up, played the same three songs, argued and went home. Wally didn't care. He had long since buried the dream of making it big. Now he was only concerned with making a living. Like a jaded driving instructor, he didn't mind the useless pupils as long as they kept coming back and didn't expect a discount.

"So what are you two planning? Looking at the fun pub circuit, the holiday camps, the X-Factor or what?"

Martin explained his predicament and how in order to avoid running up hills in the rain, he had accidentally created an enormous rod for his own back. Wally laughed. That wasn't a regular occurrence. In fact, he couldn't recall ever having seen him laugh before.

Considering their conversation complete, Wally's attention

returned to the broken amplifier and continued to poke aimlessly around inside with the multimeter.

"Maybe I can help you with that?" ventured Martin.

"What do you know about amplifiers?"

"Judging by the way you're randomly prodding stuff, maybe a little more than you do. I'm an electrician and I've fixed a fair few in my time. Why don't you make us a coffee and I'll take a look?"

Wally looked doubtful, but in reality, knew he hadn't got a clue. He usually just tested the fuses and looked for anything obvious before he dragged it round to the repair shop, hoping it wouldn't cost a fortune. People lived out their fantasies with his equipment, which often led to it getting broken when desire quickly outstripped their skill. But then what had he got to lose? He passed Martin the meter and went to put the kettle on.

Martin quickly got to work and discovered that the problem lay in the power supply unit. As Wally looked on he quickly fixed it with parts from another scrap amp that he found in the storeroom. When Martin had finished Wally reached into his office to grab a guitar, before performing a shaky rendition of Layla on the newly repaired amp. As the final chords reverberated down the corridor, he looked suitably impressed with Martin's handiwork.

"What are you doing about a PA and engineer for this forthcoming musical extravaganza then?"

"We haven't got that far ahead yet. My boss Nigel thinks we're already a fully functioning band. So I guess that we'll have to hire one as it will look a bit suss if we ask the firm to cough up for it."

"Would you consider using me then? I have a PA system I can let you use and I can double as your engineer if you'll have me? One good turn deserves another as we say in Wales."

"They say that pretty much everywhere else as well, Wally. I don't think it's strictly a Welsh thing."

"Are you sure, because my mom always said it and she was really Welsh."

"Take my word on it. My mom said it too, and she rarely set foot outside Oldbury."

"Well, that's me told. So how about it then?"

"Can't see why not? Yes, please, that would be magic!"

Just as the words left his mouth Craig appeared at the top of the stairs looking like Michael Buble on his day off.

"Wally has agreed to provide us with a PA and engineer for the gig," said Martin.

"That's magic" enthused Craig who wasn't even out of breath after a thirty-two step cast-iron staircase.

"Suppose we better get some work done then?"

"Might be an idea if we're hoping to get another three songs worked out tonight."

As Martin followed Craig along the corridor Wally called out after them.

"Have you got the quid for the coffee or do you want me to put it on your tab?"

Room seven always smelt of damp until the ancient two-bar electric heater they weren't supposed to have in there got warmed up. As rehearsals rooms go it wasn't that bad. It had appeared to be quite spacious upon Martin's initial inspection. But now it was full of keyboards, amps, the PA system and two mike stands, it was erring on the snug side of tiny.

"What do you want to kick off with today?" said Martin, furiously rubbing his hands together for warmth as his question formed a steamy white cloud in front of him.

"Why don't we work out one or two newer ones. Just to give the set a bit of relevance. Then run through everything that we have so far and tag them on the end for good measure?"

"Sounds like a plan. Considering we've only been at this for a week, we've done well to have got so much sorted."

"As long as we keep our heads down and carry on chipping away, no one will ever be any the wiser that The Cheesy Dips didn't actually exist until you had that conversation."

"Is the name growing on you then? As that's the first time I've heard you call it that."

"It's not what I'd have picked, but it has a certain something. It doesn't pay to take yourself too seriously at this age."

"So what's the recent stuff that you're thinking of?"

"I heard something on the radio the other day called 'Air Space'. I was driving and had to stop the car to listen. I reckon that it might sit well with the earlier stuff and give us a bit of relevance with the kids. Otherwise, anyone under thirty won't know any of the stuff we're playing. I've worked out the chords and found the lyrics online. See what you think."

Craig pulled out a sheet of A4 paper and balanced it on the improvised music stand in front of him and started to play. As the song progressed Martin began to ad-lib some strings in the background.

Sky gazing on your back
Is a simple pleasure
Ever-changing, endless blue
Clouds pass upon the wind
Ten-second Picassos in the air
Glimpsed, then they're gone
Birds swoop and soar
Planes leave a trail
While just lying still

Sun warms my face
And I do absolutely nothing
But be grateful I can.

"I like that, so whose song is it?"

"It's by a band called Electric Fondue. I'd never heard of them, but they have some decent stuff on YouTube if you look. Been going a few years by all accounts. Might be worth doing a couple more of theirs as I reckon we have a similar style."

"Are they the pair that wear the animal heads on stage? I saw something a few weeks ago someone put on Facebook. I thought I was watching the Banana Splits for a minute until the music started."

"Yes, that's them. Except they don't razz round in six-wheel buggies crashing into everything!"

Chapter 8

Abigail Robertson sat staring into space in the beautifully appointed restroom at Our Lady of Laburnum Sixth Form College. It was an amazing space in which to spend five idle minutes. The ceramic tiles were over one hundred and fifty years old with ornate light fittings designed by William Bancroft and the china on which her £7,000 per term arse sat, was imported from France just before the First World War. Until now, she had never stopped to consider what a sumptuous room this was. Worry certainly helped you to stop taking things for granted!

The first three minutes ticked slowly past as she considered her future options. She could run off to France, join a convent and dedicate her entire life to God. Stowaway on a cruise ship and see the world from the little round window in a lifeboat. Or last but not least, confess all to her parents, who would almost certainly go ballistic. Before bringing the wrath of the Robertson Crew down on a hundred heads until they found the right one. She decided that none of these options were particularly appealing. One far less so that the other two. The vision of her father bouncing around London with his goons working their way through a back catalogue of her casual encounters was an idea she certainly didn't relish.

Sobered back to reality by the terrors of her imagination, she forced herself to study the little side window of the pregnancy test, which had sat beside the sink since she had peed on it nearly four minutes ago. Her heart lurched as she saw that there was still only one line showing in the window. Another sixty seconds and she would be in the clear. No confession, no tearful mother, no vengeful father, no embarrassment, no van kidnap, no torture and no weighted body dumped in the Thames from a borrowed tug boat at 2 am. She could just carry on with her double life. Dutiful daughter and convent schoolgirl during the week. Coke hunting morally bankrupt party girl at the weekends.

There was still no additional line as the sweeping second hand passed the five-minute mark on the Tag Heuer that was a gift from her father for her seventeenth birthday. She silently punched the air and performed a little dance before replacing the negative test in its box and pushing it deep into her bag. Disposal on the way home would be a simple matter. Abigail promised herself that she would be more careful in the future. The Thames already had enough dead bodies in it, and her dad's pacemaker certainly didn't need the exercise.

Her last lesson was French, and the hour sped by far quicker without the nagging worry that had consumed her every waking moment for the last seven days. Everything seemed much lighter and brighter. If this newfound high ever came in tablet form, she vowed to make it her drug of choice. As usual, she skated through the lesson with the usual minimum level of effort and it wasn't long before she was walking towards the bus stop for the ride home. Remembering that the negative test still occupied a place in the murky depths of her Mulberry Bayswater, she made its disposal a priority in the first rubbish bin she passed. Soon discovering that was easier said than done. Most were overflowing with cans and burger boxes from the lunchtime salad dodgers. It would be foolhardy to risk being spotted dropping a used pregnancy test on the top and digging around to make a space in ketchup stained chip papers and half-eaten kebabs was also out of the question. Now it was only a matter of yards to her bus stop. Discreet disposal would either require a detour into the park or walking on to the next stop, hoping to find a bin that the council actually regularly emptied. Just as she was seriously considering turning into the park gates, a familiar black car pulled up beside her. The passenger side window lowered and her father's voice boomed from within.

"Hello Princess, had a pleasant day at school? Get in the back, there's a love!"

Abigail did as her father asked without protest, yet puzzled why he had decided to collect her from school in person. Nine times out of ten she got the bus as he always made a big deal about her living a normal life and enjoying her independence. On the rare occasions requiring her to be chauffeured, he always sent a 'civilian' driver. Ever paranoid that his 'business rivals' might discover an excellent way to exert leverage on him during the periods of 'change' that were sometimes necessary in his line of business.

This modern relaxed attitude to parenting had allowed her to gad about town at all hours of the day and night at weekends. Flitting from pubs to clubs and parties in a haze of booze, coke and taxis. All financed by the generous allowance transferred into her bank account from a shell company in the Cayman Islands once a month.

"Where exactly are we going, Pop?" she probed sweetly.

"Just going to drop you off at home so we can have a little family chat about things with your mother. Not long till you finish Sixth Form. So we thought it might be an idea to talk about what university you're thinking of and the courses on offer."

This statement didn't ring true. Something in her father's voice made her feel that there was a hidden agenda. She tried hard, without success, to recall a time when he had previously played a direct role in her upbringing. Yes, he paid for everything, but he didn't make any of the decisions. That had always fallen to her mother, who had been an eligible debutante raised by aristocratic parents. Before taking the regrettable decision to run away from home and wound up working as a hostess in one of her father's clubs. Theirs had been an infatuation that shone brightly for just a few short months. Then predictably crashed and burned when they reached a stage in the relationship where monogamy and commitment took precedence over sex and freedom. By then they had married and her mother was heavy with her only child. So practicality replaced passion, and they struck a deal. Her father voluntarily took a step back. Allowing Abigail to be raised in a mews property he bought in a desirable part of Chelsea. A home in which she had enjoyed the privileged upbringing worthy of a titled young lady. Blissfully unaware of her father's notorious exploits across the river, until she was old enough to read all about it in the newspapers. A man whose bitter sneering persona promised pain and suffering in exactly the same way asbestos dust heralds cancer.

Private schools had given her the right accent, and lessons in etiquette guaranteed her place in high society. But as Abigail reached her mid-teens, the family genes had begun to surface. Soon enjoying late nights and the seedier side of life, which always felt rather at odds with the world which she inhabited during the week. She knew she would never study fashion in Milan or marry a stockbroker and raise a family in Surrey. So maybe now might be the right time to come clean with her parents about her plans for the future.

Minutes later they swept into Cranbourne Mews as the cobbled street drummed rhythmically through the suspension of the large BMW. Eventually drawing to a halt outside the largest property in the street. Easily identified by the well-planted flower tubs that always garnered much admiration from their neighbours. Theo Robertson stepped out and glared up and down the row of neat Edwardian houses. Before opening the rear door to allow his daughter out without feeling inclined to meet her eye as he did so. Cecelia Mountford had the front door open before they reached it and ushered them both inside. Leaving their driver stood dutifully beside the car. Which always spoke volumes to any neighbour watching from behind their net curtains. Everyone in the mews knew who Abigail's father was and what he allegedly did for a living. Consequently, she never had a problem getting her ball back, and her mother rarely experienced any parking-related issues. When she did, it was simply a matter of introducing herself with a little name-dropping and her space was miraculously vacated. She threatened no one, but then she didn't need to. A simple internet search soon brought the uneducated right up to speed on the folly of risking her displeasure.

Once inside, Abigail made a lame attempt to go up to her room, which Cecelia instantly curtailed. With every passing moment, this felt less like a family chat and more like the Spanish Inquisition. Instead, she was forced to follow her mother into the large dining room with her father close behind. Cecelia sat at one head of the table with her father at the other, leaving Abigail no option to sit between them. Presuming they were all about to play 'pissed off parent ping pong'. She placed her bag on the floor beside her and waited for the storm to begin. Her mother then upped the tension by placing an envelope on the table in front of her. Then paused for several seconds in an apparent attempt to gather her emotions before she began speaking.

"I saw Melinda's mother in Waitrose the other day, who wished to be remembered to you. I thought that strange, as I know you spend a lot of time at their home at weekends. So we went for coffee at Il Bragantino. Imagine my surprise when she said it was months since you had stayed at their house and that, in fact, you had very little to do with Melinda these days. Odd, because that's where you had told me you were, every past weekend for as long as I can remember."

"So digging deeper, I was understandably dismayed as she regaled me with several tales of lewd behaviour that had reached her ears via her daughter. Who, from what I can gather, has become rather alarmed by your associations outside of school and your general attitude to your studies when in it."

"Armed with this fresh information regarding your movements and nocturnal habits, I took the liberty of securing a few stray hairs from your brush for analysis at a laboratory recommended by a dear friend on Mumsnet. This report confirms that you have been regularly using cocaine amongst other things in the recent past. At which point I alerted your father, as this is more his field of expertise than mine."

As the last of those words left her mother's lips, her father stood and reached over for her school bag. As she stammered words of protest, he turned it upside down and emptied the contents onto the table in front of him. After her school books, phone, hairbrush, makeup and body spray, the last thing to fall was the pregnancy test. Theo Robertson reached down and picked up the unfamiliar box as Cecelia watched open-mouthed from the opposite end of the table. She had expected to see cigarettes, weed or worse still, a little snap bag of white powder. A pregnancy test really couldn't have been further from her mind.

Theo looked at his daughter with doleful eyes as reality dawned. His little girl that he had tried so hard to protect from the nastier side of life was clearly in it over her gumboots. He had never wished to play the heavy father as his daughter had always complied with his wishes, or so he thought. Now before him was the evidence that she was not only fooling around with drugs but also putting herself in harm's way in every other sense.

"It's a friend's" wailed Abigail.

"Do you even know when you're lying anymore?" said Cecelia, who had now dropped her school governess persona just ahead of going completely mental.

Theo said nothing. Opening the packet, he took out the test and studied the little window intently. He wasn't massively familiar with such items, but he knew enough to know that a single line indicated a negative test.

"It would seem that your friend isn't in the family way then?" he stated calmly.

A large part of his success as a gangster had always been knowing when to lose his shit and when to remain rational. He prided himself on his restrained approach even to the point where he discharged a 20kg fire extinguisher right up someone's jacksy. It was his signature execution method and made nervous men scan a room for surplus firefighting equipment if they had any reason to be fearful. Rumours in London's underworld said that only one funeral director would make arrangements for his victims. Which was always a burial, rather than a cremation for obvious reasons. Fixing his daughter with the same stare that had dispatched several men to their maker with a fire retardant digestive system, he phrased his next utterance most carefully.

"So when do I meet the lucky fella?"

Abigail knew her father well enough to know this wasn't an invitation or even a polite enquiry. His use of the word 'meet' in this context implied torture or at the very least, a severe beating.

She heard herself stammer, "It's no one special…" and then

really wished she hadn't. That just made things far worse. Perhaps Theo might have come to terms with a homework based puppy love scenario. Or maybe a one-off tipsy liaison following a school disco, involving the teenage classic of booze doctored soft drinks. What he hadn't expected was a blasé admission of multiple drug-fuelled casual encounters.

The Guinness Book of Records requires their representative in attendance for any world record attempt to stand. Had there by some stroke of coincidence been one present during the next sixty seconds, then the record for freestyle profanity would easily have fallen to Theo Robertson. In less than ten minutes his angelic seventeen-year-old daughter had gone from convent schoolgirl to coked-up concubine. He vowed there and then when he found out who was responsible for his little girl's fall from grace, he would experience death so grisly it would require extensive photographic evidence to prove it was even possible.

Chapter 9

Dominic and Declan were making solid progress in the studio thanks to Hugh's robust work programme. Each morning he woke them at 7.30 am and insisted that they were down for breakfast by eight. This was either bacon and eggs, a cheese omelette or scrambled eggs on toast. Hugh called it brain food, but the obvious intention was to put some meat back on their bones. With drugs now firmly out of the picture, their appetites had returned. Slowly but surely, the twins began to resemble the bright young things that he had always enjoyed working with in the past. Instead of the dull-eyed, hollow-cheeked slackers, he had taken charge of just a matter of weeks before.

Each day after breakfast, weather permitting, they would take a stroll across the beach or around the village itself. Those in the know would always greet them enthusiastically anytime they ventured out in London. But in Lindisfarne, the locals weren't quite so easily impressed. There they were tourists, just like any other and nothing to get excited about. Which was grounding for two brothers who had become lost in the bubble of their own stardom. By nine-thirty, they were drinking coffee around the kitchen table before trooping into the studio at ten sharp. At one o'clock they broke for lunch, which was usually a quick sandwich or a toastie. Then back on it until dinnertime at six. After which they worked on loose ideas for the following day or finished off anything they had on a roll. Thanks to these long days of good food, bracing walks and creative camaraderie, they had five rough tracks ready to send to Tony. It was just like old times. Electric Fondue was finally functioning again!

Tony walked to the window to enjoy the view whilst again being serenaded by the first of the tracks that Hugh had e-mailed to him that morning. He had never been a music fan. He was more of a money enthusiast with business interests in music. But even he had to admit that these were very catchy tunes that had an instant appeal on his first run through. Perhaps all the hassle had actually been worth it? Finally, they were spending their time making great music instead of concentrating on shortening their life span. When the track ended he turned the volume down, sat at his desk and buzzed through to his secretary.

"Jenny, get me Robin Sparrow at Blue Sky Records, please."

It made a pleasant change to ring him with positive news instead of endlessly dodging his calls. At last, he had firm proof that the 2Ds were writing again and that they would be able to fulfil their contract with their sixth album. Moments later his desk phone buzzed and Jenny informed him that Robin was on the line.

"Hello, Robin! How are things?"

"They'd be a lot better if you have something good to tell me about that overdue album!"

"Well, it just so happens that I have. I felt that Declan and Dominic needed a new working environment to get the creative juices flowing, so I packed them off up North."

"What? Instead of half a pound of self-raising powder?"

"All rumours, Robin, I assure you. Absolutely none of it is true."

"Yeah right! I heard that Pete Doherty went round for a cuppa and stopped there for five days."

"Apparently he had an asthma attack and had forgotten his inhaler."

"So they improvised, and that's how he ended up back in rehab?" laughed Robin.

" Total bull shine, a mere bagatelle. Anyway, more to the point, I have some rough tracks for you to listen to. Could I possibly pop over and we could listen to them together? Then maybe I could take you out to lunch?"

"What about the Mersey Hen House? I really enjoy their Scouse Chicken Chango…"

"Wherever you like it's on me!"

"OK, say 1 pm then?"

"Perfect, see you then!"

Tony replaced the handset and allowed himself a little one-man Mexican wave to celebrate. At last, he had things back on track. Now all he needed to do was schmooze Robin, keep the 2D's noses firmly against the grindstone and well out of the Columbian. Piece of piss!

The cab ride to Blue Sky Records should have only taken ten minutes, but Tony had woefully underestimated the traffic. So it was five past one when he finally stepped out onto the pavement and paid the driver. Blue Sky records occupied two floors of an enormous skyscraper in the financial district. They could easily have got away with one, but status demanded two. So even the charlady had her own office. The one that Robin occupied was like the bridal suite in a luxury hotel. Tony always enjoyed meetings there, as Robin was a flash bastard and ensured the very best of everything was always right at hand. That was the principal reason he always got a taxi. His glass was never empty. Once again he checked the data key with the new tracks on was still in his pocket and punched the button for the fifteenth floor. These would give him a little breathing space. Time to prepare for the twins' return and get everything ready for the launch of their new release. Then all he had to do was sit back and watch the wonga come rolling in, lovely...

As the lift rose through the floors, he listened to a well-heeled group in business suits discussing something incredibly dull involving the money markets. That's what this office block was really all about, money! If the music thing ever dried up, he could make a good living robbing people in lifts. By the looks of it, they had about five grand worth of phones between them.

Finally, it stopped on the fifteenth floor, which brought Tony back from his lift-based robbery enterprise as the doors opened to reveal the reception of Blue Sky Records. The girl sat at the desk, looked up as he stepped out. She was fairly typical of a female record company employee. Dressed to kill with more slap on than a drag queen at a circus clown's funeral. On the other hand, the blokes all wore suit jackets over jeans like a uniform. The old business up top the party's in the basement cobblers! She smiled warmly as Tony approached, the excess of lip gloss and derma fillers making her mouth resemble a pair of sweaty sausages on a white china plate.

"Good afternoon. Welcome to Blue Sky Records. How can I help you?" said Miss Bangerlips.

"Hello, I've got a meeting with Robin Sparrow at 1 pm."

Miss Bangerlips sizzled him another smile and made a point of looking at the clock. Tony hated her already. He knew he was late. He didn't need it rubbed in. She wouldn't be so fucking smug when he took her phone off her at knifepoint in the lift. Raising the switchboard phone, she rang through and announced his arrival. Seconds later, Robin exploded into reception and held his hand out in greeting. Tony knew from experience that this would be another strong handshake competition. The smarmy twat had a grip like Sindy's little sister, but he let him win every time. That always got things off to a good start. Robin enjoyed winning on every level, and if that kept him sweet, that was fine by Tony. He wasn't disappointed as the pint-sized pinstriped knob end tried hard to crush his fingers whilst slapping him even harder on the back.

"Great to see you, Tony. I was starting to think you were avoiding me?"

"Never the case, Robin. But you know what these artists are like. We should build a crèche and stick them all in it. Be far easier to see what they were up to that way."

"I don't fancy the nappies though, do you mate?" said Robin, laughing loudly at his own joke.

Shit! Robin just called him mate. That had never happened before. They had always had a master and servant sort of relationship. Suddenly being elevated to mate status put Tony on his guard.

Robin led the way into his office that looked more like a sultan's bedroom than a workplace. It was a wonder he didn't dress like a pantomime genie. Perhaps he did when he worked late?

"Drink Tony? I have some amazing Delamain cognac that I know you will just love!"

This was becoming highly suspicious. It was feeling like he was the one being schmoozed, instead of the one doing the schmoozing.

"That would be magic Robin, I've never tried it but it sound's great!"

"It's three hundred and fifty quid a bottle so you can be rest assured it's fairly special. Fancy a cigar to go with it?"

"Again I'm humbled by your hospitality, Robin. That would be most agreeable."

"Help yourself and take another one for later on if you like."

Tony opened the large wooden box on the coffee table and was confronted by an array of the World's finest cigars. Tony knew very little about them apart from they made your teeth look like you've been eating liquorice if you smoked too many. Ignoring the massive ones that resembled an Amsterdam stage prop, he plumped for two mid-sized offerings. Hoping to see them finished before smoking them became a chore. He tucked the spare into the inside pocket of his suit jacket and used the cutter beside the box to prepare the butt of the other for smoking. He had just lit it when Robin walked over with two brandy glasses that were large enough to breed fairground goldfish in. He handed one to Tony and chose himself an enormous black cigar from the box.

"Right make yourself comfortable. Have you got the files and I'll put them on for a listen?"

It surprised Tony. He expected a whole sycophantic team of

industry experts to be present when the tracks were premiered. Sat around bopping their heads along to the music and giving each other slow, knowing nods while biting their bottom lip. Before moulding the final verdict to mirror the expression on their boss's face. But instead, it seemed it was just going to be him and Robin. This was getting odder by the second!

Robin took the pen drive and pushed it into the USB slot in the Bose sound system on his desk. Tony felt his arse twitch as the first track began. If Robin didn't like it, he couldn't rely on one of the kids in the jury to smooth it over in exchange for a bung at a later date. As the music rushed in, Robin pushed back into the silk-upholstered sofa and closed his eyes. He didn't tap his foot or wag his finger. Giving no outward sign whatsoever that he was even listening to music, let alone enjoying it. Three tracks in and Tony would have been wondering if he'd gone to sleep. Were it not for his regular sips of brandy and long pulls on the black mamba that smelt like a turd filled tractor tyre burning on a farmyard bonfire.

As the last chords of the last track faded out, Robin reanimated and stood up. Tony couldn't read him at all. This was his biggest problem with working in the music industry. Everyone tried so hard to be mysterious and cool. Instead of just saying they liked something or playing imaginary bongos on their knees like your dad at an engagement party. He felt strongly that whatever was behind this odd behaviour was about to be revealed. Like a one-man jury, Robin was building up the tension. So that whatever the verdict, Tony would be grateful that it wasn't worse.

"Frankly Tony, I love it! It's a real return to form. Probably the best stuff that I've heard from them in the last five years. I can hear it playing from a million cars in a hundred different countries. Its appeal will transcend languages. It feels almost religious, like an aria for a new generation. A sensory backdrop for the new Utopia that will save the planet…"

Tony listened as Robin continued to ram on like a wanker. At least he liked it, but he felt there was something else coming. He took a big celebratory glug of his brandy and prepared for the onslaught. He had long since left his cigar in the ashtray. Remembering that he enjoyed the smell far more than the taste. At last, the miniature philosopher was finally getting to the point.

"So tell me. Have you got any festivals booked for the Summer?"

Tony thought this was an odd question as clearly Robin knew that until recently the 2Ds hadn't been in a fit state to put their name down for karaoke in the pub. Let alone hold a global audience spellbound with a medley of their greatest hits.

"Nothing at present. We were just concentrating on the album and then maybe looking at something big for next year."

That was utter bollocks and the last thing Tony had planned. The notion of Declan and Dominic let loose on five hundred acres of groupies, drugs and dealers was laughable. He would have to spend half the fee on personal security just to get them on the stage. Then they would need airlifting back out again before they got their hands on anything remotely pharmaceutical.

"Well, I might have a golden opportunity for them to promote their new album before it's even released! What would you say to that?"

In a perfect world, Tony would have said fuck off. But he was between a rock and a hard place. If he rebuffed whatever amazing offer Robin was about to lay before him, it didn't bode well for the new album. If he accepted, he risked his easily distracted, test tube reliant twins stuffing up the entire thing in front of a global audience.

"Well under normal circumstances, I'd take your arm off, you know I would. But I've only just got them back in the saddle. If they fall off again so soon, it might be the end of the whole rodeo."

He had absolutely no idea where the cowboy metaphor came from, but he was desperate. He could sense that Robin was lining him up for the sucker punch, and if he didn't do something soon, it would undo all his good work.

"Nonsense. They'll be fine. What if I told you it was headlining Glastonbury? Would that change your mind?"

"Whilst I appreciate the offer, I would still respectfully have to decline. I can't risk them relapsing either in private or public."

"OK, let me put it another way. Michael Eavis rang me personally to asked if they would do it, and I assured him they will."

"Without speaking to me first?"

"It was Michael fucking Eavis, I panicked. You don't say no to him unless you want a cow's head in your bed. Apparently, he had Justin Bieber all set to headline but they couldn't agree a fee and negotiations went on for that long, he can't get anyone else to do it because they're all booked up for the summer."

Glastonbury! That was the end of June. So they had roughly three months to get clean, finish the new stuff, put a set list together and rehearse it ready to play live on the world's largest stage.

"Tell me you didn't sign anything?"

"I didn't, but I have the contracts here ready for you to sign."

"I can't do it to them. They'll freak! They need careful handling, otherwise the wheels will just come straight off again."

"Fuck 'em. They'll be fine. Who are you, their dad? Let me put it another way. If you don't sign, Michael Eavis will have my balls as earrings and in return, I'll drop them straight off the label. No problem, you say, we'll just find another label. Well, you can try. But I'll snare you in a legal battle over intellectual property so vicious that no one will touch you. And by the time it's settled, their fans will be so old they'll be mail ordering zip-up boots out of the paper and glueing their teeth in for the week on a Sunday evening."

Tony clenched his fist. What he would really like to do, he knew he couldn't. When he first knew Robin, he was buzzing about all over London scouting for talent at crap gigs. A man utterly desperate to make a name for himself in the music business. And now he had one, except no one ever used it to his face.

"I wondered what all this soft soap was about and why we weren't sat here with your little gang of boyfriends hanging on your every word. Doing your thumbs up or thumbs down Roman emperor routine. I ought to throw you out of the fucking window and watch you hit the pavement like a sock full of warm jam."

Robin noted Tony's clenched fist and decided it was time to switch tack and add the second slice of bread to what was a fairly impressive shit sandwich.

"Tony, Tony... Let's try to look at the positives instead of the negatives. The deadline will obviously inspire creativity and a sense of urgency to finish the new album. The resulting pressure will leave no time for recreational narcotics. Instead, anticipation will be their new drug. For one day in June, they will become the biggest band on the planet and their record sales will soar. Not just the forthcoming one, but the older ones too. It's a well-recognised fact that fans backtrack through earlier material when they witness an amazing Glastonbury performance. A few months later we will all be riding a tidal wave of money. All you have to do is keep them clean and get them there. After that, you can lock them up in the Tower of London for all I care!"

As tempting as it was to pummel Robin's face until his brains ran out of his ears like greasy grey porridge, he had a point. After this, he could retire and entirely free himself from the music industry. Buy a nice little pub down by the coast and live his days out selling lager tops to tourists. Instead of endlessly stroking egos and listening to music that made his teeth ache.

"OK, you win. Give me the contracts and a pen. But you can forget your Scouse Chicken Chango lunch, you sneaky prick!"

Chapter 10

Martin was planning to enjoy a rare night off from rehearsals. Tonight he would treat himself to a takeaway and a film on Netflix, which was as much of a treat as his severely depleted finances could run to at present. Their set list was growing by the day, and last night's run through had seen them tip the hour mark. So Craig suggested that they have a break as he had a funeral booked for an Italian chap the next day and apparently their massive families could be quite a handful when in mourning. So he needed to be on his game, rather than knackered with ringing ears.

Martin hadn't objected, as three weeks of learning new songs had taken its toll. He'd fallen asleep on the toilet at work a few days ago. It was only the repeated calls on the tannoy that raised him from his slumber. His head balanced against the toilet roll holder and his trousers round his ankles. The deep mark left on his face had taken some time to fade and noticeably puzzled the customer who was waiting for advice on dimmer switches when he eventually returned to his section. When he checked in the mirror, he found that it wasn't just the indent from the wall bracket that had caused the intrigue. He also had "Now wash your hands" written backwards across his forehead in red ink.

As he crossed the car park, thankful that the working day was now firmly in his rearview mirror, the only dilemma was what takeaway to order? He liked Indian, but sometimes it didn't stay with him for too long. Rising at 3 am for whitewater rafting down the Rogan Josh Rapids would not see him raring to go in the morning. Pizza was also a contender and if he ordered big, it would provide him with lunch for the next day. Although the downside of that was pizza often had the opposite effect and settled in his middle-aged digestive system like a bag of Blue Circle cement. The sensible option was definitely Chinese, as at least that had a few vegetables in it and resembled something along the lines of normal food. Rather than a foot-wide cheese topped scone or brightly coloured meat in a molten lava sauce. Just as he had decided, he heard fast footsteps behind him and turned to see Debbie from the coffee shop right behind him.

"So are you rehearsing tonight?"

"No, I've got the night off. Thought I'd watch a film on Netflix, order a Chinese and get my head down early."

As the words left his lips, he thought he detected a hint of disappointment in Debbie's demeanour. As if his plans for the evening had somehow clashed with her own. Then he remembered the frequent gazes they had shared across the coffee shop over the last few weeks. He had never been successful with women, which his inability to pick up on body language and seize the moment when opportunities arose just made worse. He didn't respond well to subliminal messages unless they broke over his head like a thrown vase. For once Martin grasped that this might be a pivotal moment in life's journey.

"Why?"

That really was the best he could manage. But it did the trick. Debbie's face instantly brightened. Lifting her tired makeup back to where it had started the day. Regrettably, Max Factor didn't market a foundation formula suitable for smiling at builders all day whilst huddled over a grill plate in clouds of steam.

"I thought you might like to come out with me? There's a comedy night on at the Bear Hotel. It doesn't start till nine, so we could go for a curry in the Standard Tandoori beforehand if you like?"

Martin couldn't believe his luck. As tired as he was, he knew that this opportunity wouldn't come again. Debbie had probably spent days working herself up to asking him out. He knew from experience how that felt. Looking for your opportunity to separate your quarry from the bulk of the herd. The clammy hands, words that stuck in your throat, the fear of rejection, the point-blank refusal, the endless piss-taking when she told the rest of the heifers. It was all still there, as if it was yesterday. If he just stuck to the mixed grill and salad, he shouldn't have to ride the rapids later.

"Fuck yes! Sorry, I mean I'd love to. I'm not assuming anything. I mean, if that happened it would be lovely, but it's not mandatory. We don't even have to kiss unless you really want to…"

He tailed off as Debbie dissolved into fits of laughter and his cheeks blazed.

"I'll see you in the Standard at seven. I haven't booked a table, but it's hardly likely to be busy on a Tuesday night. The comedy club is at nine, so don't be late. Otherwise, I'll pull a waiter and go with him instead."

With that, she gave him a saucy smile and walked over to her car. He watched her go. He wasn't 100% sure, but he thought she was swinging her hips slightly. Admittedly, it was hard to tell in her safety shoes and sexless tabard.

He unlocked his car and climbed in as his heart banged like the door on Oliver Reed's drinks cabinet. This was unprecedented. A woman he fancied had actually asked him out. He tried to recall a previous occasion when he hadn't had to do all the work, and couldn't. God, life was wonderful!

At 6.50 pm Martin sat in the Standard Tandoori which was a precious relic of a bygone age in British Indian Cuisine. The burgundy flock wallpaper, matching carpet and the waiter's short jackets embroidered with the restaurant's logo all added to the nostalgia. Here existed a world of traditional British Curry. Long before some chancer over on the Stratford Road stuck two handles on a tin hat in the 1980s and Britain went mad for Balti .

He had eaten here countless times when he was a younger man. Vividly recalling the theatre of brightly coloured starters brought from the kitchen still sizzling on piping hot skillets. Spicy dishes that had once sounded so exotic but were now like dear friends to old school curry lovers. Often followed by red banana fritters coated with sweet sticky cinnamon sauce and garnished with squirty cream. Back then he ate what he wanted without fearing the consequences.

Martin studied the menu with a lager while he waited for Debbie to arrive. The waiters guessed correctly that he wasn't dining alone and obligingly left him in peace to do so. He oozed nervous energy and had the aroma of a man waiting for a date. Standing in his bedroom dripping wet from his shower, he had channelled his inner Craig. Initially, the look he was going for was effortlessly cool. But after laying his best clothes out on the bed, he wisely downgraded this to penniless tool. And instead concentrated his efforts on simply smelling good and being on time. Just as he was marvelling at the inclusion of the classic Bombay Duck in the starters section, he heard the door open and a waiter say "Good evening, madam". He lifted his eyes and there she was. She looked amazing! He watched closely as she wobbled down the aisle between the closely packed tables. There was no denying she was swinging her hips now, and from his expression, the waiter had noticed too. But then it was hard to miss as she was almost knocking the chairs over as she passed. She was much taller in heels and had shapely legs that filled her jeans perfectly. And judging by the waiter's admiring gaze, the rearview was equally as good. The long workday ponytail had gone and now her hair fell across her shoulders in gentle blonde ringlets. Framing a face that had clearly undergone a complete repaint following their conversation in the car park. Once she was almost at his table, he realised that perhaps it would be more gentlemanly to greet her upstanding. So he shot to his feet like a guilty schoolkid when the headmaster enters the classroom. Clumsily knocking over his drink in the process. Which promptly smashed against the cruet set, sending a shower of lager and broken glass everywhere. Debbie took a step back and laughed as a tidal wave of Cobra cascaded onto the carpet and the flustered waiter rushed forward to mop it up.

"You look lovely would have been nice, but I'll take a calamity fanfare if that's all you've got."

After ordering their meal from an alternative table as their waiter noisily vacuumed lager out of the carpet at the other end of the restaurant, Martin learned Debbie was a widow. Her husband had died two years previously in somewhat bizarre circumstances. He had taken to feeding a fox in their back garden and over some months the animal had become tame enough to hand feed. Unfortunately, late one night after a rather 'indulgent' evening out, screams from the garden alerted Debbie at feeding time. He died in hospital two weeks later from the vicious mauling he received from a prowling African Jackal who had escaped the day before from nearby Dudley Zoo. At the inquest, the coroner agreed it was a simple mistake to make in the dark after several pints. Recording the verdict as misadventure, he declared it had been a brave move to rub his ears but an utterly fucking foolhardy one to tickle its belly.

Martin was secretly relieved to hear that they never had children. So there was no danger of him failing the family entry requirements set by a traumatised ten-year-old who desperately wanted a pony. Instead, she lived alone with a mental cat called Barney who seemed to feature quite heavily in the stories she told him about her life. She seemed lonely, and Martin knew all about that. The band had given him another reason to function apart from going to work and paying the bills. Now it had brought him a girlfriend. The Cheesy Dips had their first groupie!

The meal was just as he remembered from his twenties. Timeless tastes from the East that just couldn't be replicated by the Johnny Come Lately Asian grills that seemed to spring up in every closed down pub. These were time-honoured dishes marinated in cultural heritage and passed down through the generations. Rather than dodgy red chicken soaked in a bucket and cremated on a gas grill.

When they finished eating, he lamely attempted to do the manly thing and pay the bill, but fortunately, Debbie was having none of it. So after a little playful discussion, they settled on halves. Which came as a great relief to Martin. Because a sneaky look at his banking app in the toilet had informed him just fifty-nine quid separated him from absolute destitution. Once they had both paid their half by card, he fished around in his pocket for a cash tip. The tired little waiter lingered expectantly, with high hopes of being handsomely rewarded for his impromptu carpet cleaning duties was crestfallen when Martin handed him just under a pound in loose change. So once again Debbie got the rise out of him as they walked over to The Bear Hotel arm in arm.

The bar, as you might expect, was full of larger-than-life characters and they could hear the banter before they even pushed the doors open to enter. It surprised Martin when she didn't go to grab them a seat while he got the drinks. Instead, she remained by his side and greeted some of the people stood at the bar by name. He was a little inhibited by this as he honestly didn't know a soul in there. Yet it soon became apparent that Debbie knew many of the regulars and they, in turn, knew her.

Eventually, Martin and Debbie moved away from the bar with their drinks. She suggested going up to the function room to ensure decent seats before the gig began. They paid on the door at the top of the stairs and went in. Once again, he found many of the people already settled on the rows of crimson-coloured metal chairs arranged in crescent-shaped rows in front of the stage warmly welcomed Debbie. He decided she must be a bit of a dark horse. Perhaps they had a book club or something else up here she regularly attended? He had noticed no posters for Zumba or slimming clubs, so surely it couldn't be that. Then thanked God he hadn't said that out loud and ended the night early with a lager rinse.

The room quickly filled up, and as Debbie had predicted soon, it was standing room only. Bang on nine the PA system played some dynamic opening music, and the compere bounded on to the small stage from the wings. He had a local accent and did a short warm-up routine about his mother's atrocious cooking when he was a kid. He got some good laughs before introducing the first act. This turned out to be a Canadian chap who did 20 minutes on how our version of the English language adversely affected his relationship with his British wife. The main of which focussed on our ability to turn telling the time into an impromptu maths lesson. He did really well, and the audience lapped it up.

Once again the compere leapt on from the wings to pump up the applause and to bring on the second act. Which was a young lady in a woolly hat who told several stories about her toddler son and his insistence on loudly telling the truth about everything. Which climaxed in him loudly declaring another mother's newborn child to be "Yuk!" and steadfastly refusing to remain in the same room as her. Her earnest deadpan delivery connected very well with the audience, and she left the stage to rapturous applause. Just as her routine was coming to a close, Debbie whispered to Martin that she needed the loo. Luckily they had selected aisle seats, so it was no problem for her to nip out. During her absence once again out came the compere to introduce the headline act, who judging by the reaction of the audience was more local talent. Martin hoped that Debbie would make it back in time so she didn't risk a ribbing about her bladder capacity from the stage. Shit, too late! Now the compere was giving the next act the big build-up.

"… and now put your hands together ladies and gentlemen to welcome to the stage our very own Debbie Dixon!"

Martin couldn't believe his eyes as his shy date cooly walked out onto the stage and took the applause like a pro. The seemingly fragile widow that he'd just spent the last couple of hours with, was now leaning on the mike stand. Poised to launch her latest comedy assault on the chuckle muscles of those assembled.

"As some of you probably know I'm from the less fashionable side of Birmingham, the Black Country. Pretty much the same crime rate as the posh side of the city, but the houses and the takeaway food are far cheaper.

Just like Cornwall, we have our own dialect, and now we even have a flag too. The Cornish Flag looks like something you'd see flying from the mast of an old pirate ship. Ours looks like something you would see hanging off a Toyota Land Cruiser full of angry Arabs with a 50 calibre machine gun stuck on the back.

My dad was German, which made growing up in an area that was heavily bombed during the war quite challenging. I told everyone at school that he was Danish and only spoke like that because he was deaf in one ear. Which worked a treat until he grew 'that' moustache for parents' evening and loudly told my language teacher a sausage based joke in German that made her cry.

We were poor and only went on holiday every four years. Coincidentally when the World Cup was on. Then when we came back, my dad would make cleaning all the graffiti off the house into a game for us. But it wasn't all bad. As we were the first family in our street to get a jet-wash.

Tell me, why do people still try to make a living doing Ann Summers parties? What's the point? They have stores in every shopping centre now! You wouldn't have an Aldi party, would you? You can't expect someone to believe that waiting naked in the dark, covered in own brand tikka masala cooking sauce will bring the spark back to their relationship. Or sell them a bargain-priced angle grinder based on the fact it feels a bit tingly on their top lip. Then guaranteeing it will leave them absolutely fucking breathless on a Wednesday night when hubby takes the kids to judo.

But don't they have some amazing stuff on that centre aisle, though? It's like an assault course for people with ADHD. One minute you're perusing an exceptional selection of cooked meats and olives. Then you turn around and impulse buy a jet ski and a polka dot wardrobe organiser.

Aldi literally has the power to make you want to buy anything. You'll stand there for ten minutes trying to decide if you will ever need a Lion King potty. When you eventually decide that you don't, you try to think of anyone that might? Why? Because it's a fucking bargain at only 99p! That's why!

Then when you finally convince yourself you need one, it comes up on the till as £2.99! Because someone else got a grip on their sanity halfway round and dumped it in the wrong section. So now you have no option but to style it out. Because a forty-seven-year-old childless widow getting a price check on a Lion King potty will set a warning buzzer off at social services.

Stranger Danger - Sector 8 - Aldi Oldbury!

I wouldn't even make it halfway across the car park before two women in flat shoes and excessive wooden jewellery took me to the floor like a really fucking compassionate version of Starsky & Hutch.

What do you want the potty for weirdo?

I bought it for the young girl over the road?"

How old is she, you sick bitch?

She's 27, but I saw she's put on a bit of weight and bought a bigger car. So I thought she might need it soon...."

For nearly thirty minutes, Debbie kept the audience rolling in the aisles. When she eventually pushed the mike back into the stand and took her bow, the applause seemed to go on forever. Now Martin understood why Debbie was so well known there. He felt like Denis Thatcher as he waited for her to make her way back to him through the throng of half-cut well-wishers. He just hoped she didn't expect him to do her hair.

"That was amazing! I had no idea you did stand up comedy?"

"You're the only one that knows apart from the people here. I've had the odd customer in the coffee shop give me a double look. But they've said nothing as I reckon they can't place me."

"So how long have you been doing it because that obviously wasn't your first time?"

"After my Gary died, I was lost. I just wont to work each day, then got home and cried. I realised that I couldn't go on like that, so I started coming here for the comedy gigs to cheer myself up. One night I got talking to the chap that runs it and he told me there were evening courses you could go on. Gary and me were always messing about and making each other laugh. So I thought I would give it a go. It was hard at first, but I soon got used to telling gags on stage at the course. Then I started jotting down material in between serving coffees and it just sort of took off. Now I do a regular monthly slot here and the odd gig in town."

"Well, good for you. Are you thinking of going pro?"

"I don't think so. I don't fancy dragging my ass all over the country late at night. I'll just stick to what I know and carry on doing the local gigs."

By now they were back in the downstairs bar where the customers were thinning out as it was almost closing time.

"One for the road?" said Martin, who was enjoying being Mr Dixon for the evening and the reflected minor celebrity status that came with the title.

"No, I'll just get up with a thick head in the morning. I better get off now."

Martin immediately appeared crestfallen. She wasn't giving a lot away about how she felt their date had gone. She sensed his disappointment, and so squeezed his hand before kissing him tenderly on the lips.

"Why don't we split a taxi back to my place and you can tell me more about the band. Naturally over some great coffee?" she said, winking.

Martin could only manage an enthusiastic nod, like a five-year-old who'd just been offered a free Happy Meal. As he desperately tried to remember exactly which underpants he had on.

"I didn't know your dad was German."

"He wasn't, he was from West Bromwich. But I doubt that would get a laugh…"

It took a few seconds for Martin to remember what had occurred when he woke up in Debbie's bed at 7.15 am the next morning. They had sealed a brilliant night with a rather energetic session of noisy sex that had started the moment they shut the front door. With the preliminary heat taking place in the hall, the semi being held in the lounge and the final taking place in the bedroom. Now he could hear Debbie singing in the shower. Which presented him with a few minutes' grace with which to locate his shamefully ancient underpants and study his unfamiliar surroundings. Judging by the amount of furniture and accessories that he recognised as product lines from work, she obviously made good use of her staff discount. Her bedroom was neat and functional, with no sign of ever being shared by a man except for a can of Brut deodorant that stood on the dressing table. Martin was just considering the implications of Barry Sheene's favourite deodorant being present in a widow's boudoir, when Debbie appeared in a towel, picked up the can and gave herself a liberal all over spray. Seeing the puzzled look on his face, she informed him that Brut had been Gary's favourite. She began using it after his death, so she felt he was always there with her. Martin was relieved. Better that than he had a rival to contend with. Perhaps he would treat her to an Impulse gift pack from Superdrug if this was going places. He wasn't keen on his bird smelling like Henry Cooper, but at least she wasn't 'splashing it all over' with another bloke.

After Martin made a half-hearted attempt to drag away Debbie's towel and make best use of his morning glory, she pushed him in the direction of the bathroom and got dressed. As he stepped into the shower he heard a creak as she went downstairs. At least she knew how he liked his coffee! It amazed him that there was no awkwardness between them now alcohol wasn't a factor. But then he had known her for so long that there was no danger of being disappointed how she looked the morning after, unlike the cousin he pulled a few years back at a mate's wedding. That was possibly the worst hotel breakfast he had ever eaten as her entire family stared and nudged each other whilst she ate her weight in bacon and eggs. Before broadly hinting she was saddle sore and announcing to everyone present that he was 'the one' and 'watch this space'. Martin had ducked out of a fire escape without checking out and made his mate promise to withhold his phone number under pain of death. Eventually, she had tracked him down on Facebook and he'd blocked her. After being rather relieved to find she lived in Telford and thankfully didn't own a car.

As they pulled away from Debbie's house in the Brut mobile, the music that suddenly blared from her car stereo deafened him. As they drove, she happily sang along to "I'm in Synch with You" by Electric Fondue. She knew every word and even sang the chorus harmonies. Martin didn't join in. Instead, he mimed playing the keyboards and fantasised about playing it live for her at Tool Aid.

It was only a short ride to Martin's egg box sized flat, and the traffic was surprisingly light for a Wednesday morning. When they drew up outside Martin wasn't entirely sure what etiquette demanded from him. So he went for "Cheers for the lift!" and tried to jump out. But as he went for the seatbelt release, Debbie pulled some sort of Judo move and gave him a long lingering kiss. Then said, "Now get out and don't be late for work!". With that, she pushed him out, cranked the music back up and roared away. Leaving a shocked Martin kerbside feeling like a trampy one-night stand. Which when given a moment's reflection he decided he quite liked in a horny sort of way.

A little later, on arrival at his section, he was pleasantly surprised to see a steaming hot mug of coffee waiting for him. Along with a bacon bap that definitely contained more rashers than specified by head office. As he turned to offer silent thanks in Debbie's direction she mimed a strongman back. Magda laughed too, clearly in on the joke. As he took a large bite from his breakfast, Martin wondered once again how his life could get any better!

That morning, putting away the day's quota of incoming stock seemed far easier. Even the constant interruptions from customers seeking advice on tedious electrical matters didn't irritate him at all. In fact, things were going really well right until Nigel rocked up for a mid-afternoon matey chat.

Chapter 11

Theo Robertson was perplexed. He wasn't getting anywhere with his daughter. Once she took to her room, he couldn't get another thing out of her. This annoyed him greatly as information gathering was one of his greatest skills. Sadly, stripping his daughter naked and hanging her upside down in a bitterly cold warehouse wasn't an option open to him. Theo needed to find a more creative approach. So he phoned a contact in the Met for advice. He was told that in order to find the man responsible for interfering with his daughter's virtue, he would need to build a picture of her movements from around that time. In Theo's day cash was king, but amongst the younger generation that was no longer the case. They carried very little actual money and used their bank cards to pay for most things. If he could get a look at her bank statements for the last few months, her spending history would be a helpful place to start. He wanted to kick himself for not working that out. But admittedly, his expertise wasn't in the subtle end of the market.

Following their enlightening family conference, Theo had arranged for a civilian driver to take Abigail to school each day and collect her again at home time. This unenviable task had fallen to a barman known as Cooch. Who had experienced the indignity of a prolonged grilling regarding his sexual preference. Before having the job forced on him when Theo was 100% sure he was gay. Now each day Cooch collected her at 8.30 am in the little Peugeot gifted to him as a perk of the job. It meant getting up early, but he didn't really mind. As now, he could travel to see his old mom in Southend at weekends and go cottaging in the week.

Theo sat moodily stirring his cup of coffee in the café immediately opposite to the entrance of Cranbourne Mews. London's underworld was enjoying a few days' unexpected rest from his attentions. Nothing was as important to him as finding the slag that had groomed his daughter. So the late payers, skimmers and grasses could wait for the time being. This was personal...

Bang on 8.25 am, the little Peugeot bobbed into sight and

turned left onto the cobbled street. Exactly six minutes later, Theo watched as it departed with his daughter in the passenger seat. He swigged off the last of his coffee and thanked the owner as he left. No payment was necessary. The patron was just happy to survive the unannounced visit without injury. It's not every day that Theo Robertson walks into your café with a face like thunder. He had spent the first five minutes desperately trying to recall anything he might have done to offend him. But when your life mainly revolves around frying eggs and pigmeat, it doesn't leave a lot of time for crossing gangland bosses. So a free coffee and twenty minutes where you didn't sell a lot seemed a small price to pay. As it would seem the sight of Theo Robertson sat in the window did little to encourage passing trade.

Theo crossed the road and strode up the mews towards the property he paid the mortgage on but rarely set foot in. Cecelia must have been waiting behind the curtains as once again the door opened without him ringing the doorbell. Abigail's parents had a cordial relationship rather than the acid flavoured one that you might expect. Cecelia had never openly sought the company of other men once Theo had decided that monogamy was not for him. Instead, she had contented herself with raising their daughter and appearing to hope that one day he might tire of barmaids and strippers and return to her arms. But then, she didn't really have much of a choice. As there weren't many men who would knowingly swipe right for the ex-partner of a psychotic underworld kingpin. So for the last seventeen years, she had been a pitiful example of a bird in a gilded cage.

"Coffee?"

"No, thanks just had one in the cafe at the end of the road while I waited for her to go."

"So what do you want to look at?"

"Her laptop. I want to see her bank statements."

Cecelia nodded without fully understanding. But she knew that when Theo had that look on his face it wasn't always a wise idea to ask too many questions. So she led the way up to Abigail's bedroom. The late Winter sun filled what had always been a very pleasant room. It was a long time since he had been in here, and even longer since he sat at the side of the bed reading bedtime stories to his little girl. Often leaving to bring unspeakable pain to someone else's daddy on the other side of the river when she'd finally dropped off to sleep. He looked around at the pop posters on the wall that were now just relics of those innocent times, or so he thought. Beaming down at him from the one right above her bed was Electric Fondue. Pictured leaning against a large American classic car on their 2013 US breakthrough tour. Cecelia booted up Abigail's laptop while he passed the awkward delay, looking out of the window to the pretty cobbled street below. He blamed her for letting their daughter run wild across the capital while she sat watching Strictly Come Dancing and Monty Don's gardening programs. If she had paid more attention to where she was going he wouldn't need to be snooping around to find out who with.

Teenagers can be secretive, but also reckless. Abigail's laptop had no password protection, and the login for the banking app was easy for them to guess. As across the room sat on her bed was the fluffy toy rabbit that she had since she was a child. 'Flopsy' got them in and soon they were combing through her purchase history. As they moved back through recent months paying close attention to weekends, one entry kept recurring, 'Blue Lagoon'. It would seem that whatever this was, Abigail regularly spent quite a lot of money there. Theo sat back and pulled out his phone. A quick internet search revealed 'Blue Lagoon' to be an exclusive cocktail bar in Bayswater. He decided that would be as good a place as any to start his enquiries. So Cecelia powered down the laptop, ensuring that she replaced it exactly where she found it. She doubted that Abigail would notice any slight movement of her things, but it always made sense to be careful.

"Right at last I have something to go on. I'll pop round there and see what they know about who our daughter is hanging about with. Then I will furthermore provide them with instruction in relation to serving alcohol to minors."

"By instruction, I take it you mean violence, destruction and mayhem?"

"Not really. Just a little up close chat. If I make too much fuss, it might get back to whoever I'm looking for and that would be counterproductive when they go to ground!"

With that, he scrolled through the contacts on his phone and lifted it to his ear.

"You'll see. I can be a man of the people when I want to be… Hello Barney? Yeah, pick me up at Cecelia's as soon as…"

Fifteen minutes later a familiar black BMW turned into Cranbourne Mews and drew to a standstill outside. Theo was in the passenger seat before Barney had any need to announce his arrival. Leaving Cecelia readying her lounge to host that morning's Cranbourne Book Club.

"Where to, boss?"

"Queensway in Bayswater, a cocktail bar called Blue Lagoon. Do you know it?"

"With respect, do I look like someone that hangs around in cocktail bars in Bayswater?"

Barney had a point. He was a six-foot-three muscular ex Para with a shaven head and a penchant for black leather jackets. At the last count, he had eight. When asked, he would always reply that they were wipe clean and durable. Making them a popular choice for the gangland enforcer about town. His presence in a cocktail bar would shatter the ambience to the point of him being the only person in there five minutes later. Once again Theo pulled out his phone to show him the location on Google maps as they swept out of the mews. Barney didn't ask why they were going there or who they would see. His position in the structure of Theo's enterprise didn't encourage curiosity. He just drove, held, threatened or punched on command.

It was a little after ten-thirty when they pulled into a parking space on Queensway. A busy street in the heart of Bayswater that was home to a wide range of bars and restaurants. Blue Lagoon had an inconspicuous black door with only a small sign above it to announce its presence. If you didn't know it was there, you would have missed it. Theo rang the delivery bell, and they waited quietly to see if they could hear movement within. Seconds later they heard a murmur of voices and feet climbing stairs before the door opened. Revealing a short pale man in a Hawaiian shirt and white cotton shorts with sunglasses set on top of his head. Never one to be unduly taken aback by unseasonal beach wear, Barney grabbed him by the throat and hurled him back down the stairs. As Theo quickly followed in his wake, closing the door behind them.

The man now lay in a dishevelled heap at the bottom of the narrow set of stairs as his two unexpected guests calmly descended to provide him with much-needed detail in relation to the reason for their visit. His sunglasses now lay beside him in a way that strongly suggested they might require extensive repair before he next wore them.

"So who the fuck might you be?" inquired Theo, squatting beside him.

"It's my bar. People call me Cocktail Kevin or CK if you prefer"

"Is your name Kevin?"

"Err yes…"

"And you make cocktails I presume?"

"Err yes…"

"Then I would consider that to be a true classic in the vast and eclectic world of nicknames. Following the unwritten rules to the letter. Accurate, descriptive and catchy. As a traditionalist, I'm not fond of the American habit of shortening names to initials. I see it as disrespectful to the time and effort that goes into naming a child. So if it's OK with you, I will address you as Kevin during our visit. Who else is here?"

"No one, I was talking to the radio."

Sensing the critical need for absolute honesty at this point in the conversation, Barney placed his booted foot on Kevin's genitals. Grinning as he found the sweet spot and the little barman gasped.

"I was doing PopMaster on Radio 2 with Ken Bruce. I do it every day while I'm bottling up. I thought you were the bloke delivering the mixers. So I was cursing you for arriving while it was on."

Satisfied with the further detail he had provided and seeing no need for increased pressure, Barney relaxed his foot. In the background, Nadine from Chipping Sodbury was struggling with the first question.

"The Real Thing…" said Kevin.

"What's the Real Thing, Coke?" replied Theo.

"No! Who sang You to Me Are Everything in 1976…"

"Wasn't that Hot Chocolate?" said Barney.

"A common misconception, but no, it was The Real Thing," corrected Kevin

"Sorry Nadine, unfortunately that was The Real Thing," said Ken Bruce.

"Told you so" retorted Kevin cockily.

"Are you really going to take issue with us over a point of pop trivia while Barney's boot is poised to turn your meat and two veg into the world's tiniest novelty haggis?"

"Sorry point taken, but I take my pop trivia very seriously. I'm in a travelling pub quiz team and we go all over London competing."

"Kevin, as pleasing as it is to hear you have a social life away from your labours that promotes the work of recording artists from a bygone era. Frankly, I feel that you are failing to grasp the gravity of the situation. Barney is six foot three and tips the scales at around sixteen and a half stone of ball crushing muscle. Whereas your cobblers have all the structural integrity of two softly boiled quail's eggs wrapped in a slice of Parma ham. So should I lose my patience with your inability to afford me what I consider to be an adequate level of respect. And instead, continue to insist on prioritising the ramblings of an admittedly entertaining bald-headed veteran Scots broadcaster. Then I will have no option but to instruct Barney to bring his full weight to bear on the matter. Whilst I plainly possess no formal qualifications in urology. It's fairly safe to say that from there onwards the continuation of your family name will almost certainly fall to one of your male siblings. If by some enormous stroke of bad luck, you are an only child or raised in the bosom of a family unduly dominated by the fairer sex, your bloodline will die right fucking there."

"So, why don't we make ourselves more comfortable and we can explain the reason for our visit? But if at any point I feel that you are not answering the questions truthfully or are being in any way evasive. I will instruct Barney here to further re-apply his large boot to your adult entertainment area. Am I making myself clear?"

Kevin nodded energetically, but Barney knew that like a Pantomime dame, Theo preferred to hear his audience roar. Once again, without words passing between them, he renewed his pressure on the unfortunate barman's groin.

"Yes, yes, perfectly clear. More than happy to help!!!" screamed Kevin.

Barney removed his foot, allowing his victim to climb slowly to his feet. The reverse skydive from the top of the stairs had taken its toll, and it was some seconds before he was fully upright. Kevin led the way through into the bar as his tormentors cautiously scanned the room for any sign of threat before entering. It was a well-designed space with a great deal of seating for what was after all just the repurposed basement of a high street shop. The décor was bright and breezy with a cheery tropical vibe which fitted its name perfectly. The bar area itself being entirely constructed of bamboo poles which loosely resembled the Kontiki. Evidently, much thought had been given to colour and lighting to create the illusion of a sun-kissed beach bar in the Caribbean rather than a dingy shop cellar in London.

"Ah, now the Magnum P.I. workwear all makes sense," laughed Theo, taking in the décor and selecting a booth close to the bar that still allowed him an unobstructed view of the stairs. Barney went behind the bar to turn the radio off and indicated that Kevin should also take a seat. Then hovered menacingly, hands clasped in front of him like a bald choirboy with a growth hormone imbalance.

"OK, so let's get to the point. I believe that my daughter has been frequenting your establishment on a fairly regular basis at weekends. Whilst I understand that you can't be expected to ask for the I.D. of every adolescent girl who comes in here. I'm still a little upset to discover that you have been allowing her to drink alcohol whilst underage. Are you with me so far?"

Again Kevin nodded enthusiastically, but hearing Barney shift his weight beside him, blurted out, "Yes, yes…"

"Now whilst I'm obviously disappointed that your apparent lack of civic responsibility has led to my little girl making some rather poor life choices. I'm willing to overlook this if you can provide me with information regarding any of the gentlemen that you might have seen her in the company of."

Theo placed his phone face up on the table, displaying a picture of Abigail in her school uniform. Deliberately chosen to convey her appearance whilst further enforcing the fact that she was still a minor.

"Yes, I know her. You're right, she comes in a lot. She can't get enough of my Pink Parrot."

"She can't get enough of your fucking what?!" hissed Theo.

"My Pink Parrot, she says it's the best she's ever had! Coconut

Rum, Raspberry Liqueur, Fresh lime juice topped with four raspberries."

"So now not only have you been selling my underage daughter alcohol, but it's a cocktail with a name based on a double entendre for a man's rampant appendage?"

"Whoops see your point. I never thought of it like that. It was in a book of famous cocktail recipes, and as it fitted with the theme of the bar, I put it on the menu."

"So setting aside my daughter's predilection for drinks with dodgy names. Can you remember who you've seen her drinking with?"

"In fairness, she's a very popular girl, and she has made a lot of friends in here."

"Boss with all due respect, might it be appropriate for me to say something at this point?" interjected Barney.

Theo nodded glumly and put his phone away as Barney punched Cocktail Kevin hard in the face. Who screamed as his nose made an audible crack.

"I thought you were just going to say something?" he screamed.

"I did, but it took the form of a mime. It's a work in progress which I have loosely entitled Be More Respectful When You're Answering the Fucking Questions."

"Sorry I neglected to mention that Barney here is a big fan of Marcel Marceau. Though you might also be a lover of classic French mime artists. I would strongly discourage you from saying anything else that might mistakenly offer the impression that my daughter has been somewhat free with her favours. Otherwise, he might decide to give you his full tribute act. Which could very well leave you having to add a cocktail to the menu called the Beach-coma."

Cocktail Kevin now had blood streaming from his nose, which

was adding a new edgy dimension to his Hawaiian shirt as he tried to staunch the flow with several paper napkins.

"Let me put it another way. Can you think of anyone in here that she is particularly close to?"

"She spends a lot of time with the 2Ds."

"Ah good. Now all thanks to the art of mime, we're finally getting somewhere,. And exactly who might the 2Ds be?"

"They're famous pop stars. I've got two CD's of theirs behind the bar."

Barney moved to allow Kevin to rise out of the booth and with one hand still clutching enough napkins to block King Kong's toilet, he disappeared behind the bamboo bar. Emerging moments later with a CD and a signed photo.

"Surely you must have heard of them? They wear animal heads on stage. They've been in the charts for years…"

Theo wasn't a fan of popular music. He was more of a Radio 4 man. He enjoyed lively discourse, documentaries and political satire. Even as a younger man he hadn't bothered with the clubs and bars favoured by his peers. He was too busy learning the gangland ropes so that one day he could simply own them instead. When you were a face on the manor, women came to you. You didn't need to bop around all night buying overpriced drinks, hoping for a knee-trembler on the way home.

"No, sad to say their work has passed me by," he said taking 2014's 'Standing Out In A Crowd' from Kevin's outstretched blood-stained hand. The cover showed two men that Theo estimated were in their mid-twenties riding matching Raleigh Choppers through a packed market. Whilst the market goers recoiled with varied expressions of freeze-framed shock as they passed by. However, the signed photo was a studio shot, possibly taken some years earlier. The 2Ds were back to back looking at the camera, each with an outstretched arm making a gang-style hand gesture. The photo was signed in the blank space under the image and dedicated to "Cocktail Kevin, the best barman in London!".

"So tell me, which of these two talented minstrels has my daughter shown the most interest in?"

"Search me. I can't tell them apart. They would usually come in at about nine and stop till closing time. Then all leave together."

Realising at once what that might suggest, Kevin cowered expecting another visit from Barney's fist. But ever the skilled interrogator, Theo waved it away. Instead, allowing the flow of information to continue unimpeded.

"So when was the last time you saw them?"

"That's the odd part. They were as regular as clockwork until a couple of weeks ago. Then they just vanished and I haven't seen them since. Your daughter has even been in looking for them. So chances are she doesn't know where they are either."

Theo didn't enjoy mysteries, he liked hard facts. But as it was fairly certain Kevin had now told them all he knew. There didn't seem much point in getting Barney to work him over for anything further he might have forgotten. In his experience, one mild slap was enough to focus the mind of most civilians. Further treatment just encouraged them to make things up to stop getting whacked. After which it left you with the problem of working out what was the truth and what was fist talk.

He turned the CD case over in his hand and read the small print on the back. Taking two fifty-pound notes from his wallet, he pushed them across the table towards Cocktail Kevin.

"Right, we'll get off now. Here's a ton for a new shirt and sunglasses. Mind if I keep these?"

Cocktail Kevin shook his head dejectedly. It didn't seem wise to refuse.

"Right then we'll see ourselves out. Oh, and remember to review your underage drinking policy. The Old Bill might not be quite so accommodating if they decide to pop round for a chat."

Kevin watched them climb the stairs and listened as the door to the street outside closed behind them. If he was lucky, he might just catch the second round of PopMaster.

Chapter 12

Hugh had long since relaxed his iron grip on the wayward twins when he saw how well they were responding to the tough love therapy. Now their youthful exuberance had returned. He needed a brief respite now and then. The album wouldn't mix itself, and having them on his shoulder throughout the entire process was grating. Their grasshopper minds made getting anything finished an uphill battle with constant interruptions and "let's just try this" light bulb moments.

Life on Holy Island was growing on the 2Ds. Thanks to the long walks, good food and sea air, they considered themselves to be making great music once again. At first, they were totally disorientated outside the London bubble. But as their resentment calmed and resignation took over, they saw the benefits of living in a small island community. When they first arrived, no one had given them as much as a second glance. One tourist looked very much like another and the selection of waterproof clothing that Hugh had provided, gave no hint of the millionaire pop stars that lurked beneath the brightly coloured nylon. But as the climate gradually improved, and they could venture out without wet weather gear. Their metropolitan sense of style marked them out from the walkers and twitchers that formed the backbone of tourism on the island. Gradually the younger islanders noticed the two Cockney lads staying down at Priory Studios, and it wasn't long before they worked out who they were.

Just like the rest of Britain, Lindisfarne had seen an explosion in the popularity of coffee in the last few years. Since the cast of Friends sat on odd sofa's in Central Perk drinking from enormous cups, an instant brew really wouldn't do. Now holidaymakers expected to find the same great coffee that they drank in the big chains at home. So the old greasy spoons were long gone. Replaced by bijou coffee houses with funky décor, a fair trade ethos and enough sourdough toast to build a life raft. Steam pressured roasts with exotic Italian names made going out for coffee a holiday experience for sharing on social media just like any other.

Now when they felt the friction factor climbing in the studio. The twins would adjourn to their favourite coffee shop, The Village Idiot. Which was essentially a covered atrium between two old stone buildings with a clear plastic corrugated roof supported by thick honey-coloured pine beams. Underfoot, uneven sandstone flags added to the overall artisan nature of the structure. So when the rain pounded down, which it often did. It was entirely possible to marvel at mother nature's fury from beside the roaring log burner. Whilst enjoying a flat white and a Pain au Chocolat fresh from the oven that morning.

This quirky establishment was run by Zab and occupied a prime spot in the centre of the village. Here they were amongst friends as the little eaterie served as the unofficial headquarters of Lindisfarne's thriving artistic community. Who it was safe to say had taken the multi-platinum selling keyboard kings to their hearts. There they would hold court on the long wooden benches and tables. Telling tales of London and the famous people that they knew. Sometimes even being a little indiscreet without revealing identities and holding everyone spellbound as they tried to guess who they were talking about.

Zab was a fast-talking Asian entrepreneur with a history of dubious 'get rich quick' schemes. The latest of which was selling dried medicinal seaweed to tourists whilst loosely claiming it had mystical healing properties. This had become so lucrative he had bought a small fishing boat with which to harvest it from the more inaccessible places where it grew along the coast. He then landed this back at an old fisherman's hut that he had rented down on the shoreline. Here it dried on racks aided by the biting North Sea wind which whistled through the gaps between the ancient blue planks. Before taking it up to his house, a bread crate full at a time, and grinding it up in a rather primitive industrial coffee grinder. Somewhere during this process, it went from being plain old red seaweed to Zabga Tea at £10 for a 20-gramme sachet. Which he shamelessly peddled to tourists who displayed any obvious physical ailment. And in the three years, it had been available, claimed success with everything from Glue Ear to Jock Itch. Aided by his resident band of truth-tellers who would enthusiastically endorse his sales pitch by claiming to know someone similarly afflicted who saw enormous improvement with its continued use.

But it wasn't the clientele, the coffee or even the Zabga Tea that kept the 2Ds coming back. The credit for that went to a rather sassy young waitress called Daisy. Who kept the place running while Zab did very little except talk. But she didn't seem to mind too much as she zipped around between the long pine benches, taking orders and delivering coffee. Occasionally poking Zab into life when there was too much work for one. Knowing that he would soon drift back to idleness amongst the artists, potters and musicians who sometimes seemed to be the actual reason for The Village Idiot's existence.

The speed at which Daisy moved and her no-nonsense attitude to the customers made her a hard person to get to know. Declan had become rather accustomed to his fame making the introductions. But this would not be the case with Daisy. There weren't any VIP night club booths on Holy Island and no flunkies to deliver the invite. Instead, there was just what there had always been. Eye contact, body language, and stolen smiles. It would be a long job, but then he had the time to invest.

After one particularly tortuous recording session, Declan ventured out for a coffee alone. Dominic was feeling a bit out of sorts and was spending the downtime lying on his bed with a book. He was having a few problems with his voice and had wisely deduced that an hour's solitude would be a better remedy than two shots of espresso and laughing about the hair products in Elton John's bathroom with the Lindisfarne Massive.

So it was a surprise to the lone Declan as he rounded the corner into Marygate with nothing on his mind other than the choice of what cookie to have with his coffee, to run into Daisy coming the other way.

"Hello, Pop Star!"

It had never been Daisy's way to provide either of the brother's with any form of adulation. Instead, she spent much of her time poking fun at their London ways and referring to them as Cheese on Toast instead of Electric Fondue. But then her irreverent approach to life formed a significant part of the attraction, with her long legs and curvaceous figure providing the rest. She had no airs and graces and happily said what she thought. If that meant telling her boss he was a slacker, then that's what she did.

"What's up? Where are you off to?"

"Got an urgent pick up at the secret bakery. I've left Zab holding the fort while I'm gone. So if you want your coffee done the way you like it, I'd wait for me to get back before you order."

The twins had long suspected that Zab's bold claim his grandmother made all the biscuits and cakes in The Village Idiot to a secret family recipe was a lie. Firstly, he was the only Asian they had encountered in the several weeks they had been in residence. Secondly, they had seen very similar cakes for sale in other establishments and it seemed unlikely that any octogenarian baker would have sufficient output to supply the entire island on a daily basis.

"Mind if I tag along then?"

"As long as you promise to take the location of the secret bakery to your grave. If Zab found out you knew, it could see you end your days swimming with the fishes."

"OK, duly noted, I'll take my chances and hope I don't break under interrogation."

"So how's the recording going?"

"Pretty well to be fair. We've got eight tracks finished and mixed with four more roughed out ready to record properly."

"So you have been doing something other than drinking coffee and eating?"

"Not stopped working since we got here. Our producer is a slave driver."

"So back down South soon to see your supermodel then?"

That comment delighted Declan, but he tried hard not to show it! This was the only obvious sign of interest that he'd ever got from Daisy. She was surely fishing for detail…

"Nope, there's no one waiting for me down there. Dominic has a girlfriend, but he only sees her at weekends because she's cabin crew and always on long-haul routes in the week."

"You honestly expect me to believe that?"

"Why not? It's the truth."

"So no Mrs Cheese on Toast or any little toasties?"

"I think you're stretching the cheese thing a bit now."

"Getting too stringy for you?" she laughed. Pushing slim fingers through her shoulder-length chestnut hair as they turned into Lewins Lane.

"So what do you do for fun at night around here?"

"In the Winter we mainly just drink. In the summer it's more varied. Then we sit outside and drink. What do you do in London?"

"Pretty much the same…"

"So are you going to ask me out for a drink then?"

"I would, but there's a bit of an issue with that. I'm not allowed to drink."

"Says who?"

"Our manager. We came up here to get away from the temptations of London so we could record with no distractions.

So we're banned from anywhere that sells booze. Maybe we could go for coffee?"

"Never touch the stuff! I can never understand how people drink it. It's like dirty water that slugs have drowned in. Besides, it's what I do all day. I go home and shower to get rid of the smell. It's like working in Lush, it just sticks to you."

"What about if we went for a walk?"

"A walk?"

"A walk with a bottle and two glasses, maybe?"

"Let me guess, I'm in charge of acquisitions?"

"Unless you want me confined to barracks and chained to a keyboard, then I'm afraid you are."

"OK, Mr Romance, you're on."

By now they had ambled most of the way down Lewins Lane when Daisy pushed open the gate of a fairly ordinary-looking bungalow and walked up the crazy-paved path. Declan followed, looking puzzled as it didn't look much like a bakery. Secret or otherwise! He expected her to ring the doorbell. Instead, she followed the path to a side gate and ushered him through before shutting it behind them. As they made their way round to the back of the house, he noticed a frantic banging. Which seemed to come from a large corrugated iron shed that occupied most of the scruffy backyard. It looked more like something for keeping chickens in, rather than a food production premises. However, a large open wheelie bin confirmed to him it was, in fact, a bakery. As its contents were almost exclusively screwed up flour bags and empty catering tubs of margarine.

As Daisy pushed open the door, the noise got louder. Through the dusty air, he could make out the rotund figure of a rather short man throwing around an enormous lump of dough on what appeared to be an old school desk. As they entered, the man looked up, and it stunned Declan to see a cigarette dangling from his mouth.

"Afternoon Doris! I've come for Zab's order."

"It's there on the side in the blue tub. Make sure I get the tub back or I'll charge him for it. I saw him lugging his shitty fucking seaweed in one of my tubs yesterday. He's nothing but a thieving piss taker!"

As the conversation progressed, Declan deduced two things. One, as the name suggests, Doris was actually a small angry woman. Two, she swore an awful lot.

Thanks to The Great British Bake off, he had always assumed that baking was solely the pursuit of students, yummy mummies, bored O.A.Ps and rather flamboyant men. Now faced by a Yoda lookalike with nicotine-stained fingers and filthy white overalls, he hastily revised this misconception. Obviously, the more authentic looking entrants got weeded out at the audition stage. Perhaps when they lit up a B & H in the middle of making creme patisserie and scratched their arse with the handle of the spoon?

At 6.45 pm that evening after dinner, Declan announced he was going for a walk to clear his head. He was fortunate in that Dominic had again sloped off to read his book and Hugh was showing all the signs of a man about to doze in front of the fire. So when he put his jacket on and slipped out into the night, he didn't face an inquisition regarding his intentions. A popstar that didn't possess a mobile phone had amused Daisy. So Declan just made out that it was normal practice when they were recording. To prevent unnecessary interruptions, impeding the artistic process. So they arranged to meet by the Priory Ruins at 7 pm. There was only a sliver of a moon as he walked along Church Lane and turned left into Lewins Lane for the second time in a matter of hours. It had rained about an hour ago, so he kept to the official path when he reached the ancient ruins to save getting his feet wet. There were quicker paths to take, worn into the grass by successive generations of tourists. But recent experience told him that these quickly turned to mud at the first sign of rain.

He settled on a damp bench and waited for his date to arrive. Realising that he felt skittish and maybe a little sick. Nerves weren't a familiar sensation to him as he rarely did things on his own. It had always been so easy to be bullish when there were two of you against the world. But now sat there alone with all the trappings of fame stripped away, he was just a boy, waiting for a girl...

He could hear Daisy long before he could see her. The bottle and glasses making a clinking sound in her bag with every step she took as she progressed along the same path towards him.

"Hello, Popstar!"

"You've got to stop calling me that. It's embarrassing."

"But it's what you are, isn't it?"

"I suppose, but since I've been here I've been thinking about that."

"In what way?"

"I dunno. It's all I've known since I left school. I'm starting to wonder if there's more to life than an endless cycle of writing, recording and touring."

"Well, let's not get too deep yet, eh? Why don't we drink this on Zab's boat? He's got a little heater on there and we can listen to the radio while you tell me all about your fancy showbiz life and I play Eliza Doolittle listening enthralled at your feet."

She had a point. It wasn't the warmest of nights and the damp from the bench was slowly penetrating his jeans. A romantic night out of the cold on an old fishing boat was a far better option. So arm in arm they clinked off into the darkness.

Chapter 13

Robin Sparrow was on the phone when he noticed the raised voices coming from reception. He was holding for Richard Branson, who had failed to return his previous six calls. But then he was all about the planes and trains these days. That's when he wasn't trying to kill himself in a hot air balloon or flogging cheap cola.

Robin had spent the last couple of days ringing everyone that he knew in the business to brag about Electric Fondue being booked to headline Glastonbury. He had also been in talks with the CD manufacturers to ensure that they had adequate re-issues available to flood onto supermarket shelves when the fans went mad for their old stuff following a triumphant comeback. He had even arranged for Amazon to promote their back catalogue with an e-mail campaign, literally the moment they stepped off the centre stage. This would be a money waterfall and Robin would make sure he was right under it, lathering his balls like a teenage virgin preparing for a first date.

Like most music moguls, he chose his reception staff carefully. Preferring the nosey Rottweiler type that you sometimes encounter at doctor's surgeries. Handpicked to protect Robin from the great unwashed. He didn't offer a walk-in surgery; it was strictly appointments only. It had to be that way, otherwise you would get nothing done. If you entertained just one throng of foppish kids wearing homemade stage clothes and clutching a supposedly sure-fire No1, word spread. Next thing you're knee-deep in hopeless hopefuls and forced to put additional security down in the foyer to weed them out before they got anywhere near you. Leading to bitter complaints about the disruption from the building's management, who might further demonstrate their displeasure with a rent rise in time to come.

Branson was evidently banging another air stewardess and therefore couldn't be disturbed. Reluctantly, Robin put down the phone. Not for one second did it enter his head that he was an odious little turd that no one further up the food chain wanted to speak to. He could hear the disturbance was getting closer and decided that he would make a rare appearance in reception. Sometimes just appearing and offering a few words of encouragement to a ginger kid in glasses who couldn't grow a beard, was enough to get them back into the lift. Admittedly, he should have taken the time to play Ed Sheeran's demo CD, but then every self-respecting pop Svengali had an 'I turned down the Beatles' story.

Just as he reached out to twist the handle, the door flew inwards bending back his wrist and causing him to yell in pain. In trooped Theo Robertson and Barney, followed by Mindy, Robin's secretary. Who usually formed his second line of defence but on this occasion had been about as useful as the Maginot Line. Two-nil to Blitzkrieg.

"I'm very sorry Robin, they just barged past me. I have nothing down for them in the diary, and they're being very forceful. Shall I call security?"

Robin had spent little time in the company of gangsters, but he instantly recognised Theo Robertson from the newspapers. From what he had read, he felt sure that his head would resemble a crushed pork pie before security was even in the lift. Then he relaxed. At least the building had a sprinkler system, with absolutely no fire extinguishers close to hand. This was bound to be about some waitress in one of his clubs who had got up to do a bit of Whitney Houston on the karaoke. All he needed to do was take the CD and look encouraging. Then get her a support gig somewhere shite and he would eventually lose interest.

"No need for that, Mindy. I can always make time for important people with exciting news about breaking talent. Please, Mr Robertson, make yourself comfortable. Can I offer you and your associate a drink?"

Mindy looked doubtful, as they certainly didn't resemble talent scouts. But did as her boss said, quickly retreating from the room and closing the door behind her.

"That's very gracious of you. Would you have any ginger beer? Or ginger ale at a push?"

Robin selected mixer sized bottles of Canada Dry Ginger Ale from the drinks cabinet, pulled off the tops, emptied them into three tumblers and added ice. Theo and Barney took a tumbler each and Robin sat down on the opposite sofa.

"So what can I do for you gentlemen?" he said turning the corporate charm up to its maximum setting.

"We wondered if you might tell us the whereabouts of these gentlemen?" replied Theo taking the signed photo out of his pocket and passing it to Robin.

That caught Robin entirely off guard. He was expecting to endure three minutes of some Eliza Doolittle murdering an 80s classic or some less than gifted warbling from a favourite niece. What he hadn't expected was a missing person enquiry involving two of the best-selling artists on his label.

"Might I be so bold as to inquire of the nature of your business with Declan and Dominic before answering your question?"

"I'm afraid I was rather hoping to keep that on a need to know basis for the time being. It's a personal matter and I would prefer to speak to them about it directly."

"Naturally whilst I entirely respect your need for discretion. You must understand as a businessman that I can't allow one of my best-selling acts to have their creative flow interrupted whilst they are working."

"You're absolutely right, it would be a great shame to impede their creative flow and I anticipated your understandable reluctance to reveal their whereabouts to us. No doubt based on the sensationalised accounts of my business activities that appear from time to time in the popular press. However, I think you would probably prefer that to Barney here impeding your urine flow for the foreseeable future. I often find that the realities of pissing through a catheter for six months can quickly make one man reassess his confidentiality obligations to another."

Robin didn't like the way the conversation was going. Judging from the flecks of dried blood that he could see on Barney's hand, he hadn't been their first call this morning.

"Well, when you put it like that, I gather we are not talking about a minor misdemeanour. If it's a simple matter of payment for a debt, however excessive. I would be happy to arrange remittance within the hour, paid directly into a bank account of your choosing. Or perhaps in cash, if you prefer. Should you be able to give me a little longer to secure the necessary funds?"

"Once again, I assure you that the matter in question is not related to finance. As previously stated, it's rather more personal than that and not something that can be dealt with by proxy. So if I can be slightly more direct. Tell us where they are or Barney here will pummel you like out-of-date Play Dough until you do."

Mindy had very little interest in the often dodgy business dealings of her pint-sized boss. But she had stretched her legs far enough around the block to know when he was way out of his depth. After shutting the door behind her, she had quietly opened the intercom line into his office. She often did this to see if she could pick up any titbits from his phone calls that she could sell to a contact from the Sun she sometimes met in a bar at lunchtime. But it was clear this wasn't about a defaulted payment. It was far more serious than that. Robin was obviously stalling for time while he tried to work out exactly what Theo wanted. There was a slight tremble in his voice that she hadn't heard before. Robin Sparrow was scared, and she was probably the only one that could save him.

It would be difficult to decide who was the most surprised when Mindy walked into Robin's office singing Happy Birthday with a borrowed birthday cake and the entire staff of Blue Sky Records behind her. Robin, who by this time had run out of 'clever dick chat' and was playing an alternative game of kiss chase with Barney around his desk. Except the kisses were in fact punches, and they definitely wouldn't be going to the end of term school disco together. Barney, who by now, was listing in breathy detail the unspeakable things that he would do when he caught him. Or Theo, who was reclining on the settee enjoying his ginger ale and watching the spectacle with growing amusement.

Theo was realistic enough to know when he had been outsmarted. Everyone in the room knew it wasn't Robin's birthday, including him. Sometimes a few spectators could be desirable. Especially if they knew they were next in line to get a pummelling. It focussed minds and loosened tongues. However, seventeen was a little beyond the pale, so he reluctantly accepted that it was time to go. He called Barney to heel and rose from the settee.

Robin had the relieved look of an asthmatic hare who had just outrun a homicidal lurcher. He had been on the cusp of blurting out that the 2Ds were somewhere up North in a recording studio when the cavalry had arrived. He doubted that would have sufficed and feared that further violence would have only revealed his complete ignorance of their exact location and the geography of Northern England in general.

"Well, be sure to have a nice birthday Mr Sparrow. We can see ourselves out. Hopefully, we can reconvene at a later date when hopefully you will be better equipped to assist with our enquiries?"

Then as the seventeen brave souls crammed into Robin's office parted like a very nervous Red Sea, he walked out of the room followed by an extremely sweaty Barney. Who now fully understood exactly why tracksuits weren't available in black leather.

"So what now boss?" said Barney slowly recovering his composure as the lift took them back down to main reception.

"Truth is Barney, I'm not sure. A rich man like Mr Sparrow will almost certainly have a team of highly trained personal bodyguards on hand should we be stupid enough to revisit him in the near future. But then I'm sure if he knew where they were, he would have told us as soon as we put the frighteners on. I've met a lot of Robin Sparrows in my time. They're rarely brave men, nor are they loyal. So we can only assume that he doesn't know where they are either. Presumably, there's a reason for that. Once we know what that is, then I'm sure we'll find them."

Robin was slowly recovering on one of his vast sofas with a medicinal cognac and Mindy massaging his shoulders. She had worked for Robin since the early days and knew that she was too old to find such another well paid cushy number. In all honesty, she had found the idea of him getting a few digs initially strangely appealing. Until it was apparent that abduction and murder were also on the cards. Ultimately leading to unemployment for her, which wasn't so enticing.

"So what was that all about?" she asked as the tiny impresario's hyperventilation finally subsided as she ground deep into his shoulders.

"I honestly have no idea whatsoever! It would appear that they were looking for the 2Ds. They wouldn't even tell me what for. I thought at first given their recent cocaine intake that it might be a drugs debt or even a gambling tab that they hadn't coughed up for. But they weren't interested in money, they just wanted to know where they were. Believe me, I would have told them if I knew! There's more sophisticated bridgework in my mouth than spanning the River Forth. One good smack in the trap from that goon and I would spend the next two years in the dentist's chair..."

Mindy set her face to 'listen' as Robin provided a lengthy potted history of his dental work. She knew exactly where the 2Ds were, but she definitely wasn't going to tell him that…

Chapter 14

Nigel's persona leaked from his every pore. So it was easy to see that he wanted something when he sidled up to Martin's section straight after lunch. The unusually informal conversation and frequent use of the word 'mate' gave him away. Martin listened as he rambled on about the preparations for Tool Aid and how excited everyone was at head office to have such a talented musician as an associate. This was surely the leverage to show what great pals they were before he got hit with a week's worth of graveyard shifts. Or a section pre stock take, just before the actual stock take. So the counts could be 'massaged' as necessary to make Nigel look like the supervisor of the year when the figures went in.

"While I'm here I was wondering if you might be willing to do me a favour?"

"I will if I can…" Martin hoped to God that it wasn't running up hills in the rain again.

"I've noticed that you and Debbie have become rather close in recent weeks. As you might have gathered, I have a soft spot for her colleague Magda. So I wondered if you could put in a word for me? Perhaps we could go on a double date or all have dinner together one night?"

Martin was aware of Nigel's interest in Magda as it was a source of great amusement within the workforce. He also knew that Debbie's Polish colleague had a strong preference for rather tall black men, and therefore presumably little or no interest in weedy white fell runners who still lived with their mother. Plus, as an evening out, it had all the appeal of a trip to a nose picking dentist with a hand-washing phobia.

"Wow… erm… OK. I wasn't expecting that. Are you sure? I mean, the last bloke she went out with was a six-foot-three cage fighter."

He was actually a photocopier engineer and part-time pastor. But Martin hoped that the possibility of being bounced off four walls might help to curb his enthusiasm. When in fact he was rather more likely to fix his printer and lead him in prayer.

"I'm deadly serious. I think she's amazing. The eyes she gives me when she twists the steam knob on the coffee machine tells me she's ready for a change."

Nigel evidently didn't recognise Magda's 'death stare'. Resulting from his regular order of a Coconut Latte with three pumps of vanilla, one pump of caramel and a micro sprinkling of cinnamon. It was more of an ice cream sundae than a coffee and took five minutes to prepare. Whilst he lingered like a sex-starved meerkat and the butty and brew crew quietly seethed behind him in the queue.

"Well, I can't promise anything, you know what women are like…"

Nigel had absolutely no idea at all what women were like. The only women he had prolonged contact with, was his mother and the rather bossy sexless nurse at the asthma clinic. Neither of which gave him any opportunity to gain a greater understanding of the female species. In desperation, he had taken to reading his mother's magazines. But as she was a firm fan of The People's Friend and Take a Break rather than Cosmopolitan. This had only coloured his dreams with tweed induced pensioner romance and nightmares regarding botched abdominal surgery. He was becoming fairly desperate to know what women were like and as we all know. Desperate men say desperate things!

"OK, let me put this another way. Get me a date with Magda or I get Debbie the sack for regularly doling you out free coffees. And if you tell her I said that, I'll get her sacked, anyway!"

Suddenly the air was clear. Nigel had stated his business in no uncertain terms. Before Martin could stammer a reply, the wheezy wanker turned on his heel and stalked across the store. Leaving an open-mouthed Martin wondering how he would persuade Magda that her romantic future lay with a man whose idea of fun was running up hills in the fucking rain.

Martin wasn't a deep thinker. Maybe if he was, he might have seen this coming. But then possibly the Cheesy Dips wouldn't have formed at all had he just remembered to buy a paper that fateful morning. But then we all play with the cards that life deals us. You can't throw in your hand mid-game and choose another. If occasionally you're a bit slow, then the chances are you will only get slower.

He needed a confidante. Someone who could understand his predicament and suggest a workaround solution. During the afternoon, he considered several scenarios that would bring the matter to a close. But as most of them ended in Nigel's untimely death in increasingly bizarre circumstances. Sensibly, he had discounted them all, but his favourite was a freak nail gun accident that left his blackmailer looking like a metallic hedgehog. Then it suddenly occurred to him that the issue might cease to exist if Magda suddenly became 'unavailable".

It had been a decent rehearsal. The set list now stood at one hour and fifteen minutes. Just three more songs and they were all set for Tool Aid. Martin had suggested that they dined in reception before going home. Craig wasn't keen, having witnessed Wally openly diving for nose oysters in the office on a previous occasion. The notion that these same hands would serve him food was not appealing. But it was late, midweek and therefore options were limited.

They stood at the little kiosk window studying the Day-Glo stars stuck to the wall that served as a menu. Wally was no restaurateur, but he made sure that they provided an accurate reflection of the dishes on offer. Several blobs of vacant Blu-tac gave away he was overdue a visit to Iceland. Craig chose a Caribbean Curry Pasty with microwave chips, while Martin plumped for a Lasagne. Then watched as Wally dug about in a decrepit top-loading freezer in the storeroom that had a large dirty patch on the front. The outline of which strongly resembled the 1980s Walls Ice-Cream logo. Finally, he emerged triumphant with two frosty boxes and with all the flourish of a man with Michelin stars, stuck one into the microwave.

"Would sirs like to order drinks and dessert while they are waiting?"

Sometimes it was difficult to know when Wally was joking and when he wasn't. Experience told Martin that it was always best to assume that he was serious. As getting it wrong usually caused enormous offence. So they wisely indulged his restaurant role play.

"I'll have a Lilt and a Cornetto," said Martin.

"I'll have a Diet Coke and a Cornetto too," said Craig, gathering the idea from Martin's compliance that Wally was entirely serious about the whole restaurant thing.

"I'll just see what flavours we have available".

Wally returned to the stockroom and spent a further minute moving boxes about in the old freezer.

"I should advise you that these are own brand Cornettos rather than the bonafide variety. I have two strawberries, one toffee and three chocolate."

Martin decided that it wasn't a wise idea to advise Wally that calling them Cornettos had obvious trade description issues.

"I'll have chocolate."

"I'll take the toffee."

Wally laid the multi-pack generic ice creams in a box near the top of the freezer ready to be served after the main course and turned his attention to locating the curry pasty and drinks in the office fridge.

"So are you seeing anyone at the moment?" inquired Martin.

"No, with the band and work I haven't really got time. How are you getting on with Debbie?"

"It's going great, to be honest. Although I get through that much coffee at work these days, sleeping is becoming a problem."

Martin laughed, Craig smiled, Wally swore as he pulled the steaming lasagne from the microwave and replaced it with the small box of chips.

"So still footloose and fancy-free, eh? What if I told you someone had their eye on you?"

Craig had left school around thirty-five years previously. He couldn't recall an occasion since when he had been told that someone had their eye on him. With the exception of Wally, it was a struggle for him to imagine anyone that they both knew that might have designs on him.

"Like who exactly?"

"You know the Polish bird that Debbie works with? Well, she's got it bad for you, mate."

"What the one I don't recall meeting or even speaking to?"

"She saw you that day we first ran into each other. Apparently, Debbie says she never shuts up about you. Craig this, Craig that. Trust me, she's hot to trot."

"Mate, I honestly don't remember her and I haven't been in there since."

"I thought you might say that. Hang on, I think I have a photo on my phone."

Martin knew damn well that he had a photo on his phone. He had spent the larger part of the afternoon trying to knock a decent one out by finding excuses to pop over to the coffee shop with his phone sticking out of the top pocket of his jacket. When that became problematic he had retreated into the racking and pushed the zoom function to its limits. Finally, he had something that was approaching flattering. But had Magda known she was being photographed that day for presentation to a prospective suitor, she might have done something with her hair. Instead, it sat on top of her head in a greasy bun which did little to draw attention from the large spot, taking centre stage on her forehead. Craig peered at the photo on

Martin's phone and then looked hard at Martin.

"Whilst I don't consider myself to be giving George Clooney anything to worry about…."

That was bollocks! He openly modelled himself on the coffee pedalling penis! Who else would turn up to a rehearsal in a roll-neck sweater, a pair of chinos and mirror-polished loafers?

"… I feel that I might somehow sell myself short should I decide to pursue your hot tip. I thank you graciously for your efforts, but I will have to decline your generous offer of assistance with my love life."

"You want to see her done up though, she's amazing!"

"That's as maybe, but I doubt that she would be amazing at seven o'clock in the morning. Unless she's nicking stock from work and doing her makeup with Dulux gloss."

Then Craig narrowed his eyes and looked hard again at Martin. Realising he'd seen desperation like this before, when they first formed the Cheesy Dips.

"What are you up to, Martin? My spider senses tell me you're in the shit again. Now tell me the genuine reason that you want me to date DIY's answer to Vicky Pollard."

Martin was cornered, and he knew it. So over a cremated lasagne and a pasty seconds from its sell-by date, he spilt the conversation that he had with Nigel that afternoon.

"So you think Nigel will back off if Magda's got a boyfriend? But won't it give the game away if he realises I'm your mate?"

"I can't see how he would know that. He's never met you and you've only been in the store that once. So if you just wander in and use the coffee shop, it will look sort of natural."

"What if she doesn't fancy me? That'll fuck things right up."

"That's a good call. We need a sure-fire introduction with no distractions."

"I suppose we could go on a blind date with you and Debbie."

Craig knew his fate was sealed the moment the words left his lips and Martin's eyes lit up like a condemned man hearing a helicopter landing on the prison roof. He just hoped that Magda improved her beauty regime in the meantime if he was going to make it look in any way convincing.

The next day at work Martin studied the coffee shop carefully until he could see a lull in the tragic traffic. Deciding it was now or never, he made his move. He knew there was no chance of getting interrupted by Nigel as he was away on a day course at head office. The entire place seemed far more relaxed in his absence. So it was an opportune moment to strike.

Debbie and Magda were shooting the breeze behind the counter with a cuppa as he approached. Enjoying the ceasefire between the bacon butty hours and the lunchtime sophistication of the cheese panini and wilted side salad. Martin decided that he would use a slightly revised version of the schoolboy chat that he had previously used on Craig. Admittedly, he saw straight through it, but as Magda went to school in Poland, they might have a different system there. Anyway, that was all he had. He wasn't Cilla Black with 'our Graham' providing the voiceover to smooth the path of true love.

"Hello, ladies…"

Debbie's antennae instantly went into their raised position Martin rarely fetched his coffee, and she had never known him to address them as 'ladies' in the past. She noted that at least he hadn't got his phone sticking out of his top pocket today.

"How's your morning going so far?" he smarmed.

"Oh, just the usual intense thrill of endless bacon, sausage and coffee. We had Gary Lineker in earlier to refresh the crisps display. Apart from that, it's been fairly uneventful."

Magda didn't get the Gary Lineker reference and looked puzzled. So Debbie explained that was the name of the jug-eared bloke who advertised Walker's Crisps and sometimes discussed the football on television. She smiled weakly as the gag continued to perish on stony soil despite a lengthy summary of his football and media career.

Although still clueless about crisp pushing celebrities she now knew that Debbie and Martin had started seeing each other outside of work. So guessing Martin wanted to talk to her workmate privately, she tactfully walked around the counter. Intending to clear and wipe down tables to allow them time to do so.

"Actually Magda, it's you I've really come to speak to."

"Charming!" said Debbie.

"Well, both of you, if I'm honest," recovered Martin altogether more tactfully.

"I wondered if you were seeing anyone at the moment?"

Debbie's misgivings instantly climbed another level. Martin was about as subtle as Quasimodo in a bell shop with a pocket full of electro magnets.

"Err no, not at the moment" replied Magda who was experiencing a dry spell in lookalike basketball players. Ever since the copier engineer decided what they did to each other twice a week, contravened his lifelong religious principles when his wife became suspicious.

"OK, what if I told you a friend of mine would like to take you out for the evening?"

"A friend?" replied Magda, who found it hard to believe that Martin hung around with anyone sporty, let alone basketball players.

"Yes, he's seen you working here and would like the opportunity to get to know you better."

Debbie was enjoying this. She was already ahead of the curve and guessed correctly Craig was Magda's mystery admirer. She had only met him on the odd occasion when he dropped Martin off at her house after rehearsals. Even so, she still struggled with the notion he had the hots for Magda.

"How tall is he?"

"Erm, I would say around six foot…"

"Six foot is too short. I like men who can change a light bulb without standing on a chair."

It seemed odd to Martin that Magda operated a minimum height restriction policy for potential new suitors. He was familiar with racist, sexist and ageist, but heightest was an entirely unknown concept. Even the police had relaxed their rules regarding the height of new recruits. Perhaps she also discriminated against tattoos, but this probably wasn't the right time to ask. He considered it must be quite off-putting the first time you saw a new partner naked and realised that they had their entire service history permanently etched on them.

"Would you like to see a picture?"

"OK, maybe I look and if he's nice, he can wear heels."

Martin made great play of casually digging around on his phone. Before showing Magda the photo he took the previous night of Martin with a half-eaten pasty and a box of microwave chips in front of him. She looked as impressed with this image as Craig had with her candid greasy bun Mount Vesuvius portrait.

"He's not bad looking, but he's white. I prefer black men, tall black men."

"Actually, he's quarter Venezuelan."

Martin had no idea of Craig's cultural heritage and exactly why he had selected Venezuela as the home of his ancestors. But he was dying on his arse. If he was going down, he might as well chuck out a whopper.

"Really? He looks very white..."

"You should see him in the Summer. He tans really well."

He could feel that Magda was softening. She was still holding his phone and taking a lot of interest in the photo for someone who had no attraction at all to the subject. Years ago he remembered selling a Ford Fiesta to a bloke who upon arrival had declared he didn't like the colour and it was too small for his requirements. This had certainly been a bargaining tactic, as the photo in Auto Trader showed the colour and it correctly stated the exact model in the ad. Perhaps Magda was about to pull out a wad of cash and make him a silly offer?

"OK, as he is your friend, I will go out with him."

Magda was obviously under the illusion she was supermodel material. On a good day, she was possibly a seven. Yesterday, barely a five.

"OK, so why don't we make it fun and all go out together on a double date?"

The look he received from Debbie for that suggestion told him he was now in hot water with her. But fuck it, he was almost off the hook!

Chapter 15

Mindy Morris sat drinking coffee after work in the kitchen of her small flat in Fulham. She had specifically chosen her coffee cup to match the rather expensive ceramic tiles that were still stacked in her hall alongside a plethora of unopened IKEA boxes. On the table in front of her was a small stack of kitchen brochures that she regularly tortured herself with. By now her kitchen should have looked amazing. A worthy film location for a smug yoghurt advert, or the centre of a stylish home for some upwardly mobile character in a weeknight three-part drama. Instead, it was a total mess. She turned her attention away from the printed fantasy and reluctantly let her eyes tour the grim reality. Bare plaster, smashed tiles, missing doors, exposed wiring and a drawer that the front fell off every time she touched it. It shouldn't have been like this.

The kitchen fitter had come highly recommended on Facebook. But then she might have been less inclined to use him had she known that it was his extended family offering the glowing testimonials. Using a well-practised manoeuvre that she now knew had snared several penny-pinching kitchen enthusiasts over the last couple of years. Had she used the slightly dearer fitter that her neighbours had recommended, her Ikea show home would now be complete. Instead, she avoided having guests, thoroughly ashamed of the chaotic mess that he had left. Further embarrassed that she paid for the work by a cash advance on only the second day. Just minutes before the shady fucker 'nipped down to the van' and vanished faster than an unattended biro in a kleptomania clinic. It was a hard lesson to learn. Now she lived alone with an endless reminder of her trusting nature blocking up her hallway that constantly snagged her 100 denier Polly Peck tights!

Before work had started, her kitchen was admittedly tired but still unfashionably functional. Largely based on a 1970s beige colour palette, the brainchild of the late vendor's even later husband. Whose eventual demise sat on the toilet had seen her get an absolute bargain in late 2009 and finally vacuum up the last of the flies in early 2010. Since then she had slowly transformed the insect's former home into something that strongly resembled a bijou show home in Ikea. She didn't really live there, she just floated from room to room, leaving very little evidence of her existence in her wake. Even to the extent she rotated the sofa cushions to ensure even wear. Smoothing out the indent left by her bony arse each night before retiring to her empty GJORA bed. She even arranged the scatter cushions with military precision in a sequence designed to appear entirely random. A look she lifted from the Swedish megastore's iconic 2012 catalogue. Which sat amongst her enormous reference pile under the SKITBOARD coffee table that took centre stage in the lounge.

The whole sorry saga had cost her £1250. Which to add insult to injury was part of a low-interest bank loan that she now had the pain of paying back each month. While her kitchen sat in boxes impeding access and steadily going out of fashion. Now the little she managed to put aside each month went towards paying the loan. Which then prevented her from saving to engage another fitter. So it was an impossible situation that required an ingenious remedy. Now, at last, Mindy thought she might have one.

Selling titbits of gossip to journalists had long since been an occasional source of extra income. No one got hurt, possibly just a little embarrassed. But then, as the saying goes, any publicity is good publicity. However, this was definitely a step up from selling band secrets and exposing messy relationship breakdowns. She had nothing against the 2Ds personally. They were like a lot of the eager young kids that came through the doors of Blue Sky Records. At first, they were nervous and would happily chat to her as they waited for an audience with the little emperor. Then as their confidence increased and profile grew, they became more and more arrogant to the point they hardly acknowledged her existence. She didn't particularly mind, as that was the business. Turning spotty kids who could hold a tune into absolute megalomaniacs. Then spitting them out like a squirrel turd in a bag of chocolate peanuts, once their time passed.

She picked up her phone with shaking hands and dialled the number for Robertson Holdings. It hadn't been tricky to find. As like all successful gangsters, there was a legitimate side to

Theo's business interests. It only rang twice at the other end before her call was answered. As she expected, Mr Robertson wasn't available, but she left a thinly veiled message with his secretary that would definitely arouse his interest. She hadn't even finished her coffee before her phone rang with a mobile number she didn't recognise.

"Hello…"

"Hello, I believe that you have some information that might be of interest to me?"

Mindy's heart was beating out of her chest. But she fixed her eyes on the drawer front that was now once again lying on the kitchen floor and kept talking. If she needed a sign that her actions were righteous, there it was.

"Yes, I understand that you are looking for the Dafoe twins?"

"That's correct and who might you be?"

"That's not important. What is important is that I know exactly where they are."

"How do I know that you're not just spinning me a line?"

"I would guess from the tremble in my voice you would know that I'm not the sort of person who would knowingly tell lies to a man of your reputation."

"That's a fair point. I do sense that you are more than a little nervous. What would you want in return?"

"Fifteen hundred pounds if that's possible?"

Mindy had decided that she might as well award herself £250 damages for all the hurt and distress that the botched kitchen had caused her. The Melltorp kitchen table and four chairs came in at £200 and she could accessorize nicely with the other fifty quid.

"That's quite a sizeable sum of money for a whisper."

"But then it's quite a whisper, as I'm probably only one of two people in London who know where they are."

"So who's the other one?"

"Mr Robertson, I might not be an experienced informant, but then I'm not a stupid one either."

"Well, you've got to try, haven't you? Would you like to meet?"

"Yes, I think that might be best. Possibly somewhere public that isn't part of your empire?"

"Do you like cocktails? If so, I know just the place."

Two hours later, a rather nervous Mindy stepped from an Uber just around the corner from the Blue Lagoon. Pasha her driver had unintentionally calmed the butterflies in her stomach with colourful tales of his childhood in Russia. He seemed blissfully unaware that his parents were possibly sadists, and that been regularly beaten with a butter paddle wasn't typical of good parenting. Russian or otherwise!

She scanned the street for a sign that anyone had observed her arrival. But as Pasha's knackered Nissan disappeared into the distance and no one leapt from the shadows clutching a black hood and a length of rope, it was so far, so good. She hadn't been to the Blue Lagoon Cocktail Bar before, as most of her social life stemmed from after-work drinks close to the Blue Sky Records offices. So as she covered the short distance to the shabby entrance, she had very little idea of what to expect. Apart from the comments left on Trip Advisor, which seemed to rate it rather favourably within its locality. Taking a deep breath, she pushed open the door and wobbled down the narrow stairs, silently cursing her choice of footwear. Four-inch heels were fine on the flat, but more than challenging down worn concrete steps. When combined with the Parma Violet Gins she'd had for Dutch Courage whilst waiting for her Uber. This was the most exciting thing she'd done in ages. Twenty years ago her life had been so different with endless album launches and award after parties. Now she was lucky if a neighbour invited her round for a Tupperware party. Even luckier if there were actually any straight men present curious about keeping their leftovers fresh for days!

She wasn't in the first flush of youth, but then she wasn't quite ready for crochet and slippers either. Meeting a powerful man like Theo Robertson had stirred something deep inside Mindy that had lain undisturbed for some considerable time. Consequently, she had gone to a lot of trouble with her appearance. Secretly hoping to mix business with pleasure.

She was pleasantly surprised as she stepped from the stairwell into the primary seating area. The grimy exterior gave no clue to the faux tropical oasis that lay at the foot of a fairly lethal set of steps. A quick look around the room confirmed Theo hadn't arrived yet. The bar's clientele consisted mainly of younger people who bore all the classic hallmarks of family money and shouty jobs in high finance. She momentarily checked her look in a mirror advertising Jamaican rum that she passed on her way to the bar. The laughter lines and crow's feet she saw in her reflection made her feel conspicuous amongst such youth. Then realising that the expensive cocktail dress that she had bought for a colleague's wedding five years ago did absolutely nothing to dispel that.

Cocktail Kevin smiled meekly from beneath his taped nose as his now heavily bruised eyes fell on the woman he had been told to expect during a rather one-sided phone call earlier that evening. He was considering a change of career and possibly even continent. Men like Theo would just keep coming back, and that was the sort of regular custom he didn't need.

"Good evening. Are you the lady Mr Robertson is expecting?" he inquired.

"Err... yes, that's right."

His instant recognition and obvious expectation unnerved Mindy in equal measure. She gave a moment's consideration to a swift heel-free departure before deciding that wouldn't get her kitchen fitted. No one else in here appeared to be an axe murderer, so she might as well calm down and see it through.

"Please take that reserved table over there. Mr Robertson has pre-ordered drinks. Make yourself comfortable and I will bring them over."

Something in the young man's respectful tone made meeting a hardened villain an even more attractive proposition. So Mindy did as she was instructed and made her way over to their table. A few minutes complex preparation passed before Kevin delivered two Pink Parrots and hastily beat the retreat before the architect of his nasal discomfort arrived. With nothing else to do, a nervous Mindy had drained half the glass before Theo Robertson tap-danced down the stairs. Effecting his entrance in the fashion of an extremely brutal Bruce Forsyth. He had given Barney the night off as the wavering voice on the phone didn't suggest any expertise with firearms. Therefore, he felt the occasion called for decorum rather than barbarity, as anyone with experience in the trade would have chosen the venue themselves. Rather than cooing down the phone and replying "lovely, look forward to seeing you" and "bye for now" when he had. Which spoke strongly of a novice, as polite telephone etiquette had never been an acknowledged strong suit of London's violent underworld.

When the unexpectedly light-footed torturer approached their table and greeted her with a smile of realisation. Mindy couldn't be sure if it was the preloaded gins and half a Pink Parrot or genuine attraction she felt. As once again she sensed a familiar stirring low down in her chest high Spanx.

"Ah, I believe we've met before."

Mindy decided it was fairly pointless to deny that she was the woman who had burst into Robin's office with a child's birthday cake. That made a second, entirely more scheduled appearance at the party of a colleague's five-year-old son later the same day.

"Was it that obvious he wasn't a Bob the Builder fan?" she smiled.

"Between you and me, he wouldn't have been much of a Barney the Die-Now-Sore fan either. If you hadn't stepped in when you did. How's the Pink Parrot going down?"

She gave his obviously well practised Barney gag a complimentary chuckle. She liked a man with a dry sense of humour. In fairness, she would settle for any man who didn't need an hour's notice and a blue pill for a bunk up and Theo didn't look like he spent much time round at the doctor's looking embarrassed.

"Very nice. I'm surprised to see that you have one too."

"Apparently my teenage daughter is a big fan, so I wanted to see what all the fuss is about. Reminds me a bit of Strawberry Cresta. It's frothy, man!"

Mindy laughed at the reference to a long-forgotten soft drink from the 1980s. Theo liked that. People usually found him intimidating, violent, cruel, unsympathetic and even occasionally certifiable. So funny made a very pleasant change indeed.

"So now I know who you are. Just give me an inkling of exactly how you know where they are?"

"As you know they are presently recording at a secret location. Prior to departure, they had absolutely no idea they were going. Obviously, professional musicians have some fairly specific instrument requirements. So the correct equipment needed to be there, ready and waiting if they were going to get anything done. They asked me to arrange the purchase and shipping of the necessary items. But obviously needed the address of the studio they were using to arrange delivery. Robin has very little to do with that end of things and had no idea at all that it was me they asked to see to it. Therefore, he was telling the truth about not knowing where they were. That's why I interrupted your, erm, meeting."

Theo looked suitably impressed as Mindy's explanation quickly gave provinence to her information.

"OK, another question. £1500 is a very specific amount of money. Which I'm guessing you need for something in particular. Call me nosey, but what is it?"

Mindy explained her own particular brand of Kitchen Nightmare that didn't involve a foul mouthed ex-footballer chef and a clueless restaurant owner. When she finished Theo looked entirely sympathetic to her plight.

"The money isn't an issue, I'm happy to help. However, as an added bonus, would you like Mr Fitter to experience an extreme customer service course? It would only take a phone call to arrange and I can have him brought to your door to personally express dismay for his actions post-training."

"Thank you for the offer, but I'm not great with the sight of blood. But if you could shoehorn my name in during what I'm sure will be a very comprehensive course. I would be more than happy with that."

"Consider it done. Listen, why don't we finish these and I'll take you to a lovely little Italian place I know around the corner? The manager is a personal friend of mine and his chefs butcher their own meat. So he serves a steak just the way I like it. But then if you prefer something lighter, he does some amazing fish dishes, and the pasta is fresh every day. I would be honoured to take you as my guest and we can conclude our business there. I believe in fate and that things happen for a reason. Unless, of course, you have other plans?"

The only other plan Mindy had involved a mug of Horlicks and a cellophane fresh Spring/Summer Ikea catalogue. This morning she had a knackered kitchen and a hole in her finances. Now she was on for a free meal, finally getting her kitchen fitted and possibly about to experience a rather fruity end to her evening. What more could a girl want? She glugged off the last of her Pink Parrot and rose to her feet faster than Theo could remind Cocktail Kevin to wipe the last hour's CCTV footage.

It would be two months later when they pulled Mindy's bloated body from the River Thames. Her Spanx having almost inflated to Big Daddy proportions to overcome the traditional concrete weights and slip free from its grisly resting place on the riverbed amongst the unexploded Second World War bombs and broken clay pipes. Sadly, for her, Theo was an equal opportunity torturer/murderer. Men, women, pensioners, LGBTQIA, animals, aliens or angels. Absolutely nothing or no one was off-limits. Agreeing to leave a well lit public area for an imaginary meal in a non-existent Italian restaurant with a man slightly crueller than Hitler's mouse hating tomcat, wasn't her greatest decision. But then neither was having the address of Priory Studios carefully handwritten on a piece of Basildon Bond within a matching envelope addressed to 'Mr Theo Robertson' in her handbag. She had hoped to end the night screaming, and she wasn't disappointed. Landing the starring role in a one-woman operetta. Her stage, an empty riverside warehouse with rafters of skittish pigeons as her audience. Before finally being martyred for her Ikea habit, hanging upside down with a minge full of fire extinguisher foam.

For a second time that night, Theo Robertson had enjoyed a slight twist to his usual way of doing things. Genuinely shocked at how bad the seal was on Mindy's lady garden. After withdrawing the extinguisher hose and standing back in amazement as her massive black pants inflated like Phileas Fogg's hot air balloon.

He rarely worked alone, but then he wasn't one for paying unnecessary overtime either. So Barney never got to meet Mindy a second time, as Theo didn't see the need to divulge exactly how he came by the address of Priory Studios on Holy Island. And naturally, the leather-clad mouth breather knew better than to ask too many questions.

Chapter 16

Craig wasn't feeling terribly motivated about his Friday night mission. He honestly didn't mind helping a mate. As after all, that was essentially what he had spent the last few weeks doing. But now driving round to Debbie's for the dinner party from hell. He was sure that an exceptionally dull evening, full of painfully lengthy pauses, lay ahead. At least he wouldn't have to drop her home afterwards. As she might get a tad pissy when he asked her to lie across the back seat so that no one saw her.

He pulled onto the garage forecourt, still annoyed with his inability to say no to Martin's favours. Quickly parking in one of the bays thoughtfully provided for people who prefer paying through the nose for provisions and find the extensive choice in regular-sized supermarkets confounding.

Craig recalled simpler times when convenience shopping at a garage meant buying batteries on Christmas Day. Usually, after some distant relative ignored the time-honoured tradition of taping the required quantity of AAs to the side of the box. His dad had loved nothing more than an 11 am Yuletide tour of local petrol stations buying overpriced power cells. Trying to prevent a cataclysmic junior meltdown when some piece of plastic tat from Hong Kong had become the centre of his world. Rather than the expensive new bike that he had spent months breaking his back to pay for in instalments at Halfords.

He stalked past the pumps, heading for the kiosk. Carefully avoiding any spilt fuel that might ruin the sheepskin over mats when he got back into the car. The kiosk doors opened automatically as he approached, making a familiar swishing noise as they did so. Reminiscent of entry to the bridge on Star Trek. Where he was immediately confronted by a rather lacklustre display of partially withered flowers. Spending literally seconds over selecting a suitable bunch of blooms from the 'I'm sorry about the porn you found on my phone' and 'mildly upset that you're dead' section. Finally deciding on some heavily discounted chrysanthemums that he hoped had no secret meaning whatsoever in the flower world. Least of all a willingness to move to Gdansk to care for elderly relatives.

Ever the gentleman, he then pressed on round to the confectionery aisle. Magda was almost certainly a chocolate fan judging by the festering bonce boil he'd seen in Martin's photo. It never ceased to amaze him just how many types of reasonably priced chocolate petrol garages sold nowadays. But if you wanted a can of de-icer or a pint of oil, a Columbian kidnap gang set the pricing.

Cadbury's Roses were on special offer, so he grabbed a 250g box and made his way to the till. He noted the cashier had a vague resemblance to Leonard Nimoy, which perfectly complimented the noise the entrance doors made. His immaculate uniform spoke of a career in the military or years spent pounding a beat. A man apparently clinging on to some degree of self-importance as middle age gradually pushed him closer to drooling and incontinence. Sensing the conclusion to his browsing, 'Leonard' lifted a trained eye and watched with interest as Craig approached the counter.

"Minor misdemeanour, sir? Unsanctioned late night in a charming hostelry with good pals and foaming beverages? Maybe the forgotten birthday of an elderly aunt? Or possibly a reluctant hospital visit to an unpopular work colleague?"

For a second 'Leonard' had the better of Craig. Then he realised he was carrying a classic 'get out of the shit' combo.

"Close but no cigar. Actually, a dinner date with a Polish acne sufferer."

Leonard instantly appeared deflated. He prided himself on guessing right as this was the only actual skill that his job demanded. Other than that, it was just about pressing a button when someone picked up a pump and stared at the window to stop the bleeping that he now heard every night in his sleep!

"Well Sir, whoever she is, she's a lucky lady!"

Craig severely doubted 'Leonard' meant that, but still appreciated the sentiment. Passed over the fiver he had set as the absolute budget limit for his entry-level romance combo and waited for the 25p change. A casual pick at the price reduction sticker on the flowers told him it would probably be a bitch to shift.

"Have you got any scissors?"

"Scissors, sir?"

"To cut the price ticket off?"

"Oh, I see..."

Leonard rummaged about under the counter and reappeared with a pair evidently stolen from a four-year-old nursery school pupil. The pink coating and rounded ends giving rise to understandable concerns about their cutting ability. Craig thanked him and said on reflection he would try to peel it off when he got back into the car. Leonard appeared somewhat irritated by this callous disregard for his efforts. Consequently, Craig felt that his "Have a great day!" farewell lacked any genuine warmth as he retreated out of the bridge doors of the Enterprise.

Back in the less pressurised environment of his car, he once again tried peeling off the 'guaranteed dead in 3 days' sticker. As he had suspected, it didn't go well. A visually unappealing female employee who saw it as revenge on mankind had probably applied it for her continued lack of floral appreciation. By now it was knocking on a bit and Craig knew that he should really make tracks to Debbie's. Then his eye fell on the cigar lighter in the dashboard. Great, he'd melt it off! Pushing the lighter in and holding it, he waited until he felt the spring release. Then held it in some more to make sure of the job. When too long seemed more than enough. He withdrew it from the smouldering socket and set about destroying the cellophane around the label with the glowing element.

Ten minutes later Craig drew up outside Debbie's neat little semi. Which hadn't required him to check the door number, due to the large 'powered by angel farts' sign in the back window of her car.

Walking to the door, he thought he briefly glimpsed Magda through the net curtains. Bouncing up at the bay window over the settee like a boisterous Yorkshire Terrier. Martin opened the door before he even rang the bell and gave him a 'thanks for this mate' look. Which further confirmed his suspicions that Magda had eagerly anticipated his arrival and was now trying to compose herself in the kitchen. Most likely to prevent her running frantic circles around the lounge before rolling on her back to perform a 'golden shower tribute' for her esteemed guest.

He and Martin endured a few moments of stunted conversation before the kitchen door finally opened and Magda followed Debbie through into the lounge. Craig was instantly taken aback. This wasn't the same Magda that he had seen on Martin's phone during their microwave dinner date at Wally's. Her hair was delicately coiffured with no sign of the forehead fungus that had previously marred her beauty. She smelt great, her makeup was faultless and a casual top and tight leggings dared his eyes to drop lower at the first opportunity. He was still marvelling at the miraculous transformation as he proffered his five quid gift compendium and went in for a continental greeting kiss. Perhaps this wouldn't be such a chore after all!

"Thank you they are lovely," said Magda. Trying hard to ignore the blackened cellophane that now stubbornly clung to one entire side of the increasingly sickly fading flora. Superheating the cigar lighter had been a masterstroke from a thermal scissoring point of view. But added very little to the overall aesthetic when flames forced Craig to throw them out of the car window and beat out the inferno on the forecourt floor. Watched by a horrified Leonard from the kiosk window. Who feared a blossom based explosion scenario might see him back on later life's scrapheap. Once again reminiscing about his glory days as a traffic warden.

"Magda has taken over my kitchen to prepare a traditional Polish meal for us all to enjoy!" Enthused Debbie, taking on the role of Greg Wallace but without feeling the need to bellow like an audibly challenged Cockney barrow boy. Craig had to admit that the smells emanating from the kitchen were quite enticing.

As the impromptu flower dance had only increased his appetite. Magda's cooking didn't disappoint. Her Bigos meat stew was an absolute triumph and thoroughly enjoyed by everyone at the table. Accompanied by homemade sauerkraut and pickled gherkins. All washed down with Polish beer. Promptly superseded by a baked cheesecake that was so good he had two slices. Magda visibly beamed as her potential new beau tucked in heartily while listening attentively to her stories of Poland and the continuing struggle to adapt to life in England.

As they cleared away the dessert plates, and coffee cups quickly replaced them. Magda pulled the final ace from her Prussian arsenal of gluttony in the form of an enormous bottle of Danziger Goldwasser vodka. Already two beers down, Craig tried in vain to dodge his shot by reminding everyone that he was driving. Unfortunately, Martin was a couple in front and, not fond of drinking alone, offered to pay for Craig's taxi home. Which destroyed his remaining resolve and saw him rapidly develop a taste for the sweet syrupy spirit. Eventually playing a major role in the demise of the whole bottle.

It was early. A semi-conscious Craig tried in vain to move his tongue, but found it firmly welded to the roof of his mouth. Opening his jaw wide, he felt the furry seal give, and it reluctantly broke free. At that same moment, the world attacked his senses. All at once he felt pain, belched garlic, smelt cooking bacon and heard singing. At first, thinking it was the radio, then realised he couldn't comprehend the words. They weren't English, but he recognised the tune. It was Abba - Thank You for the Music. Examining the bedroom through bleary eyes, he began to recall in lurid detail the previous night's events. Soon remembering why a room that was usually so tidy now looked like a bomb had hit it. An insatiable Polish blonde warhead, to be exact. Which, if he wasn't very much mistaken, was now downstairs noisily preparing breakfast in his dressing gown. The one plainly absent from the hook on the back of the bedroom door. He fearfully studied the pillow beside his head, which evidently bore heavy traces of foundation. Then noted the matching women's underwear that lay beside his shirt on the bedroom floor. Oh balls! What had he done?

Dragging his vodka ravaged body out of bed, he shambled over to the wardrobe to pull out a t-shirt and joggers. Halfheartedly searching for his slippers then guessing that his guest had probably taken those too, dug out his old pair from under the bed. Lingering upstairs just long enough to use the toilet, he slowly descended the stairs to face the music. Screwing up his face in cranial pain as the Eastern Bloc Agnetha's voice climbed to a howling crescendo for the big finish.

Silently shuffling into the kitchen, he could see Magda was plainly in her element. The table was laid for two with a cafetiere of fresh coffee brewing in the centre and a panful of sizzling food in progress on the hob. She stood with her back to him as she belted out the slow last chorus of the 1977 classic that now sounded more like a communist national anthem than a Scandinavian celebration of the gift of music.

He wanted to say that although he'd had a marvellous time, and she was a lovely lady, he wasn't looking to take a gamble on anything serious. Then offer her the classic Bullseye goodbye handshake but without the tankard, cash, and darts. Instead, he stood quietly and witnessed the sheer joy she felt from just having someone to cook for. Finding himself delighting in the effortless way she tied up her hair and the slight wobble in her bottom as she fussed over their first breakfast together. Slowly softening to the unexpected intrusion into his Saturday morning routine as the neural discomfort slowly lessened. Before finally admitting to himself that it wasn't only Magda who was lonely.

As he watched, still unobserved, unexpectedly captivated by her simple beauty Magda expanded her diaphragm to hold the last note and trumped loudly, like a three pint Guinness granny down the bingo. Rendering Craig helpless with laughter, his cover blown, and turning the soon to be de-robed chef as red as Chairman Mao's passport

Chapter 17

Martin had tried hard to keep his head down since Nigel made his intentions crystal clear regarding Magda and Coffee-gate. Striving to keep things business-like whenever he encountered his supervisor around the store. Even their previously informal section meetings now had a slight edge to them. There was definitely an elephant in the room. Martin was no longer 'mate' and they only really discussed Tool Aid when it was absolutely necessary. He wondered if he had changed his mind about Magda or reconsidered blackmailing a colleague into supplying him with a reluctant girlfriend. But having experienced Nigel's management style at great length, that was unlikely to be the case. Now At least Magda wouldn't have to face the same indignity and discover below-average length was definitely more like it!

But in his heart, he knew it was coming. At some point, Nigel would require an update on his matchmaking progress. Then he would have to play the reluctant messenger of bad tidings by informing him that Magda had unexpectedly started a new relationship. Do his best to look sorry and give him some old guff about plenty more fish in the sea and all that tripe. Hoping that the bitter disappointment would knock the hard edge off his blackmail enterprise. Then they could just get back to discussing cables and clips with the odd mention of 'Tool Aid' to keep things light.

It was a pleasant Wednesday afternoon when Nigel decided to go into bat for Team Bastard. He appeared out of the sun like a fighter ace attacking an ailing bomber. In reality, he came across from the kitchen and bathroom display. Which was unlike him as he had no jurisdiction in that area of the shop floor. That fell to another supervisor called Colin, who was popular amongst his colleagues. Rather than disliked, hated, feared or loathed. Which were four adjectives regularly used by other staff members to describe Nigel. Martin didn't spot him coming until he was almost on his shoulder.

"Martin, can I have a word?"

'Here we go…'

"Did you make any progress with that little favour I requested from you?"

"I looked into it, but there's a problem. She has a new boyfriend who I'm lead to believe she's very keen on."

"So you didn't mention us going out on a double date despite my obvious 'concerns' about Debbie and her free coffee service?"

"I understand your disappointment, Nigel, I really do. But if you saw her with this bloke, you would realise how futile it would be to try and set anything in motion."

Martin immediately regretted sharing that observation. It strongly suggested that he had enjoyed a social engagement in the company of Magda and her new fella. He could see from Nigel's growing displeasure that he had noted this treachery and was about to play his trump card.

"Well, in that case, I will have no option but to take the matter to the store manager and seek Debbie's instant dismissal on the grounds of theft."

Martin stared at him blankly. He hadn't expected things to escalate so rapidly. The scenario he had played out in his head saw Nigel crumble into tears. He would then escort him off the shop floor to the restroom and buy him a three-pack of chocolate digestives from the vending machine while listening to him blub about how shit his life was. Before maybe suggesting a more social hobby as a way to meet women, or perhaps giving online dating another stab. Later Nigel would tell him he was a good bloke, then offer a heartfelt apology for his strong-arm tactics.

Debbie getting sacked over a few admittedly excellent bean to cup beverages had figured nowhere in this soft-focus role play. Martin was fresh out of ideas. So he took the only option open to him. He twatted Nigel straight in the head. Releasing more pent up aggression than a safari park lion who'd spent the last ten years watching the piss-taking gazelles through an aging chain-link fence. Nigel hadn't banked on a physical conclusion to their chat and stumbled back into the racking. Seemingly unable to comprehend what had just happened. Never one to do half a job, Martin smacked him again.

He had only been in the store manager's office on one previous occasion. Ironically, to install a mains socket that would allow Mr Slater to charge his phone at his desk. Other than that, he had ever only encountered him during staff meetings and leaving parties. He was an old-style store manager. He didn't tour the troops solving problems and listening to their concerns regarding store morale. He remained in his office and occasionally gazed over his kingdom from the one-way window that covered much of the shop floor. But by using his eyes and ears along with trusted informants, he was conscious of pretty much everything that went on in-store. He was aware that Ross was a porn obsessed deviant that no woman wanted to work with. He knew Derek toured the sections every morning, handing out the very latest juicy morsels of gossip. And lastly, that Nigel was a universally detested hill-running mummy's boy strongly suspected of manipulating his stock figures. So when he spotted Martin giving him the 'old one-two' following what was evidently a rather terse conversation, he sent for him instantly. Even before the stunned supervisor had time to make it an official disciplinary matter. A process he knew better than anyone else on the pitch, as he filed at least half a dozen cases a year.

"Hello Martin, how are the knuckles?"

"Not so bad, Mr Slater. How's the socket?"

"Doing its job to the very letter of the regulations."

"Glad to hear it…"

"So what was all that about?"

"All what?"

"Look, Martin, drop the 'I ain't saying nuffink till my brief gets here' routine. I saw you clout Nigel from up here on the poop deck. You've worked here for quite some time and caused me not an ounce of bother. OK, you're late once in a while and your new bird in the café looks after you with a few free coffees. But your stock counts are tidy, the customers find your advice helpful and God help me, apparently due to be a star of Tool Aid. So why would you flatten your supervisor and risk being out of work in your fifties with no reference from your previous employer?"

As a statement of fact, it was beautifully weighted between 'you've been a dick' and 'I would hit him myself given the chance'. It shocked Martin that Mr Slater knew about the free coffees, but not that Ross belonged in a secure psychiatric ward.

"He made a suggestion to me I wasn't happy about."

"What sort of suggestion?"

"He wanted me to get Magda in the coffee shop to go out with him or he would get Debbie the sack over the free coffees."

"So he was trying to blackmail you into helping him force his attentions on a member of staff by using his power over another female employee as leverage to do so?"

"If you put it that way, yes I suppose so…"

"Would you be willing to accept a written warning for manhandling another member of staff, if I can guarantee the outcome of a disciplinary hearing against Nigel?"

"Guarantee?"

"Yes, no one at head office likes him either. He sends them more bits of paper than an exiled poet. It drives them fucking mad! They've been onto me for years to find a reason to get rid of him. Now I have one! So how's about it?"

"What about Debbie and the coffees?"

"What coffees? I'll even write the bacon bap off I saw you get last week. What about that? I'll write your statement, you sign it. Him and his wanky sandwich box will be out of here by tea time! I would offer you the pleasure of escorting him from the building. But it wouldn't look good and to be honest, I can get a little raffle going for that honour."

"Where do I sign?"

Later that afternoon Martin watched from his section as Mr Slater paraded a bewildered and bruised Nigel around the store getting his things together. Before being escorted from the premises by a burly bloke called Dennis who worked in the building supplies section. Who had been lucky enough to see his ticket pulled out of the hat when they held the draw in the staffroom, whilst Nigel was getting the old heave-ho in the store manager's office. Which at a quid a ticket, raised just over £50 for a cake to celebrate the occasion the very next day.

It surprised Martin at how everything had worked out. Debbie still brought him free coffees across. Magda was delighted that she no longer had to prepare Nigel's hot milkshakes under his lecherous gaze. Whilst Craig piled on the pounds as she stuffed him daily with all manner of spicy sausage and he returned the favour whenever he could manage it.

Now with just two weeks to go until Tool Aid and the plastic Geldof up the road for what was quite literally 'crimes against coffee'. Head Office realised the need to get a firm grip on the reins before the whole thing collapsed and made them into a laughing stock. Luckily a review of staff CV's held on file revealed a diamond in the rough at the Wednesbury branch.

Myles Denton wore his hair long. Primarily, to confirm his rock credentials but also to hide the fact that he was bald as Bod at the crown. A man convinced that heading up the indoor lighting section was just a temporary thing before Knebworth came calling once more. But hopefully this time he would appear on the stage with his band Cat Slayer rather than replenishing the bog rolls in the Tardis style portable toilets. But such an ill fragranced, low-level role in proceedings hadn't prevented him from telling anyone who would listen about his time brushing shoulders with the stars. Without mentioning it was mainly their toilet bowls he was brushing. But with his Cuban heels, bushy beard and ever-present mouth organ, he looked every inch the musician turned promoter. More importantly, there was no one else employed by the company with any festival experience in the greater West Midlands area. So Myles got an instant transfer to the Halesowen branch and a very generous travel allowance to boot. Tasked with the sole aim of taking Tool Aid into the stratosphere!

There were no spare offices at Halesowen. So Head Office arranged for the delivery of a mobile office in the car park. That way their new promoter could oversee every aspect of the stage build. Ensuring the whole event would be as amazing as the vision Nigel had deluged them with on a million pieces of paper. However, its arrival caused some confusion for a few days. As builders continually knocked on the door to order a sandwich until eventually Myles place a 'site office' sign in the window. Which came as a great relief to the lady who ran the burger van in the car park. Who understandably feared the demise of her tiny calorific empire.

It was a surprise to everyone, not least of all Myles, how quickly things took shape. He very much enjoyed being the hub of the whole thing. Fond of putting one foot up onto a flight case whilst jabbering away on his phone. Praying that some passing pap would capture the image for posterity. Occasionally Martin would make time to go out into in his break and marvel at the massive structure that now dominated one-quarter of the car park. All resulting from his tiny white lie.

Craig couldn't believe his eyes one evening when he collected Magda from work. The company's media department had requisitioned the staff car park for three Winnebagos and several miles of telecommunications cable. Following a head office decision to up-scale Nigel's original concept of a local concert. Now the entire event would be beamed onto enormous in-store screens nationwide. DIYers from Land's End to John O'Groats would soon take the Cheesy Dips to their hearts. And hopefully, in doing so, a shitload of home improvement supplies to their homes.

Chapter 18

It was a quiet day at South London Tool Hire. The weather hadn't been great of late. Which kept the gardeners from gardening, the DIYers from DIYing, and the builders from actually turning up at all. So when Barney pulled the large black BMW into the yard, he was entirely spoilt for parking spaces. Naturally, Theo was keen to get up North but suppressed his natural appetite for revenge to ensure a perfect outcome. As the 2Ds were still oblivious to the absolute shit storm of leather-clad violence soon to be heading their way, happily recording in their island hideaway.

Bored with inflating his victims using fire extinguishers, Theo had given a lot of thought to the 2Ds ultimate demise. Like an old TV chef with a fading profile, he needed a new signature dish. Something that would really make people sit up and take notice. He'd had a look at Holy Island on the internet and felt sure it was far enough away from London to try something fresh. That way, if it didn't work out, no one would connect it to his earlier legendary work. Allowing him to refine the idea further, or if necessary discard it altogether. But if it was a runaway success, he would ensure they added it to his legacy as the great innovator of gangland butchery. The sign that hung over the counter amused him greatly as he entered.

Proper Planning Prevents Piss Poor Performance

If he had a trade counter, he would probably do something along those lines.

Clever Killing Creates Capable Career Criminals

He waited patiently until eventually, a slack-jawed youth sauntered out of the door behind the counter in the manner of a spotty Liam Gallagher. Confident of his place in the world, he continued to ignore him. Whilst he tapped away on the counter terminal and loudly chewed his gum. Just milliseconds before the underworld slayers patience finally ran out, he turned to Theo as if he had just magically become aware of his existence. Offering him the 'what can I do for you face' without feeling compelled to actually utter the words. A perfectly executed counter jockey ensemble that would have brought him a solid row of tens were this the Superiority World Championships. Timeless moves developed by his forbears to enforce the understanding that he was the one in charge. Who, dependent on his mood, could choose to guide, embarrass or fleece you entirely at will. Unfortunately for him, Theo felt no compulsion to observe counter etiquette and babble his requirements like a stammering Maths teacher with a blocked drain. Instead, he just stared back at him, watching as the gum went round in his mouth. Resembling an errant pink t-shirt in an otherwise yellow load of washing. Before lowering his eyes to the name badge which hung loosely from the pocket of his blue warehouse coat.

"Good morning, Brandon. I sense from your rather casual opening to our transaction that you don't know who I am?"

"Nah, should I?" replied Brandon who felt no obligation to increase his level of customer service despite the loud cracking of ice emanating from beneath his feet.

"Then it would be safe for me to assume you are not someone that concerns himself with the tabloid newspapers when he collects his favourite gum from the newsagents each morning?"

"I don't get it from the newsagents. My mum buys it in value packs from the supermarket. She puts a pack in with my sandwiches each day."

"Would this be the same mum that has your tea ready on the table when you arrive home from a hard day's being surly?"

"Err yeah. How many moms have you got then?"

"I don't but nonetheless still an interesting question. Sadly for me, I never knew my mother as she passed away at the hands of my father and I was raised in care. Which saw me passed from pillar to post until I was eighteen. Whereupon, they cast me out into the world to make a living. Luckily for me, I found employment with a local businessman who schooled me in the art of self-preservation."

"I'm sorry to hear that."

"You don't look it son, but I will do you a solid and let that pass. So tell me, when you're eating your tea, do you watch the television?"

"Sometimes, not always…"

"So then I'm guessing on the occasions you do. The six o'clock news isn't your chosen source of entertainment. Mainly because if it was, you would know who I am."

"Do you read the news on telly then?" scoffed Brandon enjoying his own joke enormously.

Barney stepped forward, feeling that this 'getting to know you' session was about to reach its conclusion. But Theo waved him away, and he obediently stepped back.

"No son, I don't read the news. I'm considered more of a newsmaker than a newscaster. Perhaps I should tell you my name? Maybe you've heard it mentioned amongst your friends down at the skin clinic. Theo Robertson?"

Brandon wisely ignored the jibe and instead appeared to be giving it some consideration. However, his blank expression only continued to betray the fact that he had not a clue who Theo was.

"Still nothing?" prompted Theo.

"Nope."

"OK, I'll put you out of your misery. Some say ignorance is bliss. But in this instance, I assure you that would not be the case. I am, to quote the Evening Standard, "Possibly the most evil man to walk the streets of London since Jack the Ripper". Strongly suspected of involvement in more unsolved killings than a schizophrenic Grizzly Bear with an AK47."

Brandon swallowed, then reddened slightly. At last, realising he was tap dancing on the nose of a crocodile. Theo wasn't used to giving it the 'do you know who I am?' routine. As usually, the merest hint of his shadow across the threshold had the desired effect in most establishments. Barney was amazed at his patience. Perhaps he saw something of himself in this kid and that's why his hands weren't nail gunned to the desk? Or facing traumatic amputation with a chainsaw 'that could be yours for the whole weekend for £57 - not including petrol or two stroke oil' according to the label.

"So now you're fully in the picture about who I am, can we start again? This time with the required level of respect for my standing in the Pain Management Community. Otherwise, Barney here will hit you so hard you'll need one of your other presumably spotty mates to 3D print you a new face. Are we clear?"

Brandon instantly felt a new dawn break on his attitude towards customer service.

"Yes, Mr Robertson. What can I help you with today, sir?"

"Now Brandon, that's so much better. I am interested in the long-term hire of a piece of equipment that I saw on your website and wondered if it might be possible for me to see a practical demonstration? So I can be 100% sure it's suitable for my intended application."

Barney hadn't spent a lot of time in the North, although he had been to Blackpool several times in his twenties. The rural parts of Britain were something he only saw on BBC television programmes. One of his favourites was Coast. Where a team of soft-voiced academics marvelled at the landscape, before delving into the history that lay behind the cliffs and crags. He really wished he had an alternative travelling companion for his first time in the North East. Someone who might appreciate the changing landscape and see the beauty in their unfamiliar surroundings.

Away from work, he was a quiet man and both a gentle and considerate neighbour who greatly enjoyed feeding the birds in his garden. Delighting as the seasonal cast of the bird table slowly changed, in complete contrast to the misery that permeated his every waking hour spent on the manor. Washing the blood from his knuckles in the downstairs cloakroom and leaving the blood-curdling screams of his clients outside the front door. It was never personal with Barney, just a job. He bust heads for a living, the same way a chef cracked eggs. Except that chefs didn't do it on top of a multi storey carpark at one in the morning.

But sadly for 'Barney The Closet Ornithologist' his passenger was 'Theo The Extinguisher'. Who had very little interest in anything other than money, power and murder. Today murder was heading up the trio. Their usual BMW had been swopped for a Range Rover, which Theo considered being a more capable mode of transport. Given that their intended destination looked a little challenging from an access point of view. In the boot were two overnight bags, Barney's binoculars, several guns and Theo's brand new toy. Brandon had been courtesy personified after the formal introductions had brought him right up to speed. Once their business concluded, five minutes on the internet quickly added colour to the whole sketchy picture. Making him realise just how close his mother had come to gum-free shopping and being strongly advised against viewing his severely traumatised pimply remains.

Barney spent the journey continually marvelling at the wide-open spaces and the vast peaks of the North East. Whereas Theo just twitched and stared straight ahead, offering nothing in the way of conversation apart from intermittent expletive-laden bursts of criticism aimed at other road users. He wasn't an ideal travelling companion, and Barney suspected that the whole Abigail thing was taking a toll on his mental health. He thought back to the time before Theo became London's answer to The Terminator. Then he was totally rational and never lost sight of his objective. Making him an easy man to follow. Now it was like chauffeuring a manic Cockney Hitler around during the last days of The Reich. He was irritable and preoccupied, and they had done no proper work in ages. Other than hammering around London trying to find a pair of poxy pop stars. It felt to him like things were slipping away from Theo. Barney knew better than to question his boss. He wasn't paid to think, just act. Yet every cloud has a silver lining and he got great satisfaction from driving the Range Rover because in his own words, "it felt like a real geezer's car!"

Retracing the route taken by Tony, just a few weeks earlier, they finally turned off the A1 and followed the signs for Holy Island. As they drew closer to their destination, it became obvious that the tide was coming in. This enraged the recently awakened Theo, who commanded that Barney should just keep going.

"Is this not a fucking Range Rover? What difference is six inches of water going to make to a masterpiece of British engineering with two feet of ground clearance?"

"But boss, there are signs everywhere warning against attempting to make a crossing when the tides coming in. Apparently, the causeway floods very quickly, making it rather tricky to see the road. Maybe we should just turn back and find a little hotel until it goes back out? After all, they're not going anywhere and they have absolutely no idea that we're coming. So what's the harm in waiting up, getting something to eat and a few hours rest?"

"Fuck that! I'm not waiting another minute. I want my fists hitting flesh within the hour. These things have been through jungles and up mountains. I can't see a bit of seawater stopping it. Just put your foot down and stop being such a melt."

Barney had serious misgivings as they sped onto the causeway. He could see the waves gently lapping over the road further ahead. Theo wasn't Captain Nemo, and this definitely wasn't the Nautilus. Now he sincerely wished he was somewhere else entirely.

Chapter 19

"This coffee is beyond shit!" thought Robin as he wondered for the hundredth time that day where Mindy was? The place was falling apart without her, and he'd just wasted an entire hour trying to work out where she put things. He honestly hadn't realised exactly how much she did around the place until she hadn't appeared for work just over a week ago. It wasn't like her to not turn up. Sure they'd had their differences over the years and occasionally she had dug her heels in over things, usually money. But then they'd always eventually sorted it out. OK, he'd been a bit handsy now and again in the early days. But once the ground rules had been firmly established by Mindy's knee. They had settled into the traditional roles of the hapless tosspot boss and his ever capable, eye-rolling secretary.

He racked his brains to think what he might have done that had offended her so badly that she wouldn't even answer her phone to him? It just went straight to voice mail whenever he called. He had even tried getting the nearest thing Mindy had to a friend in the office to ring her, with exactly the same result. Perhaps she'd been headhunted and didn't have the words to tell him that their twenty-year association was over? She might be sat somewhere right now, dumping two decade's worth of secrets and contacts into the ear of one of his rivals. But if that was the case, why hadn't she taken all the fussy crap home that made her office look like a Scandinavian junior school staff room?

But then, surely by now, someone would have told him they had seen her. Or he would have had one of his less gifted warbling wankers on the phone thanking him for everything before announcing they were going to 'take things in a different direction'. As Mindy's new employer slowly picked off the unfancied stragglers on three-track contracts. Hoping to take them from the Conference League straight up to the Premiership.

Or maybe it was the hullabaloo with those goons the other day? But then she hadn't seemed unduly rattled afterwards. Besides, there were two costly ex-SAS security guards on duty now. So if they came back, they wouldn't even make it past reception. Perhaps she had something to do with the whole thing? Possibly part of some elaborate plot to destabilise his business to allow a ruthless takeover bid? That was more like it. Branson trying to re-launch his glory days in the music business by getting to his best artists. Well, if that was her game, he better let Tony Chapman know. So he could remind them of their contractual obligations and that the rights to the unfinished album lay with Blue Sky Records. If Branson wanted them, he wasn't getting their new album too! It had cost him a fortune so far to get the pair of coke monsters back in any fit state to record. So if that was going to be their last album on the label, he was having the green from it. Not to mention their fast approaching appearance at Glastonbury. If that went tits up, Eavis would see him sitting on orange boxes in a council flat by the time his lawyers had finished with him.

Robin's brain worked very much like a jukebox. Once his ego had made the right selection, there was only ever one record playing in his head. Now firmly settled on his utterly delusional train of thought and without his previously ever-faithful secretary on side calming his rampant megalomania. He decided to fire an SOS off to Tony. In the few seconds, it took for the call to connect his imagination added a few more 45's to the already shaky pile between his ears.

The 2Ds long-suffering manager was enjoying a little 'Tony Time' down on the Jurassic Coast. When his ringing mobile rudely interrupted a particularly delicious ice cream. After Robin had browbeaten him into signing the Glastonbury deal he had been giving his 'pub by the sea' retirement plan some serious consideration. He really fancied something in Dorset. Far from the madness of London and the omnipresent pressure of living in the capital. So having time on his hands with the 2Ds in the North East safely out of harm's way. He had taken a few days out of the office and found himself in Lyme Regis. The old-fashioned seafront with its pastel-coloured beach huts and ornate little guest houses made a strong case for a move this way. However, a quick look in the estate agent's windows had soon cooled his ardour. Deciding instead to relax and enjoy the unseasonable sunshine with a cornet by the harbour while watching the world go by. The nagging pest in his pocket, an ever-present reminder that he still had a business to run before he could cash in his chips and leave all the bullshit behind.

He groaned loudly when he saw the name on the screen. "What now?" he thought, clicking to receive the call. Robin was babbling away before the phone was even to his ear.

"Hello, Tony, it's Robin.."

"I know that Robin, my phone tells me who's calling before I even pick it up."

"Does it? Oh yes, of course. Mine does too. I mean when you ring me. Or when anyone else rings me for that matter."

"As interesting as that is Robin. Can I be as bold as to ask what you want? I'm taking a little time out of the office to relax before the 2Ds return to London and I have to click back into Heavy Father mode."

"Richard Branson sent a pair of heavies here last week looking for the twins. I think he must want them to sign for Virgin as I think Mindy was spying on me and now she's gone missing. So I reckon they must be heading up North to find them. If Branson pulls it off, we're both fucked! As no doubt, he'll get the new album before it's released and then they might not play Glastonbury. If that happens Eavis will sue us off the planet."

Robin's jukebox was now completely out of control, manically playing every single in its repertoire all at the same time. Turning what came out of the speakers into ten percent fact blended with ninety percent hysterical speculation. But the previously relaxed Tony soon seized on the important news that Mindy was missing. Quickly realising that other than himself, she was the only one who knew Declan and Dominic's exact location. Immediately making this his primary concern.

"Who exactly were they and what did they say to you?"

"It was that Robertson bloke that everyone is so shit scared of and one of his oppos. They had an old promo photo of them and kept asking where they were. I thought that maybe they owed on some Charlie. So I offered to settle the debt. But they weren't interested in money."

"So when did Mindy go missing?"

"The day after. I tried ringing when she didn't turn up for work, but it went straight to voicemail. I thought she was just trying to screw a rise out of me. So I didn't take that much notice as she's done it before. Usually comes in a few days later cracking on she's had a stomach upset. I tell her I wouldn't know what to do without her. Then bung her another few hundred quid a year and she settles down again. But she's never gone AWOL for this long in the past."

Tony immediately doubted Branson's involvement, as it didn't sound like his style. He would have been more likely to turn up in a limo with a giant cheque book and a camera crew.

"So why didn't you tell me this straight away, you pint-sized prat? I could have gone up there to keep an eye on them while they were working!"

"I don't know. I suppose they scared the crap out of me and left me traumatised. Then Mindy vanishing confused me even more. But I phoned you as soon as I'd worked it all out."

Tony was grateful that Robin didn't have any involvement with Bletchley Park during the Second World War, because his ability to invent absolute cobblers and enthusiastically roll it around in the facts might have greatly impeded the war effort! He cut the call, took one last lick of his cornet and dumped it in the bin. Hurrying back along the Cobb, he began to climb the steep hill to the two quid all-day car park. Loudly cursing his thrift and wishing that he'd used the millionaire's parking at the bottom as anxious sweat trickled from his armpits and over his ribs. It was a mystery to him how a total cluster fuck like Robin had made Blue Sky Records into one of the most successful companies in the British music industry. Now he had a long drive ahead of him he prayed would see him reach Holy Island before the Robertson Trio. For the life of him, he couldn't understand why a mild-mannered spinster secretary would get herself involved with a notorious gangster who had a worse track record than Harold Shipman!

When he, at last, reached the top of the hill he paused for a few moments. Gratefully clutching the wall as his chest heaved in the oxygen like a basking whale. His heart unaccustomed to the sudden speedball of exercise and stress. Slightly calmer, he fumbled in his pocket for his car keys and pushed himself away from the wall. Taking the final concrete steps up into the car park two at a time.

Heading off in the general direction of his car across the baking tarmac, he now wished he'd bought a cold drink instead of the ice-cream. His mouth was open and his tongue bone dry, as lungfuls of throat scorching air continued to pass over it in quick succession. When he had arrived bright and early, the plot was almost empty. Now it was absolutely heaving thanks to an influx of day-trippers keen to enjoy the warm weather and competitively priced seaside parking. Finally locating his car, he unlocked the driver's door and clambered in. Woefully unprepared for the black leather sauna that lay within.

Jamming the key into the ignition, he started the engine, wound down all the windows and sped towards the car park's exit. His anxiety seeing him then make an ill-advised right turn down the hill towards town. The now frantic Tony only realising his error once he was stationary in heavy traffic. Forced to gulp down chest fulls of choking, hot hydrocarbon laden air whilst trapped behind a lorry delivering large tubs of clotted cholesterol to a nearby fudge shop. Sweating profusely, he thumped the dashboard in fury and began to execute an extremely laboured three-point turn. Before promptly collapsing over the steering wheel and careering into a pasty truck crawling the other way up the steep hill.

Chapter 20

Finally, the big day had arrived. Martin and Craig sat in their Winnebago. Listening as the voice-over man from the company's TV adverts warmed up the crowd, a voice you knew but just couldn't place. And today he was really going for it. No doubt weary of smoothly announcing there was an Easter Special on fence paint or trying to tempt you to decorate your lounge over Christmas with 20% off everything.

A loud knock broke their attention as a rather stressed Myles appeared around the door wearing a flimsy microphone headset and carrying a clipboard. Craig soon realised it only held a single A4 sheet of paper and felt inclined to ask what was on it? Because as far as he knew, they were the only act due on stage. But wisely let it slide for the sake of talent/ backstage relations.

His suspicions were well-founded. As Myles had only stolen his son's video gaming headset the night before and made quick work of removing the felt-tipped 'NIGEL' from the clipboard with WD40. Desperate to avoid a return to the career graveyard of Wednesbury's Interior Lighting Department. He hoped that closely resembling a stage manager during the broadcast could only enhance his future employment prospects.

"Ready to go, lads? Sixty seconds to stage time."

Martin bounced up onto the balls of his feet as a rush of adrenalin ran down his back. The roar of the crowd steadily intensifying between each line of inflammatory drivel Mr Voiceover bellowed over the PA. His delivery style slowly morphing into an exuberant compere at a boxing match.

Martin grinned at Craig who returned it with a 'how did I talk myself into this one?' look. They hugged amidst the pile of non-recyclable rubbish that nervous boredom had created, then parted. Martin held up his hand and bawled, "Let's do this!" in a very poor interpretation of an American accent. Craig just stared back. Utterly flabbergasted that a fifty-two-year-old divorcee stood in a glorified caravan outside a regional DIY store was so drunk on proceedings he wanted to high five like Bruce Springsteen. For a second he left him hanging then thought "sod it!". Screaming "Yeah man!" in an accent that strongly suggested his last meal was also Mac 'n' Cheese washed down with a root beer. Completing the gesture with a hand whose closing speed at the point of impact could be considered ill-advised, given their musical obligation to the baying crowd outside.

Ever the rock professional, Myles had waited outside to allow 'the talent' to share this climactic moment in privacy. Sensibly stepping back as the two middle-aged adolescents exploded from the door exuding enough adrenalin to restart a Hippo's heart. Passing them their sweat towels, he led them to the side of the stage where Mr Voiceover was expertly cranking it up to a crescendo.

"… Ladies and gentlemen, they're ready to thrill you in the sunshine. So without further ado, I present to you…. THE CHEESY DIPS!"

Right on cue Martin and Craig bounded out onto the stage and a sea of Orange went completely mental! Suddenly they were no longer a store assistant and an undertaker. Now they were rock gods! It had been a long journey, but they were finally there. Martin noticed Debbie and Magda in the wings on the other side of the stage. She pointed at him and mouthed, "You're the man!" as her heart almost burst with pride. Magda appeared to try a similar thing with Craig, but he had gone to the edge of the stage to soak up the applause like a cream cracker in a dead man's mouth. As the roar slowly subsided, he walked back to take his place behind his keyboard. While Magda frantically continued in her attempt to stake a claim to her man from the wings. Finally pulling up her t-shirt and flashing her breasts in sheer desperation as Craig still failed to catch her eye. Myles gave her a wide smile from the other side of the stage, to which she responded with the middle finger. Nonetheless, secretly delighted that at least someone liked what they saw.

As Craig played random test notes on his keyboard to ensure everything was live and then gave Wally the thumbs in his raised sound booth amidst the crowd, Martin began to make a speech. Yet for no apparent reason continued in his brand new Halesowen Elvis voice.

"You know when we came up with this idea in the staff room four months ago. People said it wasn't possible. That nothing could bring the world of DIY together in one enormous love huddle. We're here today to prove them wrong!" Then he raised his fist in the air as their audience screamed back their agreement. With that Craig played the open chords to Love Is the Answer by England Dan and John Ford Coley. Which puzzled the crowd to some extent, as they were expecting Tooling All Over the World.

The lone black-clad figure's face broke into a demented smile as he heard the first notes from his lair in bushes high above the store on Mucklow Hill. As he had planned Tool Aid would be the perfect mask to any noise that he might make on his approach. It had been a simple matter to elude the lax security the company had provided to secure the car park and equipment. Just a matter of being in place twenty-four hours earlier, before the perimeter cordon had been fully established. Admittedly, lying on your back amongst the dog roses hadn't offered the best night's rest. Nor had a family pack of Twix Mini's and a bottle of Strawberry Yazoo formed the finest breakfast. But the privilege of watching two rampant foxes hump each other's brains out at 3 am had been truly magical. But now it was time to get into position once he'd had a crouching wazz.

Slowly the intruder slunk down the rose studded bank, dragging a large black holdall behind him. Totally focussed on his objective which was a spiral staircase at the very back of the store served by a concrete path and protected by a chain-link fence. As he drew closer, he saw that the guard who had earlier been patrolling this area had deserted his post to enjoy the spectacle unfolding on the stage at the front of the building. Perfect! Breaking cover, he silently bounded over the last ten metres before coming to rest against the fence. Reaching into the holdall, he took out a pair of brand new wire cutters. Spending several bad-tempered minutes wishing he had previously removed the zip clips that held the tool to its packaging. Whilst cursing the irony that a pair of wire cutters were the perfect tool to remove them. Finally with the clips defeated he set about cutting a hole in the wire fence. Soon discovering that the tool he'd seen in countless insurgency thrillers just wasn't up to the job. It had long been his suspicion that the company sold attractively packed but utterly fucking useless tools to the DIY masses, and now he had irrefutable proof. Unfortunately, Nigel was no longer in a position to put it on a memo. Because that podgy bastard he thought was his pal punched his head and somehow got him the sack. Even the woman at the Citizen's Advice Bureau couldn't understand how he had been the victim of violence at work and wound up being the one dismissed. But once Nigel had told her how to rearrange the office and strongly hinted that her personal hygiene was a little suspect, she wanted to belt him herself.

He silently seethed through the indignity. The best supervisor they ever had, attempting to break into his own store. With one piss soaked foot and a crappy pair of Chinese wire cutters that he had to travel on the bus to Wednesbury to buy. As understandably, he was banned from the Halesowen branch and no longer had use of a pool car. But to the last, a loyal company man, as plenty of other local DIY stores sold them. But Nigel wanted the CCTV footage of his purchase featured in the documentary Channel 5 was certain to make about his rightful revenge. The final two fingers to a company that had taken his best years and cast him aside like the sexually frustrated potential class-action lawsuit that he was.

The tears came quickly, but he fought them back and returned his attention to the job in hand. After around twenty minutes of solid effort, which became more about twisting until the wire snapped than actually cutting, he had a hole large enough to get his head through. By the time his hand was bleeding and the cutters had an overbite than would even make Tracey Emin's dentist consider leaving the profession, he finally managed to clamber through. Then straight back again when he realised he should have pushed the holdall through first.

By now The Cheesy Dips were halfway through their set. The crowd was bouncing along to every number. Total validation of the effort taken over their song choice. Slowly making their way from the nineties to the noughties before Martin made an impassioned but entirely scripted plea sent over from head office an hour before curtain up. Once again the area of his brain controlling speech experienced issues sparked by the intense emotion of the moment. Delivering this in an accent that crossed the Irish border several times before eventually settling on a collaboration between Jimmy Cricket and Gerry Adams accompanied by copious amounts of Ian Paisley spittle.

"I want everyone watching this to understand that just by buying an MDF radiator cover, a 12-inch oscillating room fan or a three-pack of Terracotta patio planters, they can help to change the lives of people living on the other side of the world. Families who don't have access to the most basic human essentials. Like a well-stocked coffee shop, clean customer toilets or a wide range of exotic houseplants. They need the DIYing British public to send them a message that we do care and that help is on the way. So pull out your cards, go into those aisles, choose that wallpaper, make a final decision on those wall tiles and get through those checkouts!"

Once again the crowd went bananas and Martin held his arms aloft to take their adulation. Myles, following the same script from stage side, realised that Martin had shot his bolt prematurely and ran onto the stage to bawl the omission into his ear. Madly irritated by the intrusion into the most important seconds of his previously utterly unremarkable life. Martin screamed back:

"FUCK THE WEBSITE GO TO THE TILLS!"

Craig saw this as a good time to prevent his mate saying anything further that might threaten his ongoing employment, (if screaming the 'F word' via a satellite link into pretty much every branch in the country wasn't enough) and drowned him out with the introduction to a three-song Electric Fondue medley. Leaving the man with the worst Irish accent since Mickey Rourke in 1987's A Prayer for the Dying with little option but to return to his keyboard. Before launching into Air Space, Impossible You and I Wouldn't Do It If You Didn't Like It in quick succession as the crowd swayed in unison and sang the lyrics back to them. By now Nigel had dragged the heavy holdall up the steel steps and onto the top of the store. Slowly inching his way across the corrugated metal roof before selecting his position at the far edge, looking down on the heartwarming spectacle below. But he felt nothing but hatred as he witnessed his brainchild brought to life. A spectacular vision of unity stolen from him by some halfwit electrician, an undertaker and a largely bald part-time toilet attendant. He knew what he had to do to show the world who was the real brains behind Tool Aid! He unzipped the holdall and began to assemble the apparatus whose secret development had seen him spend three days and nights in the shed. Ordering Mother to leave his Ribena and Dairylea sandwiches outside the door and only taking them in when he heard her Zimmer frame clatter back down the garden path. Testing had been difficult as understandably a nerdy bachelor riding the bus to Clent Hills carrying a bag the size of a drugged teenager made the other passengers nervous. But he had cleverly sidestepped the issue by explaining he was a model aeroplane enthusiast whose car was in for a service. Which sufficiently calmed their fears to the point they stopped whispering and taking covert photos of him on their phones.

Soon his weapon of mass destruction was in position and Nigel was all set to reclaim his glory. To the casual observer, it was a garden leaf blower with the bag removed and the addition of two bolt-on legs that were adjustable for height and angle. However, to an expert in improvised weaponry, it was a petrol-powered mortar. To further the transformation, its 'inventor' had pulled the stock stickers off and scrawled V3 down the side with the same green paint Mother had chosen for the summer house window frames. Which when viewed against the bright orange plastic wouldn't see it in a black museum next to Hitler's earlier V1 or V2 efforts any time soon. However, starting the thing had always been a little hit and miss. Bearing in mind that during testing it hadn't just spent the night lying on its side. Before being carted 50ft up a spiral staircase and onto a DIY store roof.

Now Nigel's adrenal gland was twitching like a twenty stone mermaid in a sushi restaurant. Lay prone, he moved the switch to run, set the choke to full, pressed the little fuel bulb three times and vigorously pulled the starter cord. The little 25cc motor responded with little more than a complimentary chug. Undeterred, he recharged his muscles and gave it another go with entirely the same result. Seventeen attempts later, Nigel had risen to his knees. Struggling for breath as the relentless tugging gave him more stamina issues than his fourth-year school Summer holidays. What he needed right now more than anything in the world was a double shot of Salbutamol. But stupidly, he had neglected to pack an inhaler amongst his improvised assassin's kit. As Mother was the one who usually reminded him to take it and she was still in a huff about his secret 'door shut' shed antics.

Finally, mustering all his determination as his screaming lungs noisily begged him not to, he rose to his feet. Gripping the starter cord with a similar level of determination that saw King Arthur pull Excalibur from the stone. Silently counting himself down from three. He summoned every fibre of muscle in his scrawny body to congregate in one last valiant all-out effort to get the orange and Buckingham Green bastard to start!

THREE... TWO... ONE...

Giving it absolutely everything he had, he was finally rewarded as the puny motor spat back and then roared into life. Inconveniently timing its eventual combustion with a hushed lull between songs. As a convulsing Nigel, his lungs now containing slightly less air than a bag of pound store party balloons, kicked the lot over and plunged to his death in the car park below. His terminal velocity made an absolute certainty by the now fully operational leaf blower which soon followed him from the roof. Cushioned in part by the heavy holdall which had become tangled around his ankle during the dramatic staggering of his last ever asthma attack.

Not surprisingly, the sight and sound of a man dressed entirely in black plummeting headfirst from the roof in the style of a mortally wounded gunman in a Spaghetti Western. Closely followed by a screaming leaf blower and an enormous bag of condoms stuffed with several days-worth of the more viscous offerings from Mother's commode, which instantly exploded on impact. Spraying shrapnel of a type unseen in any military conflict in all directions had a rather detrimental effect on the crowd's willingness to stay and enjoy the final fifteen minutes of Tool Aid. Instead, despite the best efforts of the ragtag security team, stampeding out of the car park onto Mucklow Hill. Leaving behind a bewildered Cheesy Dips now just playing to Myles, Debbie, Welsh Wally, a completely topless Magda and two cack splattered cameramen.

Chapter 21

It was a bright chilly morning when Barney awoke to the sound of gulls crying as they swooped and soared, searching for a stiff fresh breakfast in the waters that surrounded them. As ever, he had experienced no problem in sleeping, despite their less than luxurious lodgings. It was a talent that never left an old soldier. The ability to curl up in whatever you had handy and nod straight off. But when you could manage a solid five hours lying in a Kuwaiti shop doorway as a war raged on around you. The safety refuge on the Holy Island causeway wouldn't pose much of a problem.

Like a leather-clad King Canute, Barney knew all along it was a stupid move to try to beat the tide. So as the splashing under the tyres became aquaplaning that threatened to see them crash off the road and disappear beneath the waves. Theo finally realised his driver was right. Willingly abandoning the Range Rover and gratefully clambering up the sea-worn wooden steps to the little white hut on stilts that lay halfway between the island and the mainland. From where he watched glumly as the sea slowly engulfed Cecelia's new car that he had only borrowed that morning for their mission in the North. Of course, they could have used their phones to request help from the coastguard. But then that might have led to awkward questions about the arsenal of unlicensed weaponry they had about their person. So a night in an elevated garden shed waiting for the tide to recede had appeared to be their only option.

Unusually for the North Sea, it wasn't a windy night and if they'd had sleeping bags, it would have been a proper Boy's Own Adventure. Admittedly, it was a tad on the cramped side for two large men, with their overnight bags and a versatile selection of firearms. Barney was secretly relieved there hadn't been time to grab the electric plaster stirrer with which Theo intended to blend the twin's internal organs like a fresh offal stew. Because now he didn't have to hold them still whilst he did so. Sometimes blood-curdling screams visited him in his sleep. If Dickens had confronted Scrooge with the Ghost of Victims Past, it could well have seen the first example of PTSD in British literature.

Theo was still sleeping on his back, snoring loudly as the salty air moved in and out of his sadistic body. Asleep, he appeared vaguely similar to most other men in their late fifties. A greying, podgy mess of overindulgence, late nights and poor dietary decisions. But much like a lazy middle-aged crocodile basking in the sunshine beside a filthy stagnant river. He was inert and harmless within that moment, but if disturbed, utterly deadly seconds later.

Barney gently fished around in his bag and found his binoculars. Forcing his stiff body to move quietly, he stepped out onto the top of the staircase for a better view. In no time at all, spotting birds that he'd only previously read about in books. The onset of Spring had brought many foreign sea birds to these waters. Some to stay, others just stopping off en route to their breeding grounds. Readily admitting to himself just how much he enjoyed his secret hobby and the thrill that engulfed him when he saw something new. Alas, good things don't last forever, and the vocal dismay of his mentally unstable travelling companion soon shattered the peace.

"Oh bollocks, it's fucking ruined! Cecelia will go stark staring mad. It was a special order, and she spent an entire day in the dealership picking out all the extras," wailed Theo peering over the handrail beside Barney at the flooded Chelsea Tractor below. That now looked more like a mobile hot tub than a luxury 4x4.

At first, Barney said nothing. If the wooden structure had been more substantial, he might have strangled the prick there and then. As his pointless wailing had just scared off a Red-Throated Diver, he had been quietly observing for some time hoping it might dive for its breakfast. Eventually, though, he stopped saying nothing...

"If you had listened to me, we could be waking up fully refreshed in a little guest house somewhere nice. Enjoying the view from the dining-room window and being fussed over by some old dear who makes her own marmalade and drives past two butchers to get to the one she knows has the best sausage and bacon. Instead, because you're an impatient homicidal megalomaniac that can't wait a few hours to do unspeakable things to two kids who mess about on Bontempi organs for a living. We're cold, hungry and our transport is more fucked than the train Alec Guinness blew up in Bridge Over the River Kwai!"

This unexpected outburst took Theo aback. He was a bastard, but nonetheless, he was a fair one. But Barney was absolutely right. He had made the elementary mistake of allowing emotion to cloud his judgement. He was so desperate to avenge his daughter's deflowering that he had failed to heed good advice when it was offered. Although getting a bollocking from his driver was definitely something new. But as there was only a bunch of seagulls bearing witness, he would let it go just this once. That said, he wasn't keen on the mention of Colonel Nicholson. The British officer who became so fixated on the construction of the Japanese bridge that he forgot which side he was fighting on. That stung a bit!

It was a further hour before the waters sufficiently retreated to reveal the causeway. During which Theo sat sulking in the corner of the hut with his arms folded like a scolded child. He wasn't used to be told off. Barney just ignored him and got on with the very serious business of bird watching. Finally, it was time to make a move when a pair of plasterers sped by in a beat-up old van. Tooting the horn and shouting, "We know what you're doing!" out of the window as they passed.

Theo instantly sprang into action, realising his sulking spot hadn't afforded him the best view of the water's withdrawal. Grabbed his bag and squeezed down the steps past Barney. Who was reluctantly putting away his binoculars, having experienced the best hour's bird watching ever. Then climbed up to the hut to replace them in his bag and retrieve their firearms compendium. Quietly laughing to himself as Theo opened the passenger door and sea water poured out. Resigned to the fact that it probably wouldn't be the best of days…

The 2Ds were in a more relaxed routine now. They had completed the vast majority of the album and there was just a few days work remaining on the final mix before they returned to London to present it to Robin and Tony in person. The whole Holy Island experience had proved to be an enormous influence on their writing. Gone were the days of fast living, women and powder. Replaced by love, optimism and hope for the future. It impressed Hugh how well they had settled down to their task after such a shaky start. Now they pretty came and went as they saw fit, with breakfast at the Village Idiot appearing to be their favoured start to the day. The older man chose not to cramp their style by tagging along. Instead, he enjoyed the peace to get on with his work while they filled up on coffee and freshly baked bagels.

This particular morning Declan and Dominic had risen early after the sun put in a 7 am appearance through the roof window of their attic bedroom. But then it was always hard to sleep through the seagull's antics as they screamed to each other across the rooftops. Declan had confessed his moonlight trysts with Daisy to his brother a few days previously. But suspected that Hugh might curtail their romance if he got wind of it. So extended breakfast meetings and long walks had become their time together. Which soon led to the little radio in Zab's boat requiring new batteries. As that had often been their destination as things progressed in the way they always seem to.

"We're just off out for breakfast, do you want anything?" said Declan putting his head around the control room door to Hugh who was already hard at work at the mixing desk.

"What was that thing you brought me the other day? I liked that."

"The one with the eggs and chorizo sausage?"

"Yeah, that's the one. I'll have that."

"Spanish Eggs coming right up!"

"Thanks, kid, see you shortly…"

Hugh winced as Declan thundered back down the studio stairs two at a time and straight out of the door at the bottom. Waiting for the inevitable bang as the spring slammed it shut before returning his full attention to the loop he was working on. Safe in the knowledge that it would be an hour or more until he was disturbed again.

Back at Murder Mission Control, things weren't going at all well. The Range Rover was as dead as Sooty and Sweep's legs, and harsh realities were dawning. Theo was now having to come to terms with his brand new signature killing method being an absolute non-starter. As the plaster stirrer was rather too heavy to carry, which might make creeping up on his intended victims a little tricky after a two mile route march into the village. Plus, with nowhere to plug it in, he wasn't sure if it still worked after a night soaking in saltwater. So the time had arrived to select your favourite firearm and dump the rest.

Theo was a big fan of the Magnum 357. Like him, it had a fearsome reputation. His weapon of choice since Clint Eastwood mockingly enquired after his detainee's good fortune. Barney selected a Colt 45 automatic pistol. Preferring its ease of use, reliability and simpler loading system. Then, much to Theo's disgust, everything else went to a watery grave amongst the rock pools. Hoping to avoid discovery until after they were long gone. He knew replacements wouldn't come cheap and the cost of the whole trip was firmly into five figures already!

So it wasn't a harmonious duo that set off to walk the rest of the way along the causeway towards Holy Island. Theo was still smarting from Barney's outspoken tongue lashing, and his driver no longer felt obliged to soothe his ego by making conversation. He was far happier walking behind whilst enjoying the sea breeze and sunshine on his face, as the inhabitants from the pages of his bird book collection sprang to life everywhere he looked.

A steady stream of traffic flowed past them towards the mainland as they trudged along like an Abbott and Costello tribute act. Barney couldn't help thinking the islanders might easily recall the two dishevelled strangers once the police made enquiries into what would almost certainly be their first-ever twin sibling homicide. Not to mention that the abandoned car helpfully registered to Theo's ex-partner might also provide a fairly major clue to the identity of their suspects. But once again decided not to mention it and instead just act accordingly when the time came. Soon the Range Rover was a speck in the distance as they rounded the right-hand bend and got their first view of Lindisfarne.

Hugh was hard at work when he heard the outside door open again. He glanced up at the clock. It was only 8.40am. He rarely saw sight or hair of them until well gone nine. Then he detected two pairs of feet climbing the stairs, instantly perplexed by how heavy their footsteps seemed. The twins lived in trainers, but these sounded more like boots. As he rose from the mixing desk to make enquiries, the control room door flew open. In trudged a weary Theo, closely followed by Barney. Instinct soon told Hugh he was in trouble. He watched, still dumbfounded, as Theo and Barney gladly threw themselves onto the enormous leather sofa that covered the back wall of the control room. He deduced from their attire that they were neither locals nor obsessive fans. Either of which could usually be placated with a selfie and a bagful of eBayable promo. His alarm only increased when Theo spoke, and he heard his distinctive London accent.

"So who exactly might you be?" inquired Theo

"What the fuck's it got to do with you?" responded Hugh, surprised by his own bravado.

"Fair point."

Theo took the Magnum from the inside pocket of the now ruined brand new Crombie he thoroughly regretted travelling in. Pointed it at Hugh and whilst maintaining constant eye contact, calmly cocked it with his thumb. There was an audible click as the hammer came to rest on the trigger lever and Hugh immediately emitted the sound a beach ball makes going down at the end of a day trip to the seaside.

"Now do you feel more disposed to answer my perfectly polite question?"

"My name is Hugh Hunt. I'm a music producer and engineer,"

Hugh babbled, now struggling not to recreate last night's excellent Toad in the Hole on his swivel chair.

"That's much better" snarled Theo, who was slowly recovering from the two-mile trudge into the village and an extensive tour of its narrow streets in the search for Priory Studios.

"My name is Theo Robertson. I'm a businessman and some say a gangster. This is my associate, Barney. We would like to speak to Dominic and Declan Dafoe."

"May I ask what for?"

"It's of a personal nature, I'm afraid," replied Theo. Deciding he was rather tired of this phrase and hoping this would be the last time he would have to utter it.

It didn't take Hugh long to work out that the 2Ds were enjoying their last ever coffee in the Village Idiot if he told Theo where they were. Or that they were due back in around fifteen minutes. He guessed that this was the first recording studio that the gruesome duo had ever set foot in. As although they looked 'a bit Goth' in their all-black attire, they definitely didn't ooze previous musical experience.

"We ran out of recording tape, so I sent them over to the mainland to fetch some more. They probably won't be back till after dinner."

"That was a nice try, Hugh and I might have gone with it. Had it not been for the word 'digital' emblazoned on the desk behind you and the otherwise telltale total lack of tape recorders. So would you care to try again before I ensure you need urgent knee replacement surgery?"

Hugh gulped. He wasn't a hero. He knew his way around a desk and he'd made some great albums over the years. But he didn't have any medals for courage under fire or going above or beyond the call of duty.

"They've gone to the café for their breakfast. They'll be back soon."

"That's better. Now why don't we all relax and just wait for them to get back?" said Theo uncocking his Magnum. Much to Hugh's relief, who had seen a documentary about gangland kneecappings and didn't fancy thinking of Theo every time he bent his legs in the future. Clearly, whatever these guys wanted the 2Ds for, they'd brought it upon themselves, and anything that might happen, still would, regardless of what he did. So he didn't see the point in him becoming unnecessary collateral damage in the process. But that said, it might just be possible to warn them something was amiss. So when Theo's fickle attention span momentarily wavered, he quietly reached behind him under the desk and pressed the button that turned on the red recording warning light outside the courtyard door. Praying they might see that upon their return and therefore enter cautiously.

They didn't have to wait too long. The 2Ds had just left the Village Idiot buoyed by a hearty breakfast of ham and cheese croissants and double espresso. It was only a short walk back and soon their footsteps were crunching up the gravel drive. Theo put a finger to his lips and stood behind the control room door. Barney took out his Colt and stood flat against the back wall beside the settee.

Hugh heard the courtyard door slowly open, and some low mumblings as the twins entered. Thankfully, they had seen the warning lamp, and it had puzzled them. Otherwise he knew right now they would be thundering up the stairs before bounding into the control room in a ball of caffeine-induced energy. Then, just as he hoped, the performance area door quietly opened and unobserved by Theo and Barney the 2Ds stood staring quizzically at the control room window. Time stood still for several seconds until Theo felt their gaze upon him and realised the objects of his frustration were silently observing them from below. Instantly, he brought the Magnum to bear and cracked off a shot that passed over Hugh's head, shattered the control room window and lodged itself in the sound insulation board six inches to the left of Dominic. Who responded by dropping Hugh's eggy breakfast and pushing his twin back through the performance area door. Just as Theo's second effort ricocheted off a keyboard in A-sharp. Neither brother had any idea who Theo and Barney were or why they were being shot at. But it didn't seem sensible to take the time to discuss it as they exploded back out of the courtyard door and pelted down the drive. Followed moments later by Theo and Barney. Leaving Hugh lying on the control room floor bearing a nasty head wound but still posessing two fully functioning knees.

As they ran past the Priory ruins, Barney managed a good effort which spat dust up from the path just in front of Declan as it missed him by inches. By now Theo having trouble keeping up, bitterly regretting never having considered the prospect of adding a gym to his criminal empire.

Having no vehicle with which to escape or phones with which to call for help. The 2Ds had no option but to attempt to evade capture. Which could only mean getting off the island? As surely it was only a matter of time until one of those rounds connected? Suddenly Declan remembered Zab's boat and bellowed for Dominic to follow him.

It was only a matter of a few hundred yards and soon they were at the water's edge, as a relieved Declan saw the little fishing boat still afloat on the very last of the outgoing tide. They ran across the sharp rocks, slithering on the wet seaweed. Still hearing the angry voices of their pursuers making breathless threats far behind them. Their lungs gasping for air, struggling to cope with the unfamiliar exertion, and their unsuitable footwear making progress slow over the tough terrain.

Salvation in sight, the exhausted twins splashed through the shallow water and gratefully clambered aboard. At once Declan began a desperate attempt to make sense of the embossed tape labels that gave purpose to the knobs, switches and dials that covered the bare plywood dashboard. Far less familiar with their transport. Dominic set about untying the thick weatherworn rope that secured them to the beach and ultimately an untimely demise at the hands of Theo and Barney.

With only seconds to spare the red heater plug light finally went out and as Declan cranked the starter, the old diesel engine lazily clanked into life. Instinctively, he slammed the throttle lever fully forward. Provoking a chokey cough, as within its oily chambers, tired pistons struggled to respond. Unaccustomed to such a heavy demand for power so soon after starting. Then they were away. And not a moment too soon, as the splashing of clumsy feet loomed louder behind them. It was a time for celebration. But neither twin could muster the strength. Chugging slowly out to sea as desperate bullets cut through the air surrounding them.

"Where should we head for?" gasped Declan.

"Search me! I've no more idea than you!"

"Maybe sail along the coast a little way, look for a harbour and head toward that."

"Sounds like a plan. Then if we can get to a phone, we can ring Tony to come and get us."

Granted, it was an excellent plan for a pair of landlubbing Londoners whose only previous experience of boats had been the glass fibre ones on a kiddy's carousel. One that just might have worked had the engine not spluttered and died just a few short minutes later. Starved of fuel by their complete ignorance of the need to open the main fuel valve.

Back on the beach, Theo was incandescent with rage. He had been within a hair's breadth of avenging his daughter's deflowering. Instead, he was now ankle-deep in the North Sea, watching helplessly as the 2Ds made good their escape. Barney looked on impassively as the homicidal maniac screamed and bellowed like a spoilt brat watching his older siblings board a coach for a school trip. He'd never seen him like this. But then things usually went to plan. People just looked scared, paid-up or died. Failure was an entirely unfamiliar experience for his boss and it was clear they wouldn't be easy bedfellows.

As Theo stood, head in hands, sobbing. A large gull watched with increasing interest from a nearby buoy who had taken it upon itself to bear witness to the whole sorry saga. The pitch of his shrieks and sobs must have sparked something in the enormous bird's psyche, as it suddenly squawked loudly and began wildly flapping its wings, without seeing any need to take off. Once again, Theo tore his tear-soaked hands from his face like a hateful child as the seabird's deafening call rang in his ears. Then one last time, aimed his enormous hand cannon and promptly shot it in the head. Which immediately disintegrated on impact as the bullet pushed its beak back into the space formerly occupied by its skull. Leaving it still momentarily erect, before tidily folding into itself and dropping from its perch with a pathetic splash as it landed amongst the waves.

Barney, the closet twitcher, stood aghast at the senseless slaughter of the first marine bird he had ever had the privilege to marvel at up close. Nothing from the television had prepared him for the sheer size and power of the unfortunately inquisitive fish powered spectator.

"What the fuck did you do that for?"

Theo was tiring of having his actions questioned by Barney. Admittedly, he might occasionally comment, soothe or respectfully suggest another course of action. But he had never employed him as a life coach or an anger management practitioner.

"Because it was fucking laughing at me!" screamed Theo.

"What do you expect, it's a fucking seagull? You were making a mental amount of noise and it probably just thought you were a massive female looking for a mate!"

Without further ado, an enraged Barney raised his gun and shot his petulant boss straight between the eyes with his last bullet. Watching without emotion as the greater part of his brain matter left by the back door before he crumpled face-first into the surf with a splash of crimson foam. Over the years, Barney had faithfully followed Theo through all manner of unnecessary slaughter. But even he drew the line at murdering innocent seabirds.

Coincidentally, he had been considering a move into self-employment for quite some time. Now it would seem he had all the contacts, experience and expertise required. Making it the perfect time for a little private enterprise. Seeing as how the king had just unexpectedly abdicated leaving him in charge of the keys to the castle…

Chapter 22

When Tony opened his eyes, he had a bigger audience than the Pope sometimes gets on a rainy Christmas Day in St. Peter's Square. There were paramedics, firefighters, police, two lorry drivers and around a hundred curious holidaymakers. Plus several people who ran the shops on the hill rubbernecking out from their shop doorways. All watching with a mixture of anger, pity and intrigue as a still dazed Tony was skilfully manhandled from his car and transferred to the back of an ambulance. Where he now sat bare-chested, answering a lot of questions while they checked his vital signs.

Had this happened before? Was he on any medication? Had he experienced any undue stress just lately?

He truthfully answered 'no' to the first two and lied about the third. In the time-honoured tradition of middle-aged men everywhere vigorously denying he was under any pressure of any kind. It was just the walk up the hill, the heat, the sunshine and the long drive. Anything but discovering his best act was being tracked down by two nasty hard cases and that he was at the wrong end of the country to do anything about it.

He found it hard to take the young paramedic with rolling Rs and badly drawn triangular eyebrows seriously. She repeatedly insisted that he should go for a full check-up in A&E. But now the lights were back on and he felt reasonably OK, he didn't feel inclined to agree. Frankly, he was more embarrassed than anything else. But Groucho Marx firmly stood her ground, and as Tony continued to protest, he felt woozy again. So that just proved her point. Next stop, Axminster Hospital!

Tony managed another little snooze as they blue lighted along the narrow hedge-lined lanes. Occasionally slowing at a pinch to squeeze past the many campers and delivery vans going in the opposite direction. As they sped along he dreamt that Theo Robertson signed as his new act and played the washboard at Glastonbury while he watched from a helicopter above. Holding the crowd spellbound, belting out Cockney music hall favourites dressed as a pearly king. Until Michael Eavis walked on and Theo killed him with a miniature fire engine while everyone clapped. He'd had more restful dreams on Christmas afternoons after a wedge of Stilton and half a bottle of port!

Suddenly he was awoken by a loud clanking and opened his eyes to find he was on the move. The back of the ambulance was now wide open, and his noisy metal bed was squeaking its way towards a white single-storey building. That even through sleepy eyes looked more like a library or large garden centre than a hospital. The cheery red-tiled roof and pebble-dashed walls no doubt seriously at odds with the illness and suffering waiting for him inside.

Hospitals in London were unmistakable. Tall, miserable and grimy, like seedy budget hotels that saw more Mr & Mrs Jones's pass through them than Cardiff Registry Office. Victorian towers of damp with bits haphazardly built on as the need arose to create an ugly warren of annexes and mobiles plastered in a thousand dreary NHS signs. Often requiring a map and compass just to find your way to a shabby outpatient clinic the size of a broom cupboard. Whilst everything you passed along the way vaguely smelt of shit, disinfectant, or last night's boiled cabbage dinner.

But this was something else. Inside it was light and airy, like an oversized doctor's surgery. Peach painted walls complemented by a cheery floral border set just above a purposeful flat white dado rail. Clearly intended to protect the perfect plaster from even the most hapless of trolley pushers. Waiting rooms that boasted comfy settees and framed art of well-known local landmarks. Instead of the usual mishmash of back-breaking, wipe clean, orange plastic chairs and dreary public health posters. Skilfully positioned to hide the missing paint taken by the Sellotape holding up last year's public health crisis. But Tony was way past caring about regional inequalities in the country's health service. He just wanted to sleep and forget about his problems for a few hours. He had the ideal excuse. He was evidently ill.

As the paramedics handed over to the hospital staff in the neat, well-equipped cubicle, he noted that nurses no longer wore paper hats and everyone seemed to have pastel coloured pyjamas on. They looked like presenters on a kid's

TV programme and spoke to him in slow measured tones as if he was simple or very elderly. Groucho had driven them in and been at the back of the trolley as they made their way to A&E. Surprised by her eyebrows for a second time, they still seemed comical to him. Which he had to admit was an odd reaction considering the potential gravity of his situation.

"This is Tony. He passed out and crashed his car in Lyme Regis. His vital signs now appear to be stable. We haven't given him anything apart from oxygen, but he was still a little dazed and fell asleep again on the way here. So we insisted that he came to get fully checked out."

Tony just listened. For once he wasn't in charge. Just a new patient dropping on to the start of a very long conveyor belt. As the paramedics retreated to rescue another overwrought tourist, more in-depth questioning began. As a manager, he was more used to posing questions than providing answers, but surprised himself with the level of honesty in his responses. He could always rip the tubes out of his arm later and turn the place over, looking for his clothes. The way they always did in action films. Before escaping out of a fire exit disguised as a doctor a split-second prior to the arrival of the cops or an assassin. But for now, he would just sit tight and have a good kip when they finally shut up and left him alone.

"Hello Tony, I'm Roz and I'm a nurse practitioner. You're at Axminster Hospital and we will admit you for observation. Can you tell me when you last had a check-up at the doctors?"

"Check-up?"

"You know a Health MOT or Well Man Check. Height, weight, blood test, urine test, that sort of thing"

"Err never... I got a few letters, but I slung them in the bin. I felt all right, so that was good enough for me."

"Derr... wrong answer!"

Roz was bored. It seemed she had very little to do that day and if she wasn't careful could end up helping on the geriatric ward. That was the Russian Front of nursing. Never having been a fan of bedpans and adult nappies, she took it upon herself there and then that Tony would get the works and she would save a life! Not immediately, but six months from now. When her timely intervention would prevent a blood clot the size of a pound pack of Lurpak terminating his heartbeat like a ping-pong ball disappearing up a Henry vacuum cleaner. Regrettably, for Tony, it would now be a while before he could get his head down.

After four hours of exhaustive testing, involving being poked, prodded and generally violated via every orifice. It became clear that Tony's heart was in genuinely tip-top condition with blood pressure to match, and his prostate remained the ideal size of a supermarket mini-ring doughnut. Rather than the more generous fat engorged variety often found at the fair. On the downside, he possessed blood cholesterol levels consistent with a man slightly too fond of red meat, and yet more critically, his urine contained marginally more sugar than the luminous effluent flowing out of Willy Wonka's Chocolate Factory! Tony finally had his label. He was now officially a Type 2 diabetic. A man about to experience the never-ending joy of questioning the sugar content of just about everything he put in his mouth from this day forward.

Following this revelation, he sat for a further hour listening politely as Roz delivered the gospel according to insulin. But at no point felt any obligation to engage as she enthusiastically thrust booklets and diet sheets towards him at regular intervals. Patiently reading the highlights aloud when he showed no genuine interest in looking at them. Weary Tony quietly watched her lips move as she droned on and on about glucose, dextrose, fructose and sucrose. Informing him of the dangers of added, hidden and natural sugars. Imploring him to say goodbye to fizzy drinks, cakes and confectionery. Then hitting him with amazing facts such as some jars of pasta sauce contained upwards of four teaspoons of sugar. All the time her earnest, sun-ripened face and 'I'm wacky!' bright orange dyed hair clashing rather heavily with the mustard-coloured cotton two-piece that willingly betrayed her preference for striped cotton maxi briefs every time she bent over. Please God, make her stop! For the first time in his life, Tony was in total denial. All he really needed was a little peace and quiet for a good think followed by some quality shut-eye and he'd be all set to split in the morning!

At last, the health lecture from Hell was over. Roz had completed her shift productively and once again successfully avoided a miserable day wiping up after the coffin dodgers. Now left alone on his bed on the ward wearing a paper-thin peekaboo gown with remnants of KY Jelly still lingering around his anus like trace evidence from a public school initiation ceremony, Tony finally came to terms with the revised lifestyle that he had spent the last hour hearing all about. Beside him on the well-worn bedside cabinet were his new tablets and a little machine that he had to stick little strips of blood smeared paper in, every day, for the rest of his life. Sod it! He'd deal with it all tomorrow. Now, at last, he could shut his eyes and enjoy the Roz-free peace.

Just as he was drifting off the buzzer sounded for visiting time and the ward's double doors flew open as the stampede for the 'good chairs' began. Followed by more clanking and scraping than an infant school dinner hall blended with the excited jabber of a dozen harassed housewives dragging their freshly scrubbed offspring behind them. All pre-threatened during the car journey there not to draw undue attention to sudden foul smells or interfere with the electric bed controls. Kids that were no doubt far happier to spend the evening playing on their games console rather than risk letting their mother down in public and suffering for it all the way home.

With no visitors to entertain and more chance of nodding off in a Formula One wind tunnel, Tony's sleep-deprived mind chewed over the facts as he saw them. He quickly dismissed Robin's Richard Branson theory as an absolute non-starter because it made no sense at all. Nowadays the bearded Peter Pan of transport was all about trains, planes and spacecraft. His days in the music business were far behind him.

If the issue was simply money, then Robertson would have been more than happy to settle up with Robin. It wouldn't matter who paid him as long as someone did. So then it must be something very personal indeed. But what exactly? He could only guess at some form of sexual trespass, possibly a spousal incursion? That's the only thing he could think of that would make a thug like Theo Robertson leave the safety of London and travel all the way up to the North East of England. He gave a moment's thought to which of the twins was stupid enough to forge a liaison with a female connected to one of London's most notorious villains. Granted they were reckless, but they weren't suicidal and presumably any love interest of Robertson's would be well outside their target age range. During their ten-year association, he'd never known either of them to display a thing for older women. So possibly it was a dancer from one of his clubs. But why would that bother Robertson so much? If they danced semi-naked around a chrome pole entirely for male titillation, then they were hardly likely to be a part-time Sunday school teacher. But then where did Mindy fit into all this? He couldn't imagine her willingly taking part in a gangland manhunt. So that could only mean that either she was acting under duress or Robertson had a thing for frumpy cardigan loving secretaries with their best years behind them.

Pleased with his rationale, he began rooting around in the clear bin bag that now contained his belongings, looking for his phone. Why hadn't he just rung ahead to Hugh and warned him? It seemed logical now. But when his blood contained slightly less sugar than a mixer can of Diet Coke, his only thought had been to scream straight up the motorway and try to head them off.

Up North, Hugh had also experienced a recent brush with the NHS. The local doctor's surgery had kindly stitched his gaping head wound while a detective from Northumbria Police waited patiently to interview him. The force had never considered Lindisfarne a crime hotspot. So when multiple reports came in of 'shots fired', at first they assumed it to be a mistake. The most noteworthy happenings on the island could usually be attributed to tourists. People sometimes did the strangest things on holiday, but early morning fireworks seemed to be stretching it a little. So when a call came in from an ex-marine who specified the weapons he suspected he'd heard. An armed response team was finally dispatched from the mainland, along with a solitary detective. Closely followed by a van full of regular coppers in the event a crime scene needed to be secured. As this convoy sped along the causeway towards the village, it was forced to give way to oncoming traffic by an abandoned Range Rover. Just as the newly unemployed Barney driving a recently acquired plasterer's van passed them going in the opposite direction. Not the vehicle Theo would have chosen for his forthcoming private burial. But as he was currently lying in state with most of the back of his head hurriedly shoved in the pocket of his Crombie. Surrounded by buckets, dustsheets and half bags of cement. Understandably, he had very little say in the matter.

Now, much later, a shellshocked Hugh sat in the kitchen of Priory Studios feeling very sorry for himself. His bandaged head still throbbed from his pistol-whipping despite there being more than enough prescription painkillers in his system to see Prince and Michael Jackson through a double speed rendition of Swan Lake. He'd told the detective everything he knew, which was in reality very little. Then repeated that to another more senior officer and once again when a rather attractive lady appeared from the National Crime Agency. Predictably, they all asked the same questions and got much the same answers.

"Who were the gunmen?"

"I don't know apart from they had Cockney accents."

"Any idea why they targeted you?"

"None I can think of"

"What did they tell you?"

"Very little apart from it was personal."

The only positive news he'd had, (obviously apart from his skull, was seemingly thicker than Humpty Dumpty's) that there was absolutely no evidence of anyone being shot. So apart from a single decapitated seagull, there appeared to be no fatalities. Which given the number of shots fired seemed to be nothing short of a miracle. The unwelcome news, however, was that the twins were missing, feared abducted and that a local plasterer's van was stolen during the resulting chaos. It was difficult to believe that something connected the two, as according to its owner it was a heavily corroded fourteen-year-old transit that rarely covered more than ten miles a day. Nonetheless, it too was nowhere to be found and Plastered in Grit now found themselves without transport, materials or tools. Meaning a rather pissy Mrs Osborne would have to wait a while longer to get her holiday cottage rendered. Hugh was just getting his battered head around the implications of the day's events, intending to phone Tony and update him on events when his phone rang. He winced when he saw it was the 2Ds manager calling him before he had anything upbeat that might soften the blow.

"Hello, Hugh! I should have rung you earlier, but I've had a bit of a bad day."

"I've honestly not had the best one myself, but you go first."

"I'm in hospital because it would seem that I'm diabetic."

"How did you suddenly find that out?"

"When I passed out and crashed into a pasty truck."

"A pasty truck? Where are you?"

"I'm in Dorset. But I'm not ringing to tell you that. I'm ringing because there are a right pair of nasty bastards on their way up to find the twins."

"Ahh... too late. They already found them."

"Oh fuck! Are they all right?"

"To be honest, I don't have a clue because we can't find them. It looks likely Robertson abducted them. But then, all things considered, that's probably slightly better than being shot dead."

"They had guns?"

"Yep, it's been like the OK Corral up here! So do you know who they were?"

With that, Tony relayed the conversation that he'd had with Robin that morning.

"So no sign at all of Richard Branson or a spinster called Mindy?"

"None at all. Just two thugs with guns. So how long are you going to be in hospital for?"

"Only overnight. Once they've stabilised my blood sugar, they'll kick me out."

"OK, well, try to get some rest and I'll speak to you in the morning. If the police tell me anything overnight, I will text you."

Once again Tony was all alone in a room full of jabbering fudge addicts. As he struggled to add the fresh information from Hugh to the hysterical cobblers, he already had from Robin. At long last, he fell asleep.

Chapter 23

The first signs of the early spring dawn were only just appearing around the curtains, but already Robin was greeting the new day slowly going out of his mind! Now Tony's mobile just went straight to voice mail and he still couldn't get hold of Mindy. Even to just give her a piece of his mind about what a deceitful bitch she was. He'd got it all planned out in his head. By the time he got off the phone, she would regret the day she ever got involved with Branson. Now he was pacing up and down his bedroom like Napoleon when his generals had all booked the same week's holiday in Guadeloupe!

Finally, tired of endlessly planning his epic phone row with Mindy, he thought about his own predicament. If Branson took Electric Fondue from him he was screwed! And if he did, how in God's name would he tell Eavis they wouldn't be appearing at Glastonbury? It was useless trying to sleep until he knew for sure what the hell was going on, and when he eventually did, he probably wouldn't sleep for a month! Taking his dressing gown from the walk-in closet, he pulled it on over his silk monogrammed pyjamas. His wife lay motionless on her back, snoring loudly, wearing her eye mask like a Gucci sweatband. She was the Goddess of Excess. Putting more cream on her face each night than James Martin keeps in his fridge. And recently, she was looking a lot like him too.

He quietly opened the bedroom door and deactivated the intruder alarm for the lower level, using the keypad at the top of the stairs. Since his brush with Theo Robertson, he'd been taking his personal security far more seriously. Varying his routes to and from work, stopping in the office at lunchtime and thoroughly screening all his calls.

Slowly descending the sweeping staircase, he admired the photos of all the famous people that he counted as friends. He really was Mr Music, but for how much longer? If he didn't get a handle on what was going on soon, he was toast. The last twenty years would all be for nothing!

He crossed the hall, heading for the kitchen. He might as well make himself a coffee if he couldn't sleep. At least he'd be able to drink it if he made his own. The girl at work he'd temporarily promoted into Mindy's position couldn't make coffee to save her life. It tasted like a coal miner's bathwater! The screen on his bean to cup machine greeted him with a digital 'Good Morning' as the grinders began their work on the unfortunate coffee beans. Just as the machine got to the noisiest part of the cycle his phone buzzed in his breast pocket. It was a text from Tony.

"Too early to call?"

Robin's frantic return call woke the rest of the ward, all except for the chap who had to lie on his stomach. But in fairness, it was difficult to tell one way or the other with him most of the time.

"Tony, it's Robin!"

"Robin, I know, we've already been through this once."

"Oh, yes, sorry. So did you get up to them before Robertson?" enquired Robin hopefully.

"Not exactly, I'm still in Dorset."

"What the fuck are you still doing in Dorset? Don't you understand that the entire future of Blue Sky Records is at stake? I slept for about two hours last night and kept dreaming about being kidnapped by a herd of Friesians. We're both utterly, utterly screwed if they don't make it onto that stage!"

"I passed out and crashed my car and they thought I'd had a heart attack, but thankfully it turns out I'm diabetic...."

"Never mind that! Have you spoken to Hugh? Are they OK?"

"I'm truly touched by your concern. Yes, last night, but it's not brilliant news. Hugh has got six stitches in his head.."

"Fuck Hugh! What about the twins?"

"Once again I'll pass on your good wishes. Well, that's a bit of a mystery, they're missing..."

"They're missing! They're fucking missing? Missing where?"

With every question, Robin's voice was getting higher and more irate. Half a dozen more and he'd be giving an eleven-year-old Aled Jones a run for his money.

"That I don't know. The police assume that Theo Robertson has taken them. They were in Lindisfarne, but they could be anywhere now."

"They could be anywhere! They could be fucking anywhere! Tell me you're on the way up there?"

"No, I'm in the hospital waiting for my breakfast."

"You're in hospital waiting for your breakfast? Are you out of your fucking mind?"

"No, just out of insulin apparently. Breakfast is a big deal for diabetics. Once I've had that and I've seen the doctor I'll get on my way back to London."

"So you're not going up North to find them?"

"What would be the point of that? If the police can't find them, what chance have I got?"

"So you don't think he's killed them then?"

"The police said that there was a fair bit of shooting done, but no blood or bodies."

"SHOOTING!!!! THEY HAD GUNS?"

"Yes, apparently it was like the Alamo. Shots were fired in anger. But it would seem no bull's eyes"

"So what are the police saying?"

"That we keep it out of the newspapers and wait to see what

happens. They think it's most likely a kidnap situation. Publicising it might make them too hot to handle and lead to an unfavourable outcome."

"An unfavourable outcome! I will tell you what an unfavourable outcome looks like. Two hundred thousand people stood in a field staring at a fucking empty stage!"

Robin, try to calm down before you end up in the bed next to me! I'm far better off in London waiting for a ransom demand or whatever they do these days. I doubt it's anything on paper or a phone call, most likely a text."

"How can you be so calm?"

"Because getting wound up is what got me in here in the first place!"

"Shall I ring Eavis and see if he will help us out?"

"How is he going to help us out? By sending his crack team of Ninja cows to get them back?"

"No, I mean by letting us off."

"Robin it's not a game of marbles or a sportsman's bet. It's a contract and he will just sue us for..."

"... breach of contract?"

"BINGO! So keep schtum and let's see what happens. We might get them back for a few quid and assuming they still have the regular amount of fingers, we could still get them there. Even if they don't, we can just get them to mime and stick a tape on. Hugh's still working on the album so we've got that and if they turn up dead in the Thames, at least it will sell like hotcakes! Now if you'll excuse me, the breakfast trolley is here and there's a bowl of porridge with my name on it. Just keep it together and wait to see what happens. We could still get out of this and make a fortune if you keep your nerve!"

With that, Tony cut the call and Robin finally stopped worrying about Richard Branson. Mainly because he had a whole new list of things to worry about! Suddenly the kitchen door swung open and Patricia Sparrow swept in, looking like the Queen of Sheba wearing a kimono and a terry-towelling turban. Robin immediately sensed her displeasure. She was never an early riser, but the combination of the noise from the coffee machine and Robin's impromptu rendition of Walking in the Air had stirred her from pill-induced slumber. If there was one person who scared him more than Eavis, it was his wife and he was instantly on the back foot.

"Morning love, you're up early?" he smarmed.

"Is it any wonder with the noise you were making? I've told you a million times to just have an instant if you get up early. That contraption makes enough noise to raise the dead! Who were you bawling at on the phone?"

"I'm sorry love, you know I'm not a big fan of instant..."

"Well, I'm not a big fan of waking up early to you shrieking like an eleven-year-old choirboy over the noise a cement mixer makes. Try to be a little more considerate in future."

"I will dear, I'm sorry. I was talking to Tony Chapman, Electric Fondue's manager. Work's stressy at the moment, now Mindy is missing."

"I don't understand the problem. Just get another secretary and move on. She's not that important."

Robin didn't think it wise to update Patricia on just how close she was to her new life in a council flat with lashings of Superdrug face cream. So for the sake of early morning marital harmony, he just nodded his agreement.

"Why don't you take the day off? Don't forget, you're the boss. We could have lunch together and maybe have a look for some new patio furniture? It would be lovely to have something new to enjoy in the garden, and the stuff we have now is so old-fashioned."

Again, it didn't seem wise to argue. She wasn't being unreasonable, and he had spent an awful lot of time at work just lately. It made sense to kick back a little and try to relax. There was nothing really that he could do to ease the situation. Now it was just a waiting game.

"OK, you're the boss," he said, willing to acknowledge the fact he was merely the junior partner in their relationship. "I'll make you a nice coffee and you can tell me what you have your eye on."

Robin was trying hard not to think about the 2Ds or work as his leased Mercedes swept into the car park of their local DIY superstore. His business was on a knife-edge and here he was about to choose garden furniture for a house that he might not own for very much longer. He hated these places. They just meant expense and hard work in that order. But he fastened on his interested face and trooped in behind Patricia, who by this time had her handbag on her arm and was navigating the store like the regular visitor she was. He found it difficult to catch a lot of what she was saying because she had effortlessly switched to her telephone voice as she often did in public. But the word 'rattan' was featuring heavily as she disappeared into the large garden furniture display and started throwing herself down onto various items before loudly reviewing their comfort level for the benefit of anyone in earshot. Robin knew that his part in proceedings was merely to rubber-stamp his wife's selection and provide finance for the project. His taste or comfort would not be a factor unless he wanted his life to become even more stressful. Instead, an enormous screen took his attention over by the tills showing what looked like a large pop concert. Leaving Patricia to her garden sofa selection, he wandered over and watched as a five-minute loop showed two middle-aged men playing chart hits on keyboards at something called Tool Aid. Despite their age, he had to admit they were pretty good, both musically and vocally. The crowd were enjoying it too, judging from the 'off-stage' footage showing them having a great time swaying and singing along in the sunshine. He was just about to drag himself away to where Patricia was now deep in conversation with a store assistant when several notes rang out in an order he instantly recognised...

It was a tense ride home. Mrs Sparrow hadn't enjoyed being interrupted mid-flow and hastened towards making her final selection. Now Robin was suffering for it as she lambasted him for not only interrupting her but also welshing out of his agreement to take her for lunch afterwards. Robin didn't care, he could take it! She wasn't saying anything she hadn't said a million times before. She was good at spending money, but she didn't understand what it took to make it. Or how close she was to a part-time job watching kids eat their dinner. As in his opinion, apart from being Kirsty Allsopp's stunt double, that's all she was qualified for.

Patricia was just getting started on her 'greatest hits medley' of things her mother had said on the morning of their wedding as Robin pulled up on the drive, flung open his door and disappeared into the house. Leaving his shocked wife mid-sentence and thoroughly outraged by his lack of remorse.

When Patricia followed him into the house to give him the closing notes of her finest concerto, she found him in the lounge. On the coffee table was the cover from the free DVD given to them at the till as they paid. Robin stood over the TV with the remote control in his hand, oblivious to his wife's entry into the room. Furiously fast-forwarding through the disc, only stopping occasionally to take in what they were playing, then off again. Until finally he found the footage that matched the brief excerpt that he had just seen in the store. Patricia thought about relaunching her tirade of displeasure, but something about his demeanor stopped her. No longer absorbed by her selfish desire for new garden seating, she took the time to study her husband. He looked far more stressed than usual and with his eyes glued to the screen. She was used to him poring over every detail of a recorded performance or a demo shoved through the letterbox by a bunch of kids smart enough to find their home address on-line, but this was different. Plonking herself down, she watched as a frantic Robin continued to search. Just as she was considering going off to make a coffee, there was a shriek. Whatever he was looking for, he'd found it as he cranked up the volume. Now booming from the home cinema speakers was a note-perfect rendition of possibly three of Electric Fondue's greatest hits. A visibly calmer Robin sat down on the edge of the coffee table to listen. Ordinarily, this would have been a crime against the state. But given his obvious fervour, she'd let it go this once. He'd just coughed a grand on a rattan three-piece, so maybe he deserved a break!

Chapter 24

Martin was rapidly discovering that he wasn't cut out to be an actor as he found just walking and talking simultaneously to be quite a challenge. His excuse was he hadn't had enough time to learn his lines, and it was hard to concentrate under the hot lights with everyone watching. However hard he tried, it only got worse. So when the director impatiently cried "CUT" for the eleventh time, as once again he fluffed his lines about the great new range of outdoor furniture and gas BBQs. A thoroughly dejected Cheesy Dip retired to his Winnebago for a coffee. Rather than waste his time listening to some luvvy tell him how talented he was.

Since Tool Aid, Martin had quickly become the public face of the company. At first, it was just endless handshakes and customers asking for autographs. But as HQ realised to what extent the concert had grabbed the public's imagination, they capitalised on the popularity of their rising star. Now Martin was beaming down from posters in every branch all across the country. He even sang the hold music for the telephone system, and every customer got a free full-length DVD of Tool Aid as they passed through the checkouts. Skilfully edited to appear that Nigel's escapade never happened. Naturally, there had been a few videos circulating on Facebook afterwards and people claiming to have suffered contamination from the contents of his holdall. But with a massive PR department and plenty of cash at hand, the company soon got those taken down and generously compensated any locals possessing photographic evidence of their colonic inconvenience. So what had started out as a silly white lie, had become the biggest DIY sensation since the electric power drill met the wall plug.

All this hadn't gone unnoticed by Craig, who was still labouring away at the undertakers. Tool Aid had transformed his life too, alas not for the better. His boss was less than pleased to discover that one of his principal employees was now a secret pop star. Like Martin, Craig hadn't realised the far-reaching effect relaunching his musical career would have on his life. He thought he would just return to front line hearse duties and play the odd gig in his spare time. However, it soon became apparent that this would not be the case. Following an awkward incident when a rather attractive female mourner asked for his autograph at the graveside. Momentarily distracted by the request, Craig almost allowed a rather heavy former member of the council to meet his maker face down, which caused a great deal of sniggering from the other less engaged mourners. Who had spent much of the day speculating on why his rather camp office manager seemed to be far more upset about his untimely departure than his wife. It wasn't long before that, and a whole lot of other whispering and pointing got back to his boss. Now the other half of The Cheesy Dips was spending his days driving the private ambulance and doing more than his fair share of embalmings. Which wasn't the way Craig had mentally mapped out his career progression. Now his hopes of becoming a branch manager and keeping his immaculate brogues entirely mud-free seemed to evaporate. A high price to pay for just doing a mate a favour.

The door to Martin's Winnebago opened and in trooped Debbie. No longer a beverage bringer, head office had elevated her to the lofty position of Martin's Personal Assistant. Which entailed being a beverage bringer for one person rather than the general public. Spending the rest of her time just hanging around reading magazines while Martin wasted more takes than Fred Astaire dancing in cut off wellies desperately trying to sell outdoor summer living.

"Cheer up love," she said, passing him a massive Cappuccino. "You almost got it that time."

"Your concept of almost and mine appear to be at two separate ends of the nearly scale. I hate all this I just didn't want to go walking with Nigel. That's all. Nothing more! Now I'm some sort of DIY monkey. When I shut my eyes at night, I can still hear that shitty tune in my head."

"Which one?"

"Hadn't you oughta, spruce up ya bricks and mortar!"

"Oh, that one..."

"It's all crap. I hate it. I just want to go back to my old life!"

"But at least Nigel's not around."

"But look at his poor mom. She's got a fridge full of Dairylea and no one to spread it for."

Debbie thought about a gag but left it on the grounds of good taste.

"But that's not your fault. You didn't ask him to stage dive off the roof!"

"I know, but it's still sad. Look at poor old Craig. He's in the backroom now, pumping formaldehyde all day in a rubber apron. The last funeral he attended a woman asked him to sign her breasts."

"Yes, but he didn't have to do it. He could have just said no!"

"I know but it's still fallout from all this. If I'd just gone running, none of it would have happened."

Martin's phone rang on the low table in what the rest of the workforce now referred to as Marty's Shag Palace. He reached out to grab it, but Debbie waved him away. All she had done all day was read Cosmo and fetch coffees. Real stars didn't answer their own phones.

"Good morning, Martin Francis's phone!"

"Ah good morning! Can I speak to Mr Francis please?"

"May I ask who's calling ?"

"Yes, it's Robin Sparrow from Blue Sky Records."

"Can I ask what it's in connection with please?"

"Yes, it's regarding his performance at Tool Aid."

Debbie was all out of questions. So put her hand over the

phone and relayed the information to Martin, who was now lying on his back like the tortured thespian genius he definitely wasn't. He was just a slightly podgy middle-aged bloke who could knock out a tune with a half-decent singing voice that didn't really suit his image. He wasn't Elton John. Come to think of it, he was a lot like Elton John!

If she had been a real PA, Debbie might have known where the mute button was on Martin's phone. But as she was a coffee shop worker and part-time comedienne, she didn't. So Robin heard his name repeated and Martin's instant reply of "Fuck me, now what?" Before there was a major amount of rustling and one half of Halesowen's answer to the Chemical Brothers spoke.

"Hello!"

"Ah hello, Mr Francis?"

"Yes."

"Can I call you Martin"

"Why not everyone else does?"

"Martin, you might have heard of me."

"Nope, sorry."

"So you've never heard of Blue Sky Records?"

"Nope..."

Robin suffered quite badly with London Bubble Syndrome. Long since having perfected the art of waving wildly at no one in particular as he entered restaurants. Knowing that this would provoke conversations about who he was and what he did on at least half of the tables. Normally he didn't take kindly to people not standing to attention when he rang. A call from him often made or broke careers. A single conversation sometimes made the difference between being groomed for pop stardom and a sick day queuing in the rain for an X-Factor audition. But today he was the one that needed a break. So with a deep inward breath, he began a charm offensive that might see Patricia still having a garden to put her new furniture in, rather than stacking it on a rust-stained high rise balcony. Reluctantly, he grabbed both handles of the barrow and started doggedly pushing uphill.

"Well Martin, I've definitely heard of you. Your performance at Tool Aid absolutely blew me away. I can't believe that artists of your obvious calibre have gone unsigned for so long."

"Unsigned?"

"Yes unsigned. I'm assuming that you haven't got a recording contract?"

Debbie was taking her role as Martin's PA very seriously. Since she had handed him his phone she had been frantically Googling Robin Sparrow and Blue Sky Records on hers. She held it up for Martin to see and began to mouth all sorts of totally unintelligible crap in a rather excitable manner.

"None that I'm aware of."

"Have you had any offers or have you got any management looking after you I can speak to?"

"I suppose you could speak to Mr Slater. He's the branch manager."

"No, I mean a management company. Someone carefully guiding your career."

"No, nothing like that. Listen, mate, I work in a DIY centre. I'm under no illusions, once the fuss dies down I'll be back to telling people how to wire up fluorescent light units and selling outdoor sockets for hot tubs."

"Is that what you really want? What if I told you you could play to millions in a few weeks and start living the life of a megastar?"

Robin remembered how hard it was sometimes trying to convince people they had star quality. For years, just the mention of his name made people turn cartwheels of joy. Now he was having to suck the plums of a bloke who had all the sparkling repartee of Kevin Turvey.

"So what exactly are you offering Mr Starling?"

"Sparrow, but call me Robin. International superstardom and maybe a star on the Walk of Fame."

"Which one?"

"Sorry, which one?"

"The real one in Hollywood or the one on Broad Street in Birmingham people drop kebabs over on a Saturday night?"

"Hollywood naturally... I think we should meet. Can you travel down to London?"

"London? Are you out of your mind? Do you know how much the train fare is?"

"OK, then we'll come to you."

Robin wasn't sure where that was. But judging by the nasal tone of his proposed new signing, it was definitely somewhere in the West Midlands.

Forty-eight hours later, Robin and a now visibly more sugar stable Tony stepped from Robin's Mercedes in Birmingham. The rain had started as they sped past Watford and had continued unabated throughout the entire journey to England's much-maligned industrial powerhouse. During which Robin had brought Tony right up to speed on his dastardly plan to hoodwink Michael Eavis and cling on to his empire. The old Tony would probably have told him, there and then, that he was out of his mind. But the new insulin-regulated model was trying desperately to let things wash over him a little more. No ransom demand had as yet been forthcoming from Theo Robertson. So he couldn't see any problem buying a little insurance in the meantime. Besides, no news was usually good news.

Martin and Craig were nervous as they along sped in a taxi to the restaurant Craig had selected in the Jewellery Quarter as the venue for their meeting. He saw no point in pressing the economy button as after all they weren't the ones paying. If this all just turned out to be a massive waste of time, at least they would get a decent meal out of it. Those in the know regarded the 'Ring Stick' to be the leading fine dining restaurant in Birmingham. An excellent venue for a marriage proposal, anniversary dinner or important business meeting. As is often the case in such establishments, the food always came stacked in the centre of the plate with a puddle of jus, squirt of foam or shower of dust on it. Which always spelt out you were somewhere a cut above the Berni Inn when you Facebooked your dinner for the peasants to see. It had pleasantly surprised Craig how well he and Magda were getting along. So it didn't seem a bad idea to do some free market research should he ask her to become the next Mrs Allen. Little did he know that she had already had a deposit down on her dress and a polka band's available dates for the following year in her handbag!

As they stepped out of the rain, the Maitre D offered to take their wet coats. Martin wasn't keen to take advantage after losing a brand new leather jacket in a nightclub cloakroom many years previously. Forced to trudge home in the snow wearing the substituted purple satin baseball jacket, he wasn't one for learning lessons twice. But when Craig apologised for his blunt refusal like an embarrassed carer, he reluctantly gave up the knock-off Barber jacket he got from a mate in the Rag Market.

Upstanding as their proposed new signings arrived at the table, Robin had to admit that in the flesh, these fellas didn't seem like the answer to his prayers. They looked more like a music hall double act than international musicians. But if the 2Ds didn't turn up soon, they were all that stood between him and a lifetime spent listening to Patricia compare him to Manny Bernstein. Her first love, who now ran a chain of cosmetic dental practices and owned a holiday home in the Hamptons.

The irony of which wasn't lost on Robin, as he had long considered him to be a total penis.

"Good evening, gentleman. I am Robin Sparrow, this is my associate Tony Chapman."

Martin just stood awkwardly whilst Craig shook hands with both men and they all sat down. He was way out of his depth. His choice had been The Struggling Man, but Craig had unhelpfully reminded him about the chronic indigestion he got from their last visit.

"So I'm guessing by now that you want to know what all this is about?"

Tony was interested to see how Robin would handle this. He guessed it would be a masterclass in truth limitation. Because if the papers got hold of the news that the twins were firmly on the missing persons list, the game was most definitely up.

Martin hadn't really given it much thought. He was tiring of being newly famous, and becoming more famous was even less appealing. Craig, however, was all for it. Even red hot twenty-minute showers couldn't shift the smell of formaldehyde and it was costing him a fortune in Kouros aftershave. The only thing strong enough to cover the lingering smell of death that didn't require a prescription.

"Well, we did sort of wonder..." replied Craig giving it his best Black Country 007 topped off by an arched eyebrow. Which owed far more to Wendy Craig than it did to Daniel.

"As doubtless you now know, I am the owner of Blue Sky Records, which is the label that Electric Fondue is signed to. Tony is their manager, and together we have made them into one of the biggest acts on the planet. However, their image has very little crossover appeal to our generation. So after seeing the great work that you did at Tool Aid. We came up with the idea to form a second similar band, but entirely geared to an older audience."

Tony had to admit, as far as shameless deceit went, it was

very impressive. That would allow these two unsuspecting dorks to sign a management contract and thus get them under a watertight confidentiality agreement before they revealed the truth behind the big Glastonbury gig.

"So what you're saying is that we would be like an OAP tribute band?" said Martin, who had an uncanny knack of popping bullshit into nutshells.

"Oh no, nothing like that," lied Tony, knowing full well that was a reasonable round-up of Robin's audacious plan.

"You'll have your own carefully crafted image, but you might share a few songs across your sets. We liked the three-song medley that you did for Tool Aid. With our eyes closed, it was difficult to tell you apart from Electric Fondue. You harmonise like brothers."

Craig responded well to flattery. Kissing his stinky, organ flushing, backroom job goodbye understandably had enormous appeal. Martin was far less enthusiastic and his face showed it. But then, that was generally his default position. The only thing he truly enthused about was Debbie and her rampant panache for lacy exotica.

"Look, why don't we all just relax, have some food and a couple of drinks. While we put everything on the table and fully explain what a fantastic opportunity, this is for you both. "

After two rather large steaks, two pints and an hour of Robin's silver tongue, (during which Martin promptly Facebooked everything, including the slice of lemon in the finger bowl) Craig rose from the table to visit the gent's. When Martin didn't take the crashing dustbin lid hint to join him, he had to text him for an unscheduled conflab by the urinals.

"So what do you think?"

"I think he's a smarmy Southern prick!" said Martin, drying his teeth with a long inward breath before replying. Unwittingly revealing exactly why posh steak restaurants offer toothpicks and McDonald's don't.

"Apart from that?"

"I dunno. I suppose it's what we always wanted when we were kids. But we're not kids now, are we? It means moving and not seeing Debbie. "

"Any plus points you miserable git? Like we might see the world. Play sell-out stadium gigs. Join the Mile High Club. Buy nice things, meet nice people. Stuff like that."

Craig wondered if Martin the Misery had heard the same pitch? For him, hanging up his green rubber apron once and for all was a dream come true. The recent treatment that he had received at the hands of his employer had made him realise that perhaps he wasn't the valued key member of staff he previously thought he was. Maybe now was the right time to spread his wings for just one last roll of the musical dice?

"Just ask yourself this. Why would two music industry heavyweights drive all the way from London to Birmingham to sign a pair of old blokes who can knock a few covers out on keyboards? There must be more to it than that. They must be swimming in gifted teenage kids they could make money out of. Why in fuck's name would they want us?". Martin had recently seen the latest Ann Summers catalogue in the top drawer of Debbie's bedside cabinet. He wasn't at all keen on a sudden return to the tool chafing loneliness of self-gratification, and it was severely colouring his judgement.

"Weren't you listening to a word he said? Because we would appeal to an older audience - double bubble! Twice the money from exactly the same songs. Probably recording back to back in the studio with a resident production team to save money. Anyway, this all started with me doing you a favour. Now it's time for you to do me one! I want to go for it and see where it takes us. You owe me that much. I had a good job until we played Tool Aid. I had my eye set on being a branch manager. Right now, I'm seeing more dead pensioners than a dyslexic pharmacist!"

"OK, you win. I'll do it. I suppose I got you into all this to start with, and I've had enough of being a DIY poster boy. You're right, it's what we always wanted. It's just twenty-five years later than I expected, that's all!"

"Right, so put your enthusiastic head on Gummidge and let's go back and tell them we'll do it!". Said Craig shooting his cuffs and checking his popstar looks in the mirror whilst Martin sighed and made a note on his phone to buy some coconut moisturiser.

Chapter 25

Things were at last beginning to return to normal on Holy Island. The police had put away their blue and white tape and removed all the stickers and flags that marked the resting place for the bullets that missed their target. Which was a relief to the publicans and guesthouse owners, who were finding it hard to sell the concept of an ancient island of tranquillity while the place still looked like a Viking longship had staged a drive-by shooting.

Eager to make amends for the twin's disappearance, Hugh was still beavering away. He had more than enough material from the previous week's recording to finish the album. So he was back at the mixing desk trying to keep things positive while they all hoped for good news about the twins.

Yet despite all this, the 2Ds favourite little coffee shop wasn't quite as it was. With the two enigmatic Londoners no longer holding court each morning, their eager audience had soon melted away. At first, there was a lot of chatter about who had come to kill them, and why? But even the most exceptional of circumstances soon gave way to the normal rhythm of village life once all the excitement died down. So the staff of the Village Idiot returned to the business of serving coffee and pastries whilst lying about exactly how homemade they were to gullible tourists.

It wasn't long before there were just Zab, Daisy and a few early bird tourists for breakfast each morning. In all the time that the 2Ds used his eaterie as the base of their ego-stroking operation, Zab hadn't needed to pay that much attention to his seaweed tea venture. Pop stars were good for business, and seemingly no one noticed the odd ad hoc price increase. If they had, they were too spellbound by tales of the rich and famous to say anything, and predictably, takings had gone through the roof. But now the Electric Fondue sideshow had vanished, things were back on the slide. Meaning Zab needed to quickly re-establish his side hustle to make ends meet.

"Do you reckon you can hold the fort here while I spend the rest of the morning on the boat gathering some weed in?". He asked, unusually keen not to overstress the plainly brokenhearted lynchpin of his business. He liked to call it 'weed'. It sounded vaguely illegal, which appealed to the dodgy side of his character. As casually contravening the Trades Description Act just didn't provide the buzz, he needed any more.

Daisy's critical eye scanned the collection of sparsely occupied benches. There was just the two of them and a family of fat, over-fussy American tourists who were noisily comparing their breakfast to 'homemade' food back in the States.

"I think I can manage," she replied, rolling her red-rimmed eyes in the drawling food critics direction. Who were really beginning to grind on her nerves with their endless biscuits and gravy talk. "I can't see them ordering anything else. But if it suddenly starts getting busy, I'll give you a ring. Hard to imagine that happening though, based on the last few days of trade."

Zab gave her a sympathetic half-smile and nodded. It was clear to him that she missed the twins more than she should. But he wasn't one to pry. Daisy was an islander. She knew that once you shared a secret; it didn't stop that way for long. So unspoken words passed between them and he went into the back to get his things before setting off for the boat. Fifteen minutes later, just as Daisy had finished arguing through the bill with a roly-poly hockey mom who didn't consider jam and butter to be chargeable extras, a breathless Zab burst in.

"It's gone!" he panted.

"What's gone? The boat?"

"No! The hut! Yes! The sodding boat!"

"Somebody has nicked the boat? Why would anyone want to do that?"

"Not a clue. But it's not there!"

As realisation dawned Daisy's face lit up and she pulled out her phone from the front pocket of her apron. Then began fishing around for the card the baffled detective had given her several days before. She placed it on the counter and began gleefully punching the number into the keypad.

Zab watched her in amazement. Then too suddenly realised the significance of the boat's disappearance. To him, it was a major inconvenience, but to Daisy it was hope.

"Hello. It's Daisy Bramall from the Village Idiot on Holy Island. You told me to call you if I had any more information regarding the Dafoe twins disappearance. Well, I think I might just have something that will interest you!"

An hour later two coastguard helicopters and boats from most of the nearby RNLI stations were crisscrossing the area of the North Sea they considered that the wind and tide may have taken a boat with an inexperienced crew. Following police enquiries, none of the harbours up or down the coast had reported a strange boat landing during the last few days. Regrettably, Zab had never thought to install a tracker which would have instantly pinpointed its whereabouts. His logic was there were far nicer boats on the shoreline. So he had never imagined that anyone would be desperate enough to steal his in preference to those. Daisy's version was he was a tight prick!

Later that afternoon, the observer of a Search and Rescue helicopter spotted the wreckage of a small fishing boat lying on an outcrop of rocks seventy miles down the coast from Holy Island. A visual inspection from 100ft revealed no sign of life onboard and a further close up report from the winchman confirmed this beyond doubt. He did, however, see that the throttle was open and its mooring ropes neatly stowed on board. Which proved that it had deliberately been taken out to sea and hadn't just accidentally drifted from its berth.

Over twelve hundred nautical miles away, the 2Ds were fast becoming accustomed to their new role as deckhands on a deep-sea trawler. The Ongonzo Perran had put to sea several days earlier from Copenhagen, heading for the fishing fields of the mid-Atlantic. By then the brothers were entering their second day aimlessly drifting out into the North Sea. Having already drunk the last dregs of white wine Daisy had hidden aboard, they were seriously considering sampling a few bits of Zab's skanky seaweed. At first, they were grateful to have escaped with their lives. But relief turned to panic as they drifted further and further out to sea. Soon regretting their forced decision to leave Holy Island by boat.

Furiously searching the vessel from stem to stern they found neither a ship to shore radio, a walkie talkie or even a phone with which to call for help. But Zab was no mug. He left nothing aboard that could be stolen. Holy Island might seem like a nice place, but it still had its rogues and thieves. So with very little else to do apart from watch the seagulls and fantasise about coffee and cake, rescue became a waiting game.

Like many deep-sea trawlers, the Ongonzo Perran ran on a knife-edge of efficiency with a large crew. Time is money and with strict fishing quotas in place, they had to be in position to lower their nets on the exact day the authorities allocated them. Being late just wasn't an option. So when the lookout spotted the tiny fishing boat bobbing up and down in some of the world's busiest shipping lanes, the captain was reluctant to investigate. He knew that any deviation from their schedule could be costly and the owners didn't entertain excuses, they simply replaced the captain. On only his second voyage with a brand new commission, this was an unwelcome addition to his stress load. He knew that a rescue meant delays, and that was something he could ill afford. So as the massive ship drew alongside the tiny wooden craft, the captain had already struck a deal with the first mate. They would stage a rescue, but whoever was on that boat was coming on a fishing trip. Whether or not they liked it!

For the second time in less than two days, Declan and Dominic had cheated death. Gratefully climbing the rope ladder away from Zab's floating tea enterprise. They were just happy to be alive. But they would soon discover that life onboard a floating fish factory was far removed from the privileged lives of recording artists.

The captain was warm and welcoming. Quickly ordering the

first mate to allocate them a cabin and see to it, they got a hot meal. The ship sailed with a crew of sixty-seven. So there was quite a support system onboard. Nothing of the comfort level that you would experience during a Mediterranean cruise. But the food needs to be good, the showers hot and the beds comfy if you want to hang on to your crew.

Although grateful for their rescue from the iron grip of the sea. Three days on a ship that continually stank of fish soon had them wondering when they might be put ashore? Would a rescue helicopter winch them from the deck and take them to dry land? Or would the trawler put into port and drop them off, ready for a club class plane ride back to London?

But unbeknown to them, the captain hadn't reported their rescue. Fearing the authorities would order him to wait for them to be uplifted, he withheld news of their salvation to safeguard his schedule. The 2Ds would stay missing, presumed dead, for the entire voyage! Just a little over six weeks!

Chapter 26

When the news reached The Village Idiot Zab's boat was now Northumberland's answer to The Mary Celeste, the previously elated Daisy once more sank back into her sorrowful fug. Firmly convinced that her best chance of true love (whilst simultaneously travelling the world) was now lying dead at the bottom of the North Sea. She couldn't believe the special times they spent together on the little fishing boat had ultimately led to Declan's death, and understandably it was a bitter pill to swallow. Tearfully resigning herself to be pawed by a procession of uncouth village youths until she finally settled for a life of fishing nets and the persistent odour of red diesel. With merely the highlight of an odd drunken night out in Newcastle to relieve the tedium of being endlessly battered by The North Sea wind.

Zab, however, was secretly relieved. It was a struggle to keep the Village Idiot going with Daisy's help, and without it, verging on the impossible! Therefore, his deep-fat fryer inferno insurance fraud was no longer on the cards and the complexities of getting a five-hundred-year-old solid stone property to burn to the ground would now cease to torment his regular Google searches. However, it probably wasn't the right time to mention that the boat was uninsured, so now his tea empire was in tatters and the place would need a replacement waitress. "Only for a few weeks. Just until Daisy gets it together", he thought as he watched the snot and tears drip off her chin.

Without bodies or a ransom demand, Northumbria police couldn't determine exactly what had happened to the 2Ds. Admittedly, kidnap situations didn't feature too highly on their hit parade of crime. Their force specialities centred more around fighting, drunken fighting and drunken football fighting. So they held a meeting at the highest level to decide upon a measured response to what was undoubtedly a tricky situation. It was decided if they were being held hostage by gun-toting London gangsters, publicising their abduction might be a stupid move. Two world-famous musicians found tied up and shot in the head would give the PR department more trouble than when Gazza turned up at an armed siege with a fishing rod, four cans of lager and a couple of rounds of chicken sandwiches. So, for now, the twins were quietly added to the missing persons list. Until their deaths were proven or they received contact from their kidnappers, there would be no official announcement or press briefing. However, if they resurfaced amidst a Saturday afternoon punch up, they were more than capable of dealing with that.

Back down South, Robin received this news as a mixed blessing. The best result of all would be the 2Ds returning to London, after being rescued or released in a blaze of carefully manicured publicity. The kind that sent old albums straight to number one when the story broke on every international news channel. Followed by a victorious comeback gig that would see them thank God for their deliverance and guarantee their place in modern musical history.

But as yet no ransom demand had been received and with no one else missing from Holy Island, it looked increasingly likely that they had drowned. Which was a win of sorts as the new album would still go to No1 and Robin could spend the next ten years remixing previously discarded tracks and selling them as newly discovered work. Whilst simultaneously allowing them off the hook with Eavis. Dead musicians can't play gigs, and no one in their right mind would sue for breach of contract in such circumstances.

But as every passing day failed to deliver closure, it became more likely that circumstances would push their Plan B into action. Two heavily disguised middle-aged men would pose as two of the world's most recognisable recording artists and play Glastonbury with no one suspecting a thing. That in itself would be quite a stunt. Getting them to agree to do it might be even harder!

Craig really enjoyed informing his employer he had pickled his last dearly departed. He was getting bored with the smell of Kouros and with a new musical career beckoning it was time to hang up the apron and kick off his wellies. But it was a blow to his ego to discover his branch manager thought it was a wind-up. Convinced that talk of pop stardom was a smokescreen for a move to the competition, he offered him more money to stay.

Waving away his indignant insistence of a London based recording career in fits of laughter. Provoking an ill-tempered exchange of views which saw Craig tell him to stick the embalming up his arse. Admittedly, not a widely recognised method but possibly a timesaving technique for the more advanced user.

Martin fared little better. Head Office wasn't happy to see their musical poster boy walk off into the sunset. Particularly when his face stared down from a multitude of in-store posters with TV commercials booked to fill advert breaks well into September. They reminded him they had made him a star and that leaving now was no thanks for the effort they had put behind Tool Aid. Martin pointed to their soaring sales figures and reasoned that his future musical career could only push things further with the reflected publicity that success might bring. It still wasn't an amicable split, but as there wasn't anything in his contract of employment regarding being the figurehead of the company's advertising campaigns, there was very little they could do.

So a few days later Martin and Craig bid farewell to Debbie and Magda. In a Jaguar piled high with bags, (Craig's matching designer leather, Martin's mainly Asda carrier) they set off for London. The previous night there had been a great deal of tears, promises and farewell sex. Craig had coped rather well and given Magda firm mid-coital assurances that once they were established she would travel the world as his life partner. In stark contrast, Martin had struggled to deal with Debbie's onslaught of emotion during foreplay. Culminating in an ill-judged remark about her and Magda being 'a bit past it' to be the next Pepsi and Shirley. Which saw the 'going away lingerie' replaced by the 'pissed off pyjamas' and a Viagra tablet wasted on a solo knuckle shuffle in the en suite at 3 am.

Martin slept most of the way down. As a night spent with a chemically induced superfluous erection had taken its toll on the quality of his last sleep in Halesowen. When he finally roused as Craig joined the North Circular, both their progress and London's obvious traffic problems surprised him. Reminding him of the jam down Mucklow Hill on the day all this had started, and he wistfully wondered how it might end?

Would they ultimately see their working friendship flounder amidst a blizzard of cocaine and heavy drinking brought on by the pressures of stardom? He had to admit that seemed unlikely. As in all honesty, there was more chance of him becoming addicted to Gaviscon and chocolate pillow mints than hard drugs. Weed just made him think he was wetting himself and the only spirit he ever drank was Baileys at Christmas, and that was only ever in hot chocolate!

The last leg of the journey took almost half the time again. Martin wondered why anyone bothered with fast cars in the capital when they'd barely got out of second gear since leaving the motorway. He found sitting in endless traffic awkward. At first, he passed the time looking around at the people in the other cars. But when his friendly smiles only earned him hard stares in return, he soon gave up. London would take some getting used to. Everyone looked so stressed!

Tony had given them the address of a rehearsal studio in the East End and with instructions to just bring their keyboards as everything else they would need would be provided. Craig had looked it up on the web and was shocked to find that it wasn't anything like they were used to. For starters, The Arches Studio Complex only had four rooms, which from the photos appeared to be of a considerable size. Filled by grand pianos, full (egg box free!) soundproofing, acres of exotic hardwood panelling and thick luxurious carpet throughout. He'd stayed in worse 3-star hotels!

When at last they pulled up outside, it surprised them to see the recently reformed members of Steps coming out. Craig played it cool and smiled knowingly as he pressed the entry buzzor. Whereas Martin went into a major tizz and begged them for a selfie that he could send to Debbie. Craig didn't see the point in joining him on the photo as Magda seemed determined to remain oblivious to popular British culture. Since the start of their relationship, he had done his best to explain who various people were and what they were famous for. He soon discovered that Poland didn't seem to share Britain's 20th Century fascination for balding men clutching ventriloquist dummies. So Roger De Courcey, Nookie Bear, Rod Hull and Emu took a fair amount of clarification. Emu's habit of grabbing men's groins with its beak particularly puzzled her (which as she indignantly pointed out was actually Rod's hand!) and exactly why was this funny? Craig had to agree that on reflection if Rod was still about he might have had some serious explaining to do in these enlightened times.

As a thoroughly bemused Steps climbed aboard their minibus with Martin still doing the hand movements from Tragedy, the door buzzed and they discovered the deep pile carpet started at the door. Until now their only proper experience of rehearsal studios had been Make It Big. This was completely at the other end of the scale. It shocked Martin to see that reception didn't double as a cooking area and there was an absence of brightly coloured stars bearing the day's freezer to microwave special. Or for that matter, any boxes of out-of-date confectionery carefully positioned just out of reach behind the glass. In fact, there was no glass at all. Just the sort of reception desk you find in a smart hotel with a rather efficient looking young lady sat behind it. She raised her eyes expectantly from her computer screen. Martin scanned her crisp white blouse for any sign of curry sauce before concluding that she evidently did no cooking at all, not even in the back!

"Welcome to The Arches How can I help you?"

"Hello, we are The Cheesy Dips," said Craig, fully appreciating for the first time how ridiculous that sounded spoken aloud in polite company.

The receptionist showed no sign of amusement. She'd heard it all before. Tesco Carrier Bag, The Shagging Cats, Itchy Down Below. Nothing fazed her anymore.

"Ah, Mr Sparrow and Mr Chapman are expecting you. They are in the café bar. Would you like to follow me and I'll take you through to them?"

With that, she glided from behind the desk and they followed her along a short corridor, through some double doors and into a well-lit dining area. Tony and Robin rose from their table in greeting. Martin was a little put out that he still couldn't see a microwave or a chest freezer, as by now he was clammed.

"Pleasant trip down?" inquired Robin.

"Not bad. The amount of traffic is a surprise," replied Craig.

"Oh well, once you've parked your car at the apartment that will be the last driving you will need to do for some time. From now on you have a car and a driver. He will bring you to rehearsals and anywhere else you need to go. I'm guessing that you're hungry, so why don't we eat? Then you can unload your gear into the room and we can start getting things together."

Robin raised his hand and a lad in his twenties wearing a blue and white striped apron and matching hat appeared from nowhere.

"What can I get you?"

Martin still couldn't see any fluorescent stars, so he left the ordering to Craig. For once he didn't seem to know what to do either, which Martin found enormously satisfying.

"Is there a menu?" he stammered.

The bemused chef turned to Robin for guidance, Craig looked at Robin for suggestions, and Martin scrutinised the kid's apron for splashes of curry sauce.

"No menu. You just ask Pablo here for whatever you want and he will cook it from fresh. Today's musicians have so many dietary requirements, food intolerances or allergies, it's just easier to make what they want."

"Chicken curry?..." suggested Martin hopefully.

"What sort of chicken curry?"

"A frozen one?..."

"I meant what cuisine? Indian, Chinese, Japanese or Thai?"

"Iceland…"

"Iceland?"

"He means the shop, not the country" interrupted Craig who could see that Pablo was finding Martin's lack of culinary finesse a little wearing.

"Please excuse my friend. Can we have two portions of Eggs Benedict with Bacon and two Cokes, please?"

"Not a problem. Do either of you have any food intolerances?"

"I'm not keen on beetroot," stated Martin bluntly.

"There's no beetroot in Eggs Benedict," hissed Craig.

"How would I know? I don't even know what it is!"

"Poached eggs, on toasted muffins with bacon, dressed with Hollandaise sauce."

"Hollandaise sauce?"

"OK, leave the Hollandaise off his please and bring him the ketchup."

Pablo walked off looking like Rembrandt about to take on a Woolworths paint by numbers kit. But at least it made a change from making egg white omelettes and juicing cucumber water.

"Right," said Tony, visibly relieved that they had settled the Laurel and Hardy food order. "While we're waiting, I thought we might go through the set list?"

"Don't we get to choose our own songs?" exclaimed Mr Ketchup.

"Possibly in the future, but for now we need to focus on getting some fast results. So we can get you right into the public eye at some big events."

"What sort of big events?"

"Major festivals…"

"Such as?"

Tony was fast appreciating that managing two blokes nearer his own age would be far more difficult than managing two coke heads with very little experience of life outside music. So far they had only ordered lunch and talked about song choice, and the barriers were already starting to go up. At this rate, he would have another hypoglycaemic attack by the time the chef poached the eggs. His partner in crime was also starting to gather that this would not be as easy as they had previously thought.

"Glastonbury…" interjected Robin.

"What on the mad old bloke's stage in a tent by the toilets?" laughed Martin

He was hungry and already missing Debbie's bacon butties, non-stop cappuccino and lunch break Winnebago fumbling. He was unimpressed with playing 'guess what you can have for your dinner?', and now the smell of Cockney bullshit was stinging his nostrils.

"No, the Pyramid Stage…"

"Isn't that the main stage where the headline acts play?" said Craig, who was also beginning to smell a rat. Dummy and Brummie are two words that people often confuse. However, history teaches us that there have been some extremely smart people who talk through their nose, but they rarely see a mention in Trivial Pursuits.

"Err yes.."

"So you think a field full of hardcore music fans will want to listen to a pair of old blokes playing covers on their keyboards?"

Tony wished they had ordered Pot Noodles. This was unravelling faster than Mike Tyson in a prosthetic ear shop.

"What time are we playing? Four o'clock in the morning?"

Robin now realised that the big reveal would have to be brought forward. At this rate, they would be back in the car and making for the M1 before their bacon was crispy. The truth was becoming a hard sell....

"You're headlining. 9.45 at night, to be exact..."

"Headlining? How can we be headlining? Only world-famous established acts with a massive back catalogue of international hits do that. Are you mad?"

Tony and Robin now had no option but to spend the next five minutes bringing Martin and Craig up to speed on the story so far. Craig immediately sensed the delicate nature of the conversation and spent most of the time trying to stop Martin shouting, swearing and repeating sensitive segments of information at maximum volume. So it was a relief to everyone on the table when Pablo appeared with their food and Martin finally had his mouth full.

"So now you see our problem," said an almost whispering Robin. "If Electric Fondue doesn't play Glastonbury, then we are both potentially ruined. All the tickets sold as soon as they went on sale. The lineup has been announced and we have no idea where they are or even if they are still alive."

"But how in God's name are we going to get away with it? We don't look like them and we've got entirely the wrong accents. We might sound like them when we sing, but that's about it!"

"Fortunately, no one has seen them in public for months. So a little of extra weight here and there might go unnoticed."

Everyone instinctively turned to look at Martin, who was busy ramming an enormous piece of eggy muffin slathered in ketchup in his podgy cakehole. He instantly returned their stares with a look of delusional incredibility.

"Regarding your facial features, they have often worn animal heads on stage as part of their act for years. So you can just wear those from the moment you're picked up for the gig. Musicians are a little eccentric at the best of times, so I doubt anyone will take that much notice. They will just see it as 'being in character!'. You'll fly in by helicopter, play the gig and then come straight back out again on the same aircraft. So the chances of anyone getting close enough to work it out will be minimal."

"So what's in it for us? We'll be Birmingham's answer to Milli Vanilli if we get rumbled. I'll be back on the hill begging for my old job back and he'll be washing hearses till he finally gets a ride in one."

"Quarter of a million quid each…"

The bacon stopped midway on its journey to Martin's molars. Craig tried to look cool, but even his best Clooney wasn't cutting it.

"Two hundred and fifty thousand pounds each?" he repeated slowly.

"Yes, that's right. If you pull it off, and we don't get sued for breach of contract. You'll be amongst the richest men in…. err…."

"Halesowen…" butted in Martin helpfully who was quite enjoying Eggs Bendydick with a side helping of Never Work Again.

"So what do you say?" pushed Robin.

"Let me finish this and we'll get the keyboards out of the car," said a thoroughly re-energised Martin, spraying eggy crumbs everywhere for a second time.

Chapter 27

Following their first day at The Arches, Martin and Craig talked long into the night about playing Glastonbury for two hundred and fifty grand each. It was decided that they should keep the deception from Magda and Debbie until after the gig. Then possibly a surprise double date Caribbean holiday might be the right time to explain their sudden new-found wealth and why Magda could now have her whole family over for the wedding!

They soon found Electric Fondue's back catalogue was extensive. Ten years at the top of the music scene demanded they became prolific writers. As their career progressed so their compositions had increased in originality and complexity. Requiring that each one be individually studied in minute detail to accurately recreate the sound of twins performing in perfect synchronicity. It was hard going, but they had a quarter of a million reasons to get it right and after two weeks they were starting to get somewhere.

In the mornings they ran through the tunes they had already conquered to keep them fresh in their minds. In the afternoons they pored over a couple more. Slowly pulling them apart and dividing the score between them. It wasn't easy, but nowhere near as boring as filling shelves full of electrical supplies. Or as grim as dressing the recently departed in their Sunday best, trying hard to conceal the coroner's clumsy blanket stitch.

Martin was enjoying his new life as a full-time musician. Granted phone sex wasn't quite as fulfilling as bed sex. But the apartment was like a hotel suite and all he had to do was play his keyboard and sing all day. It wasn't far from The Arches, conveniently situated just off Shoreditch High Street. Which gave them a wide range of possibilities for their evening meal. Allowing Martin the opportunity to sample chronic indigestion induced by firey cuisine from several continents. Even Pablo was growing on him as he slowly worked his way through his curry repertoire. Frozen meals for one were definitely a thing of the past. Now he made his order on arrival in the morning and it was ready on the table at lunchtime. It was even better than living at home!

Fortunately, the bathroom in their apartment had a bidet. At first, Martin was suspicious of it, because it had a French name and related to his undercarriage. But the morning after a rather spirited choice from the menu at Dhimashada Dab the neighbourhood Somali restaurant, he thought he would try it out. As a bum-wash first-timer, he soon learnt that carefully regulating the water pressure was critical. As was keeping your legs firmly shut and the five grisly minutes he spent wiping the back of the bathroom door stood testament to this.

As Glastonbury drew nearer, so the phone chatter between Tony and Robin increased ten-fold. Both knew that transferring stress to their artists at such a delicate stage in proceedings would be a mistake. So they kept their input to a minimum. Just occasionally dropping in for lunch to check on progress and making sure that they had all the reference material they needed to keep the project moving. All four men knew they had a deadline to hit and each had his own personal motivation to ensure the plan was a complete success.

Robin didn't want to witness Patricia crying as she packed up her silk scarf collection for a brand new life on a sprawling council estate. Tony was still making plans for retirement pulling pints by the coast. Craig was looking forward to making an honest woman of Magda. Martin had his sights firmly set on doing absolutely nothing till the money ran out…

With just a week to go, there was a flap over which animal heads they would wear on stage? One evening, Tony brought two of the most recognisable that the twins had used for them to try on. Naturally, these had been custom made by a costumier who had taken accurate measurements of the 2D's heads to ensure a comfortable fit. Craig's fitted really well considering that it hadn't been made for him. However, Martin soon discovered that his eyes weren't situated in the same place as Declan's and no matter how hard Craig and Tony rammed it on his head he could only see out of one eyehole at a time. Which wasn't altogether ideal for a complex two-hour make or break musical performance. So Tony spent the next day touring London buying up a wide range of fancy dress heads and a further home fitting session found that Craig would take to the stage as a mole and Martin as a yellow rubber duck. Not entirely ideal, but with the big day just around the corner and total secrecy still a major factor in success, it was far too late to get something custom made.

Luckily, the cover story Robin concocted had held up well down at The Arches. No one had even thought to question why two middle-aged men were learning thirty electro-pop songs to make them more accessible for an older audience? They had seen a million barmy ideas over the years, right from the Wombles to Sigue Sigue Sputnik. As long as someone paid their invoices, they would keep the lights on. But that said, the constant smell of curry around the place was beginning to wear a bit thin.

At last, the big day was almost upon them. Their final run-through went perfectly, and they bid farewell to Pablo and broke down their gear from the rehearsal room and took it out to their transport. After a shaky start, Martin had become quite fond of the kid who he could always see watching from the kitchen as he put the first forkful into his mouth. He found it quite touching that he cared so much about his customers. Pablo was simply amazed that one digestive system could endure that much curry. It reminded him of his days cooking for the Indian National Ballet Company, except Martin's portions were far bigger.

"Well, that's it. Tomorrow it's shit or bust!" remarked Craig as he climbed into the minibus next to Martin having safely stowed his keyboard flight case into the back.

"Well at least after tomorrow, either way, we go home. Hopefully with a massive paycheque."

"More money than either of us could ever have hoped to earn from music all those years ago. I just wish that I didn't have to do it disguised as a giant rubber duck!"

"Ah well, at least we will always know it was us. Better have something sensible to eat tonight. You need to be on your A-game tomorrow. We don't need you up all night with another bout of Mogadishu Memoirs."

"Fair enough, what about steak and chips that sensible enough for you?"

"An excellent choice. Then an early night ready to be uplifted tomorrow!"

For once the traffic was light and they were soon unloading the two flight cases outside the low rise block that had been home since their arrival in London. It was weeks since Craig's car had moved from its parking space and he had become quite used to being chauffeured everywhere. It would seem odd to return to their old lives where they were expected to do more than just eat and play. The life of musical royalty was a lazy one and it was easy to see how the 2Ds had lost their way. Soon it would all be over and hopefully, the blag of the century would go down in the history books for all the right reasons. No more run-throughs or final adjustments. "Tomorrow Matthew, we're going to be Electric Fondue..."

Martin kept his word and that night they dined on steak and chips in a little bistro around the corner. Even moderating his ketchup intake and just washing it down with a single pint of lager shandy. Both men were surprised how well they got on. With scarcely a cross word passing between them since leaving Halesowen. The last supper went without a hitch and they were back in the flat by 9 pm. Each taking the opportunity to facetime their partner from the privacy of their bedroom. Deliberately neglecting to mention that they would be home tomorrow or about to play the biggest gig of their lives!

Craig was already awake when his phone alarm went off at 7.30 am. That was the only part of his old routine that remained. He knew real musicians rose at midday, but then old habits die hard. He pushed the button that automatically opened the blinds and was relieved to see it was already a bright sunny day outside. It might be a gig that he could never boast of to anyone, but he still wanted his treasured memory to be perfect. With 'their' dancing fans dressed in shorts and t-shirts singing back the lyrics. Not shivering in the rain caked head to foot in mud.

When he arrived in the kitchen his bandmate was already

there nursing a cup of the caffeine stew he called coffee. Craig preferred to make his own and Martin had finally taken the hint after watching several of his efforts go cold on the breakfast island. They hadn't really talked about the money. It didn't seem wise till it was actually nestling in their bank accounts. Even men old enough to know better still firmly believed in jinx. If you don't mention it, then it won't happen. But each had repeatedly played out his own nightmare scenario in his head.

Martin's was discovering his duck's head made him sweat so much that it ran in his eyes and he couldn't see the keyboard. But Tony had anticipated this problem with a full costume run-through as the air conditioning heated the rehearsal room to 30 degrees. It hadn't been a pleasant experience but they had still managed to turn in a note-perfect performance.

Craig worried that standing on stage in front of so many people might render him speechless. Of course, there was no mock rehearsal that could allay that fear. But after officiating at some fairly large Greek Orthodox funerals and not in any way fazed by the enormous crowds at the graveside. He reasoned as he was only likely to see the first ten rows from the stage, he could just pretend the other 199,000 people weren't there.

Neither really wanted to eat breakfast, but as it was going to be a long day and tricky to eat with their heads on, it made sense to try. Craig toasted a sourdough muffin and treated himself to real butter as it was such an important day. Martin forced down two bowls of Coco Pops and a Strawberry Pop-Tart. Seeing they were individually wrapped, he decided to stick another two in his pocket. Planning to secretly chow them down during an extended toilet break. He expected more enthusiasm from Craig when he shared this intention. Instead, he slowly shook his head at the image of Martin sat all alone in a stinking Porta Loo eating cold pocket battered Pop-Tarts.

Much of the day passed watching the BBC's live broadcast from Glastonbury. Closely studying how everything was organised around the Pyramid Stage as familiarity with the setup could only add credibility to their performance. As until today the largest crowd they had ever played to was outside a

DIY store in Halesowen. Scarcely a word passed between them as they marvelled at the confidence of kids barely out of their teens holding vast audiences spellbound. Then sitting on hay bales and giving lengthy in-depth interviews regarding their mindset and preparation for the whole event. So it was incredible to imagine that in a few short hours they would be cranking out a headline set expected to eclipse every one of them. Craig decided Martin would be excellent at the whole monosyllabic sulky musician thing. While he would engage with the interviewer and give lengthy pretentious answers to simple five-word questions.

Then, at last, it was time to get ready. Tony had left them two matching designer tracksuits similar to the ones Electric Fondue wore on stage. Admittedly, the logo wasn't one that either of them recognised, but then they weren't entirely up to date with the current trends in overpriced sports gear fashion. Once back in the lounge they added the animal heads to their disguise and agreed it would take a sharp eye to know it wasn't the 2Ds underneath all the designer nylon and coloured plastic.

The two flight cases containing their keyboards were ready in the entrance hall and at 7.30 pm the doorbell rang. They knew from this moment onwards it would be impossible to speak – even to each other! Hopefully, the explanation Electric Fondue was zoning for the biggest gig of their lives would carry them through without any awkward questions. Once on stage, it was all about the music. Nothing else mattered other than their performance. The one thing they were truly confident about.

"Good luck mate!" said Martin. "Whatever happens we know we played Glastonbury!"

"Same to you. Thanks for agreeing to all this. What a mad ride it's all been!"

With a final hug and messy clash of heads, flight cases in hand, they opened the door and stepped out. Ready to undertake the greatest deception ever attempted in British Music History. Success would bring glory they could never share and discovery, worldwide front page humiliation. Now following weeks of careful planning, The Great Duck and Mole Swindle was on!

Chapter 28

When Martin and Craig arrived at Battersea Heliport thirty-five minutes later, they found Robin and Tony waiting for them like two nervous dads with a very expensive prom night limousine. Without a word, they grabbed their flight cases and allowed themselves to be ushered into the empty departure lounge. It was more luxurious than you would expect and Martin deeply regretted that he couldn't get stuck into the exotic-looking pick and mix chocolate selection. In a regular airport, you sit on plastic seats and drink coffee. In a heliport, you sit on Italian leather settees and sip champagne. But wracked by nerves, even Tony and Robin didn't partake. Even without the added complication of pouring it through a giant plastic head!

Tony and Robin didn't see the point in conversation as they waited for their flight to be called. The two impresarios passed the odd word, but other than that it was complete radio silence. Despite how it might seem, their role in proceedings was now critical. They were the blockers. Poised to prevent anyone cornering the bogus Electric Fondue asking awkward questions. Or deflecting a member of the sound crew pressing for any last-minute details that required a spoken response. Their presence also served to increase the unlikelihood of sharing their aircraft with other passengers. Further removing any chance of their intrepid plan being discovered. Right now, the last thing they needed was a forty-minute helicopter ride with anyone personally acquainted with the 2Ds. A scenario that might blow the entire thing sky high before they got anywhere near the stage. After a tense wait, at last, their flight was called.

Once again Tony and Robin led the way. Having taken more helicopter rides into packed venues than they cared to remember. Knowing when to duck, the customary waved hand signal to the pilot, which way the door handles worked and where luggage could be stowed. All minor details that frequent celebrity flyers would be acquainted with and an undertaker and a DIY store assistant wouldn't. So as agreed, Martin and Craig copied their every move on the approach to the aircraft. Once safely aboard with their luggage stowed below them, it was time for liftoff. Helicopters might be the taxis of the sky, but their pilots don't strike up conversations about last night's football or comment on the state of the nation. Like limousine drivers, they only speak when spoken to and for that, you need communication equipment. As headsets don't come in enormous sizes, Martin and Craig were safe from any intrusion during the flight. It was all in a day's work for their pilot. He'd seen enough megastar musicians to know that the more gifted they supposedly were, the stranger they came. So two grown men travelling in giant animal heads passed him by without so much as a murmur.

One of Martin's biggest reservations about the whole operation had been the helicopter ride in. He'd only been on a plane a handful of times, and even then he had dulled his senses with a couple of pints of amber nectar in Frankie and Benny's beforehand. Now he was stone-cold sober and praying that the Lean Cuisine Prawn Curry he'd found in the freezer at dinner time didn't end up sloshing around his ears for the duration of the flight. He closed his eyes as the pilot gunned the engine. The noise from the rotor blades increased tenfold and the helicopter promptly soared upwards. Then quickly opened them again, recalling all the advice he had ever been given about travel sickness. Not the stuff about putting your head between your knees, which was hardly practical at present. But keeping your eyes on the horizon and taking slow, deep inward breaths. As he began to control his breathing and focus his eyes ahead, the prawn curry stayed where it was and now his only digestive enemy was the constant smell of hot plastic inside his stupid head!

Alongside him, in complete contrast, Craig was in his element. He might only be one half of the world's most daring tribute act, but this was all he had ever wanted. Veteran of watching a thousand live performances on DVD. Drinking in every detail of how exciting it must be to travel the world as an international megastar. Particularly enjoying those that revealed the build-up to the gig. Nervous anticipation, in-jokes, vocal warm-ups and superstitious good luck traditions. He knew that mere stars rode in limos, but megastars flew in helicopters. This was the experience that his entire life had been leading up to. It was a seismic moment that forced him to put a hand through his plastic mouth to wipe away a tear. It was then that he became aware of Martin taking in air like a beached whale and sitting bolt upright as if Rigor Mortis had set in...

Once they were en route, the sensation of being airborne was greatly diminished. Even Martin settled back a little and stopped filling his chest like a one lunged pearl diver. Soon they were zipping over rolling fields, rivers and roads at breakneck speed. Such an exciting experience would have been greatly enhanced by removing their heads. Avoiding the enhanced G Force that tore at their neck muscles with any sudden change of direction. But after a forty-minute flight that passed without serious incident aside from several clashes of giant plastic skulls, they were coming into land at Glastonbury Heliport. Below them, as far as the eye could see, stretched the legendary musical carnival famed throughout the world. A place of homage for the faithful. Where many careers took off and yet others floundered. Inescapably polarized by the enormous microscope of worldwide attention.

As they came to rest, a still slightly bilious Martin peered out at the perimeter fence of the landing spot. Nervously scanning the excited faces for one that might pose a problem. But then the fans weren't their biggest hurdle, it was other VIPs. They wouldn't hover nervously, working up the courage to speak. They would just dive straight in, expecting witty replies to their playful banter. Keeping absolutely everyone at arms-length was the key to success until they took to the stage. But then, that wasn't their job. That was down to Robin and Tony. All they had to do was make it there and pump out the music. As the rotor blades slowly came to a halt, a runner ran forward to open the doors and to greet the festival's headline act.

"Doolan and Dominic, can I say on behalf of Michael and Emily how excited we are to have you here today. They know that this is going to be an amazing set and your fans will be super excited to see you back!"

She stepped back, expecting a similarly gushing greeting from the 2Ds. But when none came, she waved two roadies over to collect the flight cases from the luggage compartment. Robin stepped from his seat beside Tony and switched the bullshit from single shot to fully automatic.

"Thank you… err…" he paused momentarily to read the name on her pass, "…Mitch...can you be sure to let Michael and Emily know that Electric Fondue considers it an honour and privilege to be booked to play such an important date on the international music calendar. We have a very special set planned that will leave the audience mesmerised. In fact, the twins are so committed to producing the performance of a lifetime they have pledged to remain completely silent until it's time to perform. Even then there will only be singing and absolutely no audience interaction between tracks."

At first, Mitch looked puzzled but then recovered her composure. Smiling broadly as the Emperor's Clothes took on a life of their own.

"Of course, I totally understand they would want to safeguard their voices for such a career-defining opportunity. May I show you to your dressing room?"

Martin wondered why they needed a dressing room? When as far as he knew these were the clothes they would be performing in on stage. It wasn't like they needed their hair doing or any makeup. They were wearing two massive plastic heads and everyone was acting like it was the most normal thing in the world. Electric Fondue must be absolute fucking nutters!

"That would be amazing. Gracious thanks for your understanding," said Robin, smiling back and giving her an 'I'm just saying all this to keep them on the level, they're off their tits' sort of wink.

Mitch was experienced enough around delusional pop stars to take the hint and winked back. Before leading them off the landing pad, past a throng of screaming fans and collecting a waiting four-man security team along the way. Then continuing through the passenger lounge, gathering their VIP passes as they went. "It's not far!" she said cheerfully as they arrived at two six-seater Amphicat 'go-anywhere' buggies parked just outside the glass double doors. As the security team split between the two vehicles, Martin and Craig took the hint and climbed into the leading one with Robin and Tony bringing up the rear.

Craig instantly realised their mistake. Now there was no one to deflect attention if they were spoken to. Instead, they would just have to tough it out and risk appearing ignorant when they didn't answer. Thankfully, their security team didn't seem interested in striking up a conversation. So as the odd convoy of four shaven-headed hard nuts, two very nervous executives, a brace of Saga eligible impostors partly disguised as animals and a girl with a smile that would survive a direct hit from a speeding cricket ball set off, silence reigned.

As they pushed along through the crowds on what was the last leg of their stressful journey, Craig saw a face he thought he recognised emerge from the crowd in front of them with a camera team in tow. The constant bounce of their transport and the visual limitations of his mole disguise meant that he didn't get another glimpse until they started to slow. To his horror, he realised that Edith Bowman had used her press pass to wave them down and was preparing for a piece to camera. Intending to get a few words from the biggest act on the plot before their long-awaited comeback gig.

Behind them, Tony was slow on the uptake. Unfortunately, being bounced across a bumpy field in a glorified golf buggy immediately after a lengthy helicopter flight hadn't seen a mention in the Big Book of Things to Avoid for Newly Diagnosed Diabetics. Now he felt both queasy and tired in that order. Luckily, Robin had soon spotted the danger and was already on his feet to head the opportunist Scot off at the pass.

"Well, as if by magic, here we are making our way across to interview Jay Kay who this year is making balloon models in the Theatre and Circus field. When who do we spot? Electric Fondue making their way to their dressing room, having just flown in from London. Tonight's headline act on the pyramid stage and two very lovely men who I have always massively enjoyed interviewing..."

As Martin and Craig cowered in the back of the leading buggy looking like two VIP Banana Splits. Edith executed a perfect backwards shimmy whilst brandishing the microphone like a cattle prod and keeping her face to the camera. Unluckily for Martin, he was the closest to her and always the least capable in a crisis.

"So how are you, boys? When did we last run into each other? Was it Montreal?..."

All Martin knew about Montreal was they held the Olympics there about fifteen years before the bloke he was impersonating was even born and possibly Celine Dion's very talented dentist was still in residence. Other than that nothing! Neither of these facts delivered in a nasal whine from within an oversized bath duck was going to cut it. He badly needed a miracle!

From behind him came Robin, like Kevin Costner about to take a bullet for a floundering Whitney. Skilfully moving into shot from Edith's blindside and leaving her no option but to go along with his sudden appearance.

"Edith you old rascal! How many times do I have to tell you? You know the twins don't do interviews until after the gig…"

"Don't they? Ummm… Folks at home. This is one of the most powerful men in music. Robin Sparrow, welcome to the BBC's Glastonbury coverage."

"Hello, Edith! Hello viewers. Can I firstly say how amazing you're looking today? Outdoor living really agrees with you."

Edith bloomed as she enjoyed the gushing compliment. Tony who had now awoken to the peril of the situation began to wave his arms. Trying to attract the attention of the 'twins' driver and get him to move on.

"Yes, I think you're right. It was Montreal in 2018 on The Twins Have More Fun World Tour. The Electric Fondue you saw back then has matured like a fine wine. They're a different band to the one people heard then."

'Yep, matured by about twenty years' thought Martin who for once was relieved to see Robin.

"So what can we expect from them this evening? Anything from the forthcoming album we're all so psyched about?"

"I'm afraid not, Edith. Glastonbury is all about audience participation and singalongs. Tonight will belong to Electric Fondue's greatest hits. An absolute smorgasbord of the very finest electro-pop. An opportunity to dance yourself to a standstill and remember just why they are the biggest live act in the world."

'Fuck me! I hope we go down better than Kanye West after that statement,' thought Martin. Who now began to consider exactly how much protection his outsized duck's head would provide from a well-thrown bottle of urine. After what seemed to be a lifetime, their driver took the hint and replaced his foot on the accelerator. Hearing the first buggy moving off, Robin concluded the interview and gratefully threw himself back into the second as the crowd parted to let them through. A bewildered Bowman watched them leave before theatrically shrugging her shoulders to the camera.

"There they go. Probably the most talented keyboard duo this country has ever produced. Hopefully, they will have more to say for themselves later tonight…"

'I wouldn't bank on it' thought Tony as he swept past, praying that the bumping would come to an end in the not too distant future. He wasn't at all sorry when just a few hundred yards later, they took a left and arrived at a large clutch of Winnebagos a stone's throw from the rear of the Pyramid stage. Mitch leapt out as the odd convoy came to a standstill. Ushering them towards one that had Electric Fondue written on a whiteboard hanging beside the door.

"As I'm sure you know, your pass operates the door lock and I will leave two of the security team here with you." She said opening the door and throwing apart her arms to show the full palatial splendour of the accommodation as they trooped in behind. The floor was polished marble with ample sumptuous seating for a band and their entourage in the lounge area. A muted forty-inch flat-screen TV displayed live footage of the event taking place just yards away, and the kitchen belonged on a Saturday morning cookery show.

Martin immediately spotted a microwave and under-counter fridge. Once again he was starving and a bit of something to calm his nerves wouldn't go amiss. For most people that would mean a strong alcoholic beverage of some kind, but to him a microwaved snack and a can of something fizzy. Both of which would be a challenge to ingest disguised as a duck. He was just considering the unappetising prospect of going to the toilet to wolf down his pocket Pop-Tarts. When fortunately for him, Robin read his mind.

"Oh, there's really no need for that, we'll be fine," gushed Robin, who knew the fewer people that got close to 'Electric Fondue' the less chance there was of getting rumbled at the last hurdle. "It's no distance from here to the stage and I've seen there's tight security around the perimeter of the dressing rooms."

"I don't think Michael and Emily would like their headline act so exposed right before such an important performance," whined Mitch.

"But they aren't here, Mitch. What do you do when you're not a runner?"

"I'm a receptionist at a solicitor's in Notting Hill."

"I would imagine you're a significant asset to the company judging by the level of professionalism you've shown here today. It's not everyone who can deal with international megastars without being star struck. It just so happens that Blue Sky Records have a vacancy for a receptionist with your sort of talents. Why not have a think about it and call me next week? I'm sure I could put a package together that would tempt you from a life of divorce and endless house conveyancing."

For a second Mitch didn't look sure. But then quickly took the card from Robin's outstretched hand, with a furtive glance out of the door to ensure that the security team hadn't heard the conversation. Briefly studied it. Then for the second time that day fixed Robin with a megawatt smile and tucked it into the back pocket of her jeans.

"OK, you're the boss," and with a slight bow, she retreated out of the door to brief the security team that they were to return to the heliport and await further instructions. They looked doubtful at first. Then like most shaven-headed muscle-bound men confronted by a bossy nine stone woman with a walkie talkie and access all areas pass, they shrugged their shoulders and did what they were told. As the buggies moved off, Tony shut the door and turned the lock as Robin twisted the vertical blinds to ensure that no one could see in.

"Thank fuck for that!" spat a sweaty Craig as he heaved off his mole head. "I thought we were screwed when Edith Bowman flagged us down. Mind you, she still looks amazing for her age!"

"Do you ever think of anything else?" laughed Martin, who was also now free of his plastic head prison. "What would Magda say if she heard you talking like that?"

Craig didn't have time to answer before there was a knock at the door. Robin assumed that it was merely a runner with an update on their stage time and waved them all to one side. Expecting to have a brief conversation around the door that would only last a matter of seconds.

Fortunately, that was pretty much the only mistake he would make that day. As she heard the door unlocked, a visibly plumper Abigail Robertson put her entire body weight behind the shove of a lifetime and burst into the dressing room in the style of an extremely hormonal Diddyman. She was generally unhappy for a variety of reasons, but today she was absolutely fuming about all of them!

Firstly, she was angry that in her experience, home pregnancy tests had proved to be somewhat unreliable. Along with popstar boyfriends who failed to answer their phone or respond in any way to her daily oestrogen inspired voicemails. Which ranged from 'I'm selling my story to the papers you bastard!' to 'I want to travel the world with you and our child, just like Linda McCartney in the 1970s'.

But the reasons for her recently more bitter approach to life didn't end there. A few weeks previously her father had inexplicably decided that his long term future lay in a remote village high in the Spanish Mountains and now only occasionally replied to her texts. Whilst also steadfastly ignoring her frequent voice mails and continually having his phone turned off whenever she called. Coincidentally, around the same time, her mother had greeted Theo's sudden relocation by revealing a secret long-term relationship with Barney. Now she suffered the indignity of sharing her home with her father's driver whilst he noisily shared her mother's bed. Who was apparently 'keeping everything on the level' for when her dad eventually got back.

Robin barrelled over, unprepared for the strength of a desperate, abandoned, expectant seventeen-year-old convent schoolgirl. Who had learnt a lot from her father about forcibly gaining entry to rooms then controlling events immediately thereafter.

"Where the fuck is he?" she raged as the lonely torment of recent weeks left her in one guttural outburst.

"Who?" said Tony calmly. Just wanting a bit of peace for a kip and a Mars bar, but not necessarily in that order.

"Dominic! The lying deaf out bastard!"

"Who's asking?"

"His girlfriend!"

"His girlfriend?"

"You must be Tony. The domineering slave driver who treats them like two naughty children!"

"Granted, I answer to Tony. But I prefer to be known as the caring manager and father figure who does his best to prevent them from killing themselves in a blizzard of cocaine! The one desperately trying to keep their career alive until they are straight enough to appreciate the effort!

Since we're into name-calling, by the look of it you must be some random pregnant groupie looking for a life of luxury with her unborn child!"

With that, all the wind left Abigail's sails. That was a bit too close to the truth for comfort. She wasn't a groupie, but she was looking for the father of her child with a view to a romantic, if not financially beneficial, happy ending. Ignoring Tony's well-observed jibe, she stared at Robin, who was still sat on the floor and just thankful it wasn't Edith Bowman with yet more difficult questions. Then narrowed her eyes at Martin and Craig, who were holding their heads under their arms like a pair of comedy astronauts.

"Who are you? You're not Dominic and Declan."

Robin was running low on lies, Tony was still feeling a little under the weather and Craig had very little experience of bolshie pregnant teenagers. So for once, Martin took the reins.

"I was just going to make something to eat. Do you fancy anything?"

"What have you got?" replied Abigail, softening slightly as her new found financial independence didn't stretch to a £6 burger and quite honestly, the queue was shocking.

"Dunno, let's have a look…"

Martin opened the mini-fridge to find it resembled a showroom for Ginsters. A now visibly calmer Abigail chose a Cheese and Onion Slice while Martin plumped for a Steak and Ale Pasty. As the microwave span their flaky snacks the other three witnessed a master class in situation recovery. A skill gained from calming raging DIYers returning the wrong part for the wrong job.

"Sorry about the paper plate."

"Oh, I don't mind. I'm just glad to have something to eat."

"So you're Dominic's secret girlfriend? What's your name?"

"Abigail... Abigail Robertson..."

Suddenly a gigantic jigsaw piece clunked into place in Robin's head.

"Are you Theo Robertson's daughter by any chance?" he asked quietly.

"Yes, I am. Why? Have you seen him?"

Robin gave Tony a knowing look, who slowly placed his aching head in his hands and wished he was absolutely anywhere else in the world except here!

Chapter 29

Abigail ate her pasty with gusto, washed down by a can of Diet Coke. Which made little sense to Martin until she explained that she just didn't like the taste of regular Coke. Martin felt that was a fairly illogical point of view as clearly one was made to taste just like the other. But now Robin had filled them in on exactly who Abigail was. He didn't see the point in crossing swords with her unnecessarily. He wasn't sure if psychopathic tendencies were genetic, but he wasn't taking any chances. There were a lot of sharp implements in the kitchen drawer and he wasn't up for getting tortured to death with a cheese grater.

Now Abigail was in a far calmer frame of mind, Robin explained the situation. Being very careful to omit that Theo was strongly suspected of being responsible for the death of her love child's dad. She listened intently without interruption but looked suitably sad when he admitted no one had a clue what had happened to the twins. Then he revealed who Martin and Craig were. During which, she interrupted quite a few times. Highly amused that these two sweaty old-timers could be capable of hoodwinking the world's most discerning musical audience and ultimately saving Robin and Tony's bacon.

"Well, thanks for your vote of confidence!" spat Craig, who couldn't understand how Martin could even consider eating under such circumstances. "Remember, if it doesn't work, your meal ticket's career will be over. These two will get sued to within an inch of their lives and the only place you will ever see their records will be in the bargain bin at Woolies!"

It was the first time Craig had spoken and judging by this outburst he had a lot to learn about teenagers, pregnant or otherwise. Referencing a long-defunct high street shopping empire, vinyl records and bargain sale bins might have resulted in a complex five-minute conversation. Tedious for both parties and offering very little in the way of progress. Fortunately, Abigail focused on the first part of his statement and realised that the success of their mission might have implications for her own long term financial stability.

"Sorry, I meant good luck! Break a leg and all that."

"That's what you say in the theatre."

"What do they say at concerts then?"

"Let's do this!" interjected Martin helpfully.

Further discussion on the matter of verbal high five's was prevented by a rap at the door. Robin deducing that it was most unlikely there were any more angry pregnant teenagers hanging about, waved for silence and opened the door a crack.

"Two-minute call for Electric Fondue on stage," said the sort of stressed face Robin was more used to encountering in such situations.

"OK" replied Robin and quickly closed the door again.

Deciding this was the time for well-chosen words and channeling his inner General Patton, Robin let them have it.

"Right lads, this is it. Remember, as far as we know, nobody suspects a thing. All you've got to do is get up there and play. Pretend it's just a run-through in the studio and it will all be fine. Positive mental attitude, just lock in and give it to them."

"I feel sick…" replied Martin.

"We all feel sick, son. Just get up there and do your thing!"

"Who are you calling son? I'm the same age as you and don't you mean get up there and do their thing?"

"Does it really matter what I mean?"

"For fuck's sake just play the gig so I can have a kip and Abigail here can empty the pasty palace and watch you on the telly." Said Tony, who had experienced more of Robin's psychobabble in the last few weeks than in the previous ten years.

"Heads on and bugger off..." laughed Abigail. Cracking open another Diet Coke and settling back for the show.

Like the crew of Apollo 13, Martin and Craig put on the heads and prepared to leave the mother ship. Once they were through that door they were on their own. If anything went wrong, it was up to them to sort it. The moment they had been working towards since their arrival in London had finally arrived. Seconds later, the door was open and led by Robin they were gone. They would either return quarter millionaires or soaked in the waste of a thousand outraged renal systems.

The brief walk to the stage dragged like a condemned man's final shuffled steps to the gallows. Even from inside their comedy cranial headgear they could feel the stored human energy that would begin its conversion to dance the second they took the stage. Nothing on earth could have prepared them for this thunderclap of reality. It was Tool Aid turned up to a thousand. The tremble of adrenalin coursing through Martin's body now making him wish he'd considered an adult nappy instead of boxer shorts. Now he could finally see the opening at the side of the stage. Home free! Just a few more feet, then all he had to do was play. No more deaf and dumb routine, just get on there and do it. Suddenly a voice shouting beside him shattered his single-track thought process...

"How long is your encore?"

It was the stage manager. Yet another stressed face with an ironic ponytail, wearing headphones and holding a clipboard, was impatiently awaiting his answer. He knew it was ten minutes. But Robin had gone past, and he didn't know how to say it in a London accent that didn't sound like Danny Dyer with a head cold.

"How long is your encore?"

"Ten minutes..." said Martin quietly.

"How many?"

"TEN MINUTES!!!"

Martin's Dick Van Dyke impression instantly morphed into Barry from Auf Wiedersehen Pet due to the necessary vocal pressure required by the increase in volume. The owner of the clipboard looked puzzled, having worked with Electric Fondue frequently in the past. Granted, they didn't exchange Christmas cards, but she knew them well enough to be perturbed by the strange voice coming out of the bright yellow duck's head. Peering hard into the mouth, she momentarily locked eyes with its panicking inhabitant...

"Who the f...." was all she managed before Martin dropped the beak and knocked her spark out with a perfectly executed headbutt that saw the extracranial weight of his disguise almost break his spinal cord. Stepping over the unconscious collection of scrawny limbs, he resisted the urge to look up her skirt as he passed. Continuing to stage side with a dumfounded Craig following in his wake. The announcer greeted their presence by stoking the crowd to a baying frenzy as Robin stepped to one side to allow them clear passage. Totally unaware of the casual violence that had just unfolded behind him, as a deafening roar greeted their arrival on stage.

".... so make some noise for our headline act... ELECTRIC FONDUE!!!!"

Martin strode out and instinctively held his arms aloft in greeting with Craig mirroring the gesture close behind. At last, the nerves vanished and the good adrenalin took over. The kind that shoots lightning bolts up through your spine and orders the brain to take vivid snapshots to bore your grandchildren with in old age.

Before them, from beneath the gently flapping flags of their homelands, a sea of eager eyes stared right back. Each pair belonging to a sun-weathered face determined to dance the night away to the soundtrack of their very own adolescent showreel. All set to recall the sweet sting of love followed by the aching chasm of heartbreak. Midnight teenage fumbles and hastily copied homework. Coastal summer day trips with blaring radios, replaced by drunken weeks in the Spanish sun as the money slowly got better. This was the moment of truth!

The final digits of a countdown that began hunched over sluggish laptops in freezing January. Electric Fondue's loyal fans were waiting to experience the two strongest dance drugs known to man. A pill of nostalgia washed down by a glug of the past. Expectation and intoxication hung in the air in equal measure. Like a fat pisshead salivating for a monster-sized Friday night curry. They knew this had better be good or The Cheesy Dips were going home in a box!

The duck and mole stood for several seconds, waiting for the roar to die down. Just as the intentionally lengthy pause began to concern their security, Craig cranked up the spoken samples that preceded 'King of My Castle'. The shock power of the carefully chosen imagery projected onto the screen behind them instantaneously connected with the mood of their audience. With perfect timing, Martin banged out the instantly recognisable rising four-bar loop. Just as Craig smashed through with the melancholy lyric that until recently, had been unknown to them.

I'm the king of my castle,
A man on my own,
King of my castle,
Sat on my throne.
Now that you're gone, life's a dream,
Do what I like and say what I mean,
Don't need your input and don't miss the drama,
I don't read your texts and don't care about karma!

As they cranked out Electric Fondue's anthem to the failed romances of a generation, the words got chanted straight back at them by an army of rebuilt hearts. Side by side the doddering doppelgangers delighted them with track after track of danceable electro-pop. For nearly an hour they were completely at one with their mission. Never missing a beat. Two heavily perspiring blaggers smashing open safety deposit boxes in a vault full of greatest hits. Stealing only the really good stuff and callously leaving the crap behind on the strong room floor.

A delighted Robin watched from off stage, blissfully unaware of the unconscious stage manager who still lay just a few feet away. Back in the Winnebago, Tony stirred from time to time. Only to look up at the screen and then promptly doze off again. An enthralled Abigail sat working her way through a tub of Ben and Jerry's. Occasionally uttering "You just wouldn't know, would you?" to no one in particular. Even after all the planning and rehearsal, it was still hard to believe that not one of the thousands dancing suspected a thing. Electric Fondue was doing what it always did. Delivering the tunes that made people want to move!

It was all going so well, until inevitably, a rather dazed Andrea Bevan stirred where she lay hidden amongst the flight cases. Still groggy from the blow, at first, she thought she might have fallen. Then as her hazy memory slowly returned, she recalled being assaulted by a giant yellow plastic duck in a designer tracksuit. More importantly, she recollected that a millisecond before the bill arrived she glimpsed the face of the person inside the head. Whoever it was, it definitely wasn't either of the Dafoe twins. She sat upright and listened to the music that was now pounding through her chest. It certainly sounded a lot like them to the unsuspicious ear, but clearly, it wasn't if you listened closely.

Admittedly, after an hour on stage, things had moved back up the M1 towards Birmingham. In rehearsal, they had found it far easier to hear themselves without the added input from the fans. Making it a simple matter to alter their vocal tone in order to mimic the 2Ds. But with the added voices and the sheer volume of the music, throats were relaxing and vowels were getting flattened. And so with each subsequent song, they sounded a little more like The Cheesy Dips and slightly less like Electric Fondue.

Andrea felt the throbbing lump on her forehead. She'd been doing this job for five years. She'd experienced the nervous pukers, the intoxicated, the I'm too famous to talk to you and many forms of talentless wankers. Yet not one of them had ever assaulted her! She was incensed! So as her lump grew, so did her determination. Slowly, she rose to her feet and considered the next move. There was no point in making a complaint later. This needed tackling head-on. That fucking duck wasn't getting away with it and if that meant risking her career then so be it! She would strike a blow for stage managers everywhere. A clipboard army who sucked up celebrity tantrums every day as being all part of the job!

On stage Martin and Craig were enchanting their congregation with the 2Ds No1 ballad 'I Just Came To Try'. Now the molten Somerset sun had, at last, disappeared behind the rolling hills of the Mendips only to be replaced by a carpet of twinkling neon bracelets held aloft in the steamy darkness by dance weary arms. Their colour constantly changing in a synchronised sequence, stretching as far as the eye could see. Whilst the stage lighting bathed the two musical shamans in cloaks of purple and a spectrum of lasers danced high into the inky night sky.

I wasn't expecting it to be easy,
And I didn't dare to dream you'd care,
But I had to try just one last time,
To see if there was anything there.
Just came to try, then say goodbye,
I have to know, before it's time to go,
Had to stay, just one last day,
To make you see, it will ever be, just you and me.

As the last soft chords faded into the night, Andrea saw her chance and grabbed the announcer's microphone from its backstage cradle. Storming past a bemused Robin and out on to the stage, she waved her arms at the sound desk team in the elevated pod set amidst the audience. With well-practised arm signals she asked for the on-stage levels to be muted and the microphone she was holding to be switched on. At first, they were confused, but then obeyed, assuming that the interruption was because of an emergency announcement or had been agreed in advance with the band.

Andrea tapped the microphone and heard the sound reverberate right across the vast field. Where every set of eyes now bore right into her. She hadn't considered how daunting that would be. Now 200,000 people plus a worldwide audience wanted to know what was so important that she needed to break the spell that 'Electric Fondue' had held over Glastonbury for the past hour. Whatever she needed to say, it had to be important. If not, this would be her last moments on stage and possibly the planet.

The duck and mole stood transfixed. Their instruments and microphones now totally without audio output. They too had no option but to listen as the stage manager addressed the crowd. Martin immediately recognised her as the pushy bird with the clipboard he'd dropped the nut on. He had never struck a woman before. But caught up in the moment's drama, he had seen no other way to prevent her from scuppering their mission. She was simply collateral damage at the end of a crazy few weeks. He briefly considered pushing her clean off the stage as the ten-foot drop would shut her up once and for all. But in his heart, knew he had absolutely no chance of getting away with it. Besides appearing in court for six months solid while they cross-examined two hundred thousand witnesses seemed somewhat churlish.

In the production suite, the producer considered cutting the transmission and switching to VT. But the fear of missing something groundbreaking kept the cameras rolling. As the sense of drama rose, Andrea lifted the microphone and spoke.

"An hour ago, I asked the duck a question. I asked him how long their encore was? When I got no reply and asked again, he knocked me out."

"I'll knock you out if you don't fuck off and let them carry on playing!" shouted a wag two rows from the front. Provoking a ripple of laughter, but Andrea kept going.

"Shall I tell you why he did that? Because he knew I'd seen that he wasn't one of the Dafoe twins. The men you have been listening to for the past hour aren't Electric Fondue, they are imposters!"

At that point, Andrea expected a pantomime intake of breath. Instead, it was more of a groan. Then someone close to the stage started a slow handclap. In a few short seconds, the clap grew. It got louder and louder until it was deafening and the only people not clapping were Andrea and 'Electric Fondue'. As the tide turned against her, she began to cry. Her gut-wrenching sobs reverberating from the speakers as her composure crumbled. The tears streamed down her face and her head throbbed as impatient fans shouted insults and obscenities at her. Until there were so many being hurled, it was impossible to tell what they were. As she turned to leave the stage and possibly her entire career behind her, Craig stepped from behind his keyboard. At first, Andrea flinched, but as he gently wrapped his arm around her shoulders, she relaxed and with his encouragement, again turned to face the crowd.

The noise quickly died to a hush as expectation grew for a strenuous denial from a compassionate artist. One who had just pardoned a mad woman for ruining the most important gig his band had ever played. An image of forgiveness now pinging off a thousand satellites up in the heavens. Instantly inspiring the universe to change their attitude to mental illness, be kinder to their fellow man and more tolerant of others. The nucleus of a beautiful revolution that lasted precisely the same amount of time it took for Craig to remove his mole head and reveal that Andrea was absolutely right. Neither man was a Dafoe, or for that matter, even a twin!

As realisation spread, Craig quickly became the villain. The crowd hissed and whistled whilst the tears continued to stream down Andrea's face. Then the booing began. It was deafening but undeniably thoroughly deserved. So after taking the hate for long enough for people to vent, Craig took the microphone from Andrea and spoke. He couldn't see this being any harder than calming a volatile contingent of Irish Republicans angered by an unfortunate memorial spelling error. After all, it was unlikely anyone here would threaten to have him kneecapped and shove a three-foot-tall marble statue of the Virgin Gary up his hole!

"As you can see, it's true! We're not Declan and Dominic Dafoe. We're just two average blokes in our fifties. We're not even from London, we're from the Black Country in the West Midlands. I'm an undertaker and my mate is an assistant in a DIY store. Nobody knows where the real twins are. They've either been kidnapped, murdered, drowned, or possibly all three! We were asked to play this gig to save their manager and the record company from total financial ruin."

The audience murmured, the cameras continued rolling and Martin suddenly wanted the toilet. Craig, sensing a breakthrough, continued to speak in slow measured tones. The same ones he had used so many times before to explain exactly why a two-mile private ambulance journey costs £250.

"When we were younger, it was our dream to headline Glastonbury. So when we signed up to impersonate Electric Fondue, we let our ambition get the better of us. I admit we should never have done it. It was wrong to deceive you all, and I most wholeheartedly apologise. But then you have to admit until a few minutes ago you had absolutely no idea it was us and not them. You were having the time of your lives. So what do you say we just finish the gig and then face the music afterwards? If you'll forgive the pun?"

By now Martin had taken the yellow duck's head off and was eating a smashed Pop-Tart. He too knew the game was up with no way back. So there didn't seem much point continuing to sweat his tabs off now blabber mouth Craig had dropped them in it. He could have just legged her over when she started crying and got the bouncers to drag her off like a nutter. But no, he had to have his Jesus of Nazareth moment! Now Martin was the one ready to be dragged away by security. So he was dumbstruck when the jeers turned to cheers. He couldn't believe it! Electro Fondue's loyal fans wanted them to finish the gig!

Craig gently led Andrea to stage side where a visibly emotional Robin tenderly took her from him. Neither man knew what lay ahead, but there was a gig in progress that wasn't going to finish itself. A stunned stagehand passed him two white fluffy towels as he calmly walked back to his keyboard. He passed one to Martin, and they embraced amidst the chaos of the unscheduled interlude as the crowd screamed back their delight. Craig used that powerful moment to whisper a single change to the set list in his bandmate's ear. Martin looked uncertain. But Craig fixed him with a look that held all the reassurance a sweaty middle-aged man in a kid's tracksuit could muster. Swept along by the euphoria, he decided to trust his old friend and made the relevant changes to the settings on his keyboard. Craig held up his hands like a musical messiah and the sound team took the hint to take their equipment back to its previous levels. Using his newfound influence to milk the moment, once again he spoke.

"Thank you for your patience ladies and gentleman. We are The Cheesy Dips and this is one we wrote ourselves."

A split second later, the booing returned just as the first plastic bottle of warm piss caught him squarely in the knackers…

THE END

A Final Word From the "Editing" Team

Firstly, thank you for taking a chance on The Cheesy Dips. At the time of writing, the world of traditional publishing has so far remained completely unmoved by my literary efforts. Thus denying me a fortune for the film rights or more importantly, access to a crack team of English professors capable of deciphering the ramblings of an eight-year-old boy and correcting it accordingly. (Thank you Genever of Tetbury! I hope someone swaps your bath taps and you boil like a lobster, with my name, the last words on your lips!) I don't have a degree in English Language and certainly don't have a grand to pay someone who has.

Consequently, the task of editing falls to me, car parts bloke turned printer and part-time writer with three lukewarm CSEs. My ever-patient wife, former hotel receptionist, 16+ Music, and veteran of two traumatic births. Plus a couple of on-line writing programs, which it's entirely possible were produced by people who speak English as a second language. One utterly obsessed with hyphens, the other totally in love with commas. Therefore, the odd thing might have slipped through our net of steel. So if you are a self-appointed member of the Advanced Grammar Police, I urge you to tweak your bow tie and relax. Eighty-one thousand words is around six hundred hours of work, and it cost you less to download than half a cup of decent coffee. Lots of unpaid late nights and early mornings with no guarantee of success. So in short, please be nice, because it hurts when you're nasty...

That said, if you've spotted any howlers we've missed, drop me a line. Try to look upon it as audience participation rather than unpaid work. I'm easy to find on Facebook or you can drop me a line at allaggro@btinternet.com

Many thanks!

Eddie Lancaster

Printed in Great Britain
by Amazon